SERENDIPITY

My Story of Being a Marine, Hippie, & Teacher of The Deaf

by

JOHN READE

ISBN-13:

There are two women who have influenced my story immensely.

I would like to dedicate this book to them.

My wife of 49 years, Carol, & my sister Mary Louise, who corroborated my early life stories.

TABLE OF CONTENTS

Chapter 1: The Formative Years 1

Chapter 2: Elementary School And Dr; Nadeau Comes Through Again 7

Chapter 3: Junior High School 13

Chapter 4: Last Year Of Junior High School 15

Chapter 5: College - The First Time 29

Chapter 6: The U. S. Marine Corps 36

Chapter 7: College - The Second Time 73

Chapter 8: The Hippie 75

Chapter 9: Back To West Chester State College (Wcsc) - Third Time Is A Charm 97

Chapter 10: A Masters Degree For $1000.00 Us 102

Chapter 11: Finding Employment 118

Chapter 12: What Now? 205

CHAPTER 1:
THE FORMATIVE YEARS

3:00 PM, July 1, 1946, Easton Area Hospital, Easton, Pennsylvania. An Italian American woman was wheeled into the operating room, writhing in pain. Her first pregnancy had been difficult and resulted in a stillborn boy. The next child was also a boy, who produced one cry and died as the nurse was cleaning him up. The third child was also difficult to deliver; however, a beautiful red-haired daughter emerged, Mary. Mary was advised that she should never have any more children; it was too dangerous for her.

So for eight years, she and George were careful, but around September of 1945, they made a mistake. Mary became pregnant again. Although she was advised to abort, being a devout Catholic, that was never a choice. The frightened, pained, resentful woman heard a cry and prayed this birth would be different. She prayed this last baby would live so that she would not have to go through this agony again. I suppose this can be seen as the first serendipitous experience of my life. I lived.

Two years before I was born, George, Mary, and the other Mary (ML) Reade lived in a beautiful two-story bungalow on Elm Street in Riegelsville, Pennsylvania. They were forced to move shortly after Mary found out she was pregnant again. This was in 1945, and World War II had just ended, so the owners of the house needed it to raise their family after the father returned from Europe. My family moved in with Dad's sister on Cedar Road, also in Riegelsville. Rather than help pay their rent, Mom worked hard as a housekeeper and babysitter for her sister-in-law, and Dad helped Uncle Don fix their place up when they weren't working. Mom worked hard as a housekeeper and babysitter for her sister-in-law. She often told me that she had to do it, and when I later discovered my aunt's oblivion to dirt, I understood exactly what she meant. What I didn't understand was that Aunt Sarah was very artistic and focused her effort on those activities.

My first few months alive were shared with my cousin, Jimmy. Mom fed us both at the same time, changed his diapers as well as mine, washed all our clothes, and got her daughter and the other three girls ready for school on a daily basis. Yes, she worked hard.

A year after I was born, the family moved into Red and Evie's duplex on Pennsylvania Route 611. This was the main highway between Easton and Philadelphia. It was heavily traveled. Their house had no running water but a good well. It had no bathroom but an outhouse. It didn't have central heating but a propane stove in the kitchen and an oil space heater in the living room underneath the largest window.

Red and Evie were our landlords and really appreciated Dad's ability to fix appliances and improve our living conditions. Dad put running water, a hot water heater, and upgraded the electricity into Red's duplex. In turn, Red kept us in fresh vegetables, chicken, eggs, and water. Red and Dad would often entertain the family by playing old favorites — Red on the harmonica and Dad on the ukulele.

During the winter, we would bathe in the kitchen using a #9 galvanized tub and heating water on the propane stove. In the summertime, I was lucky enough to be able to take a bath outdoors (picture).

Red's property included a small chicken hutch and garden on the upper part of the land. When working the garden, you could look down on the roof of the two-story duplex and the pantry. To reach the garden and chickens, you had to climb a series of steps and change direction from west to north to west to north and finally west again until you got to the top. But to come down, well, that's another story.

My earliest memory is of the thrill of falling. I remember our neighbor, Dick, a WWII veteran, throwing me into the air. I'd watch his face grow small, then get large again as my belly rushed into my throat and made me giggle. My sister, ML, now tells me that I couldn't have been more than fifteen months old at that time.

One of my favorite movie serials shown on television was *Captain Midnight*. I thought it was really cool how his jet plane sped down a mountain on a ramp and soared into the night sky with a loud zoom. Since my family didn't own a television, I used to watch *Captain Midnight* at Red and Evie's. Once, after the program, I decided to play Captain Midnight, so I got my red tricycle and hauled it up the series of steps until I got to the top. This is that other story about how I came down — quickly.

On the side of the steps that led to the upper yard, Red built a terrace — three, actually. They sloped gradually from the upper yard to the bottom yard. Each terrace ended in a small rock wall a couple of feet high. I'm not sure exactly how high the first two were, but I could touch the top set of rocks on those terraces. The bottom terrace was taller than I could reach, and I used to climb that wall as if it were a mountain. What fun! Anyway, after I got to the upper yard, I sat on my tricycle, lifted my feet, and began the descent down the first terrace. At the end of that one, I flew! Onto the next slope, where I bounced, picked up speed, and flew off that one as well. Just like Captain Midnight! The rush from my stomach to my throat was just as I remembered it from Dick's tosses. Wow, it was great! I hit the final slope going a million miles an hour. When I left that terrace, I let go of my tricycle, and it went to my right, I went left, and hit the ground rolling like the Lone Ranger after he jumped off Silver and brought down a bad guy. What a great feeling! I just had to do it again. And again! And again! I became a master of that descent over the weeks during the summer of '51.

Unfortunately, sometime later that summer, just as I was wheeling down the terrace for the umpteenth time, Mom appeared with a basket of laundry to hang on the clothesline. She heard my squeal of happiness, looked up the terrace, and nearly died in fright as she saw her precious son, "Captain Johnny Midnight," fly down. She screamed! I looked up and saw her! Frozen by her yell, I forgot to let go of the tricycle. Boom! I landed square on the seat and started bawling! Mom thought I had lost control of the trike. I had, but not in the way she thought. She was very concerned about my injured crotch and gently held me as I cried and cried. Evie phoned Dr. Nadeau to see if I could have done serious damage while Mom comforted me. When I could finally speak, I told them what I had been doing—playing Captain Midnight.

Dr. Nadeau, one of the community doctors you might have seen in the movies, like Dr. Kildare, told Evie that he doubted I had seriously injured myself. Mom then proceeded to fret about how uncaring I was for causing her so much concern. Then I made a big mistake. I tried to explain that I had been playing like that for the whole summer and had not hurt myself until Mom screamed at me, implying that if she had not screamed, I would not have been hurt. But before I could let her know that I was a big boy and could take care of myself—boom! Mom's left hand, the one with the huge Reade family heirloom wedding ring, caught me across the face. How dare I blame her for my actions and getting hurt and nearly causing her to have a heart attack? Then, for the next week, every time I went outside to play, Mom tied a rope around my waist and up to the clothesline. I couldn't go to the upper yard at all, but could run around the yard and get to the outhouse. I devised another game. I'd run as fast as I could until the rope snapped me back. It was kind of fun to be thrown to the ground that way, and I pretended I was playing football.

The abrupt landing, being spanked for doing it, and then being tied to the clothesline for hurting myself almost cured me from wanting to experience the stomach thrill I so vividly remembered from age fifteen months. It did nothing to cure my imagination nor my affection for watching TV programs on Red and Evie's little Zenith television.

Special Relationship:

Red and Evie were more than landlords to me; they were my second parents. One summer morning, I woke up way too early for Mom and Dad to get me breakfast. So I tiptoed downstairs, gathered up my Rice Krispies, a bowl, a spoon, and a bottle of milk. I climbed back up the stairs (took a few trips), opened our window (ML and I slept in the same room), and crawled out on the roof overhanging the porch. I walked over to Red and Evie's window, which was open, and started to put my breakfast next to their bedroom (took a few trips). Of course, Evie woke up immediately, opened the window all the way, and helped me with my parcels. Then she asked what I was doing, and I told her I wanted to eat breakfast with them. They laughed heartily, got out of bed, and ate some Rice Krispies with me. When Mom and Dad got up and noticed I was gone, they were not worried much. They knocked on the wall (bop, bop, bopbop, bop). Evie answered (bop, bop). And my parents knew I was there. I must have been around three.

When I was around two or three, Red talked me into taking off my diaper and peeing like a big boy standing on the concrete wall and onto the passing trucks and cars. Fortunately, the trucks were loud; I never heard the men's laughter. Unfortunately, the trucks were loud; I never heard Mom scream or run up behind me. I did feel her grab my arm with one hand and whack my bare bottom with the other as she scolded me for behaving in such a dangerous manner and performing a lewd act to boot. Of course, I was just proud that I could pee like a man and had no concept of doing something wrong or dangerous. It seems I was always scaring the bejesus out of Mom. And that's part of another story about scaring Mom.

When I was around four, I decided that I should "help" more around the place. I weeded the garden with Red, chased the chickens (to give them exercise), and helped Mom and Evie with the laundry. We had one of the wringer washers at that time. It was housed in our pantry, across from the kitchen. I knew just what to do when the washer stopped agitating the clothes—take them out of the tub, turn on the wringer, put the clothes through the wringer into the clothes basket, empty the tub, and fill it with rinse water. Put the clothes back in the washer and turn it on again.

Boy, was I precocious! I was also a bit slow-moving. While putting a sheet into the wringer, I forgot to remove my hand. The wringer grabbed the middle finger on my right hand and quickly sucked me up with the sheet. "HEEELLLLLPPPP!!" I was lucky because Mom knew the clothes were done and was returning to do the rinse cycle when she saw my hand begin to emerge from the other side of the wringer. She screamed, "AHHHHHEEEEE!" (an old Italian war cry), ran to the washer, and hit the emergency release button. I was free but scared out of my wits. Not only because of the experience, but because of what I knew Mom would do. After Mom asked me if I was hurt (for those who don't know, the wringer was made of soft rubber and was capable of breaking a child's bones, and if the child resisted the pull of the wringer, the skin could become burnt—I didn't resist), and I answered, "Nope." Mom then proceeded to spank my ass really hard and told me to never ever go near the washing machine again.

I'm not sure if the spanking was to ensure that I didn't take any more chances to hurt myself with that appliance or because I scared Mom so terribly she didn't know how to handle it. Whatever the reason, I developed an aversion to doing laundry that remained with me until I joined the Marine Corps and then lived the bachelor life. After I got married, I thought that my mother's warning would be a good enough excuse to make sure my wife would do all the washing. Wrong!

Television's Influence — The Daredevil And The Serendipitous Dr. Nadeau

I loved watching the popular 1950s Westerns: *The Lone Ranger*, *Range Rider*, *The Cisco Kid*, *Gene Autry*, *Roy Rogers*, and *Hopalong Cassidy*. They were my heroes, and I liked to replay their television adventures. On one episode of *The Range Rider*, he was shot off his horse by the bad guy. Only wounded, Range Rider, played by Jock, began rolling down a steep hill toward a cliff. Thinking quickly, he pulled his large hunting knife out of its sheath and rammed it into the hill. It took hold just as his body began to fall over the cliff. Using all his strength, he pulled himself off the edge and called his trusty sidekick, Dick, for help. I thought that was one of the most exciting and cool things to do—use a knife to stop yourself from sliding down a hill.

Soooo… Red's house was next to a church, which was built high upon a hill (from a five-year-old child's perspective). I had a pocket knife that was given to me for use in the Cub Scouts, and THAT was going to be my hunting knife. After donning my cowboy hat, guns, and moccasins, I began to re-enact the *Range Rider* story. Climbing to the top of the "mountain," I pretended to be thrown from my horse and began to roll down the hill. I stopped myself, pulled out my pocket knife, opened it, and then continued to roll. I held onto the knife in my right hand and stabbed the ground where I was rolling. The knife closed onto my pinky finger—hard. I screamed in pain and wondered why the trick worked so well for the Range Rider, but not for me. Instead, my knife nearly cut off my finger.

My loud crying, I thought, would bring Evie and Mom out of the house in search of their dying son. It didn't. I hadn't realized that my everyday play voice was nearly the same as my in-pain crying yells, and Mom and Evie continued with their chores. I bravely picked myself up, and keeping the knife securely in place in my finger, ran into Evie's kitchen. I was bleeding pretty good and made a big puddle of blood on her floor, but good old Evie wasn't worried about that. She immediately assessed the situation, picked me up, and held my hand in the kitchen sink. She began pumping water onto the finger and called Mom. I screamed louder when the cold water hit the dirt-filled cut, but Evie didn't hesitate and continued with the water treatment. Mom came running into Evie's and decided that she was handling the situation perfectly, so she left to call Dr. Nadeau—again. This time she was told to bring me into his office and not to remove the knife, just wrap my finger in a towel.

Since neither Evie nor Mom drove a car, they had to enlist a neighbor to give us a lift. Evie continued to hold my hand and me in the back seat, while Mom got in the front. I don't remember who the driver was, but the drive seemed to take a hundred hours. At Dr. Nadeau's office, I was taken directly into his "operating" room. The good doctor looked me over, placed a kidney-shaped bowl under my hand, and removed the knife from my pinky. He then cleaned it up some more and decided the cut didn't need any stitches. So he placed a bandage over the cut and a tongue depressor under it to keep it from moving, then wrapped up the finger and hand. As I got older, I graduated to another favorite TV pastime: watching movies on Saturday morning. I used to watch *The Bowery Boys*, *Hopalong Cassidy*, *The Little Rascals*, and most of all, *Tarzan*. I believe I was around six when this happened.

I loved playing Tarzan. I made myself a loincloth out of a belt and towel, had a rubber knife that I'd shove into the belt, and tried to yell like Tarzan. There was a beautiful young oak tree outside Evie and Red's side of the duplex. They also had a slate and wrought-iron fence just alongside it that separated their property from that of the church. The tree was easy to climb with the help of the fence, and I climbed that tree many times, both as a cowboy, Indian, and as Tarzan—loincloth, knife, and no shoes.

Since Tarzan used to travel over the jungle floor by swinging from limb to limb on vines, I decided to create my own "vine." I got a piece of clothesline and tied it to a limb of the oak tree. The limb stretched out over the fence and up the hill. I thought it'd be fun to hold onto the rope, swing out over the fence, and drop down onto the hill. It was! And I got that stomach thrill I liked so much.

Each time I did it, I'd yell my Tarzan yell. This was done so often that Mom and Evie got used to hearing it. They checked me out and saw that I was fine, playing Tarzan. They did not see me swinging on the rope.

After about twenty swings, the knot that attached the rope to the tree became loose. Yep, you guessed it. I swung out over the fence, the rope came undone, and I hit the slate full force with my head. I had a huge cut, and the blood just flowed. Naturally, I yelled for Mom and Evie. Just as naturally, they ignored my screams as those of Tarzan. I finally got up, climbed over the fence, which wasn't very high at all, and started to walk to the house. Evie was coming out of the house toward the well and saw me walking up the lawn. Being well trained by my mother, she screamed at me and my bloody head, chest, and loincloth, ran to me, picked me up, and yelled at Mom to call the doctor's office—again.

Since this was Saturday, Red was home and drove us to Dr. Nadeau's office. The good doctor left his home and met us at the office. He checked me out, stitched me up, and then asked what happened. Since the blood stopped, the hurt dissipated by the local anesthetic, and my mother safely out of earshot, I told him about being Tarzan and the rope "breaking." He laughed and said my secret was safe. Much to his credit, Mom never found out that I was swinging on a rope, over a fence, and dropping onto the hill next door.

That was a thrill equal to my Captain Midnight game. I got hurt again, but I didn't get spanked for hurting myself this time. I guess Mom felt sorry for me because of all the blood or because she didn't know about the "vine" I created and used. I'll never know, because I kept that secret until now.

Tragedy:

Probably the most traumatic experience during this time in my life took place while I was playing Hopalong John. I used my tricycle, pretending that it was Hopalong Cassidy's horse, Topper, and wore my Hoppy outfit often, with two pearl-handled guns in my holster. While playing one day, I had to go to the outhouse and do a #2.

So I pulled down my pants, did my business, and pulled up my pants along with my gun belt and two beautiful pearl-handled six-shooters. Unfortunately, they fell out of my holster and landed on the seat. One immediately went down the hole, but the other one was sitting near the opening. Being the fastest draw on my property, I quickly reached for it, but tragedy struck—I knocked that one into the hole as well. I was devastated and thought about reaching down the hole and fishing them out. But the smell and the fact that my black cowboy hat nearly fell off my head put a stop to that idea. When I told my mother what had happened, she was sympathetic but unwilling to go down to the store and replace my guns. Yep, I cried.

Another way in which television influenced my preschool years was when we watched a movie with Fred and Ginger. They were tap dancing all over a house, including dancing on a kitchen table. I guess I was around five or six at this time and expressed an interest in tap dancing—on the table. Anyway, I was enrolled in the School of Dance and learned some tap dancing moves. I never danced on our kitchen table, but with another student, Prudence, I believe was her name, and we danced in the Riegelsville Library.

CHAPTER 2:
ELEMENTARY SCHOOL AND DR; NADEAU COMES THROUGH AGAIN

By now I had started school. In the second grade, I developed a very sore throat. This prompted another trip to visit Dr. Nadeau. Since I had had a series of infections during the school year, Dr. Nadeau thought I should see an Otolaryngologist (Ear, Nose and Throat specialist doctor). That doctor determined that my tonsils and adenoids had to be removed. This was and remains a fairly simple procedure with an overnight stay in the hospital. No big deal, right? Wrong.

I had an aversion to the smell and taste of blood (I wonder how that came about?). So after the operation, whenever I tasted blood, I quickly swallowed it. Well, that turned out to be the worst thing I could do. Because it was very hard to swallow at all, I was given ice cream as sustenance and to ease the soreness. It also helped me to swallow the blood that seeped from the operation.

After I came home, I felt really tired. Mom let me lay on our sofa in the living room and made me a hot cup of Lipton Chicken Noodle Soup. I slowly ate it, then laid back on the sofa. All of a sudden, I felt sick and called out to Mom. I told her I felt like throwing up, so she got a bucket and held it for me. Well, I did puke, not chicken noodle soup, but blood clots. To my eyes, they were BIG and BLACK, and SMELLY!

Mom knocked on the wall for Evie to come over and told my sister, ML, to call Dr. Nadeau again. Evie got a cold cloth and held it on my head, and Mom added water to the bucket. Dr. Nadeau drove down to our home and checked me out. He asked me if I had been spitting blood out of my mouth in the hospital, I told him, "No, I swallowed it." He said that I wasn't going to be swallowing it any more. He also told Mom that I'd be all right in a day or two and that the sickness, throwing up, would pass soon. He then became my best friend again by telling her to feed me ice cream, jello, or pudding for a day or two. Nothing hot or warm or irritating to my throat. Yippie! I felt better in a couple of days and returned to school the following Monday. I had a lot of work to catch up on, but, actually, was happy to be back with my buddies playing in the school yard.

Small Town Tests:

One of the rights of passage for the boys attending Riegelsville Elementary School was to climb up the outside of the fire escape. The school was only two stories high, but from the top of the outside of the fire escape it seemed as if it were as high as a sky scraper. The structure ran parallel to the school building except for the last couple of feet. Then it took a ninety degree turn and attached to the school, at the sixth grade area of the second floor.

Once you got to the top, you had to stand on the ledge of the fire escape where it turned onto the building, turn around, and spit over the side at least that was what the boys did. I'm not sure if the girls had to do the same thing or something different.

We also liked to climb up the inside. It was smooth, but had welds holding the various pieces together, so they would act as a toe hold, especially if you were bare foot. About 4 feet from the top, it took that ninety degree turn up toward the building. Then the really tricky part happened; you had to turn around and sit facing the bottom. I can't tell you how many times I wound up sliding down the escape on my belly, which was not the most enjoyable way to slide down. My shirt would bunch up around my chest and I'd get a burn on my stomach from the friction.

I really enjoyed playing football and baseball; so much so that I was allowed to join the Riegelsville, New Jersey peewee football team. (My favorite football player was Chuck. He played center and linebacker for the Philadelphia Eagles and was from Bethlehem, Pa.) We would pack our uniform in our pants, shoes at the bottom of each leg, shoulder pads in one leg, hip pads in the other, and shirt and helmet on top, practicing my punting.

In baseball, I played first base and later was the catcher on our little league team. Our best pitcher was a boy named Wayne. His father had a dairy farm on the hill above our school. Wayne had to complete his chores before he could come to baseball practice. After he showed up late for practice and a couple of games, we found out the reason why. So I decided to ride my bike up the hill and help him out with his chores so he could get to the games on time. That led to my first job at age twelve. I got to help bale hay on their farm, and Mr. Young paid me for it. I gave the money, seven dollars a week, to Mom. She opened a savings account in our names and put five dollars in it for each week I got paid. From then on, whatever job I had, I gave the money to Mom, and she put most of it into that savings account.

Our recess at school was two fifteen-minute breaks, one in the morning and another in the afternoon. We also had an hour for lunch. Some of the students would bring their lunches and eat in between playing on the swings, merry-go-round, or seesaw. Most of us ran home, scoffed down a sandwich and glass of milk, and got back to the school to continue our baseball or football game. We'd choose sides on a Monday and begin playing during the first recess. When the bell rang, we'd remember who was batting, what the count was, how many outs there were, who was on which base, as well as the score.

Each game lasted nine innings, or one week, whichever happened to come first. This story will tell you about how small our town was and give proof that it did take a village to raise each child from Riegelsville. During the morning recess game, I got a hit and was on first base. Jan, the mayor's son, was the first baseman. Our next batter got a hit, and I began to run to second base, but Jan tripped me. I fell and was thrown out at second. I was really angry and got in Jan's face. He pushed me, and at just that time, the bell rang to end recess. We challenged each other to a fight at lunchtime.

Throughout the rest of the morning, Jan and I exchanged dirty looks, and when the teacher wasn't looking, we put our fists up in a threatening manner. When the bell rang for lunch, we hurried out of the building and made our way into the cemetery that was next to the school. We faced off in front of many of our classmates. Jan threw a punch and hit me in the face. I retaliated and hit him back, then tackled him to the ground. I hit him one more time, and the other guys pulled us apart.

The fight may have taken all of five minutes. By the time I got home for lunch, Mom was on the phone and called me over. Jan's father was on the other end of the call. Mom had me apologize to him for hitting Jan and blackening his eye. I swear I was only a few minutes late for lunch, but by the time I got home, the whole town knew I got in a fight with the mayor's son, how many punches were thrown, that I tackled him, and hit him while on the ground (very ungentlemanly). To say that Mom and Dad were angry at me is an understatement for sure. Not because I got in a fight, but because I hit Jan while he was on the ground and I was on top.

In all honesty, after that fight, Jan and I became pretty good friends, and I gained a bit of a reputation as a tough guy with some of the boys, and a bully by some of the girls. That's life in a small town.

Wise Guy Trouble:

I later learned that one of the reasons Jan tripped me and thought I was a pushover was because I was still taking tap dancing lessons. During this time, my dancing partner was a girl named Karen, and we were a little bit known around town because we danced in our local Minstrel Shows. We did this for three years in a row. The last year I got in trouble. One of the men in blackface thought it'd be funny to put some of the blackface makeup on me just before Karen and I were to go on stage for our tap dance routine. I was already wearing makeup, didn't like the feel, and the blackface felt like shoe polish and smelled terrible. So when the man turned his back on me, I wiped my face clean on the back of his coat. He got really angry and threw me into the clothing rack, which had the effect of dirtying many more costumes. Karen was backstage when all this happened and helped me out of the clothing rack. She also acted as a corroborating witness when the story came out.

I was as angry at the older man who started the whole thing. After the show, I told my parents what had happened, Karen and I dancing in the Minstrel Show, and they said I was wrong for dirtying the rented costumes, which caused the town to pay extra for cleaning the costumes before returning them. The next day, Dad saw the guy who threw me into the coat rack at one of the two gas stations the town had. He pulled into the place and went up to the guy. I saw him poke the man in the chest and heard him say, "If you ever touch my son again, you'll be very sorry." I guess my father had a reputation as a tough guy because even though the other man was taller, he backed away from my Dad and said nothing back to him. I must say, I was very proud of my Dad at that time, for sure!

New House, Bad Adventure:

Around that time, we moved out of Red and Evie's home down to a two-story house on Cedar Road, just down from Aunt Sarah's and cousin Jimmy's house. We finally had indoor plumbing, a bathtub, hot water, central heating, and a flat backyard. Right after we moved into that house, Hurricane Diane struck, and the Delaware River flooded the towns on its border.

I thought it was great. I had learned to swim the previous year and believed we had a swimming hole in our backyard. Of course, my parents knew that it wasn't safe to swim in, and we moved back in with Red and Evie. This is when another traumatic event happened to me. I forgot to take my teddy bear with me to Red and Evie's and decided that I had to get it. So I walked down to a place across from Cedar Road and slid into the flood. I had no idea how strong flood waters could become and couldn't swim well enough to keep from being swept away. That was my first near-death experience, but definitely not my last. Once again, serendipity caressed my spirit.

Luckily, our town sheriff and another hero were going around the town in a motorized rowboat and saw me struggling to get back on shore. They pulled up to me and pulled me into the boat. Rather than taking me to my parents, they took me to the Red Cross Center to be evaluated by doctors. Then they told my parents where I was and what had happened. The doctors gave me a tetanus shot, in my belly. Why? I do not know, but that's where I got the shot. Then I was sent back to my parents, and they were told to keep a careful watch on me and to let them know if I got a fever or diarrhea. It turned out that I was all right, after my spanking for trying to get my teddy bear. Of course, I never actually told anyone that a nine-year-old boy wanted his teddy bear. I made up a story about falling off Red's roof into the flood waters.

Cleaning, Repairs And A Wonderful Surprise And An Angry Mom:

After the flood, our rented house was a terrible mess. The water level had gotten as high as the sixth step on our stairway going to the bedrooms. The refrigerator, stove, furnace, furniture, books, tools in the basement—everything we had was ruined. However, my Dad was a very clever man. He took some vacation time from work to fix up the house. The state declared a state of emergency and provided funding for towns to hire professional cleaners to begin the process of helping residents clean their homes.

After the worst of the debris was removed and cleaned up, Mom, Dad, ML, and I began using lye with soapy water to wash down the walls. Our basement was cleaned up by the professionals, but the furnace had to be cleaned better before we could burn coal in it. Also, all the heating ducts had to be cleaned out. Dad and Red got to work on that. Dad also completely took apart our refrigerator, cleaned each part, put it back together, bought some Freon gas for the freezer, and then we restocked food. He also took apart the stove, cleaned out all the piping and the heads of the burners, and put it back together. Then he connected the propane gas cylinder, and it worked perfectly. I believe we had to get a new hot water heater, and he connected that up, so we were able to take baths, and Mom could wash up all the dishes and pots and pans that weren't taken upstairs in preparation for the flood.

Unknown to me, Dad was secretly working on fixing up my American Flyer train set. He took apart the transformer, cleaned and rewired it. Did the same for the engine and each car. When Christmas came around, it was a pretty sad time for presents, but on Christmas morning, I woke up to a beautiful surprise. Mom and Dad set up the train set under and in front of the tree. And it worked beautifully, including the smoke stack for the engine.

My last story around this time of my life happened after a dental appointment. Our dentist was located in Easton on North 3rd Street. I was ten years old when this happened. My mother and I both had appointments to see our dentist. I had a baby eye tooth that wouldn't come out, so it was decided that it would be pulled and that would allow the adult eye tooth to drop down. That's what I expected would happen that day, but I was wrong. The dentist wasn't sure that there was an adult tooth to replace it, so they decided to take an x-ray to make sure. That's the procedure I had, and it took about five minutes.

Mom, however, had upper and lower dentures, and the upper ones needed to be replaced. That meant that she needed to have an impression done of her gum line, which took a long time. I had some money, and the Boyd Theatre was right next door to the dentist's office. The Disney movie *Westward Ho the Wagons* was playing, and I thought it'd be a great idea for me to watch the movie while Mom had her appointment. I made a big mistake though; I didn't tell Mom or the receptionist where I was going.

When Mom was done, she went to get me from the waiting room, but I wasn't there. Mom began to panic, wondering what happened to me and where I decided to go or what I decided to do. She also had a time limit. We had to catch the bus back to Riegelsville and only had about an hour to walk to the terminal, which was about four blocks away. With my mother's rheumatoid arthritis ankles, it would be slow going.

She left the office, looked around, and saw the marquee for the Boyd Theatre and knew where I was. So she told the person manning the ticket booth that she was looking for her young son and believed he went into the theatre. My parents had given me a watch for my birthday that year. It was a great watch that had illuminated numbers and hands. I was sitting about halfway down the theatre in the last seat in that row. Leaning on my left hand, my watch was clearly visible, and Mom saw it. She hobbled down the aisle, tapped me on the shoulder, and asked, "Excuse me, are you Johnny Reade?" I looked up, and before I could answer, Mom grabbed my left ear and hauled me out of the seat, up the aisle, and continued to hold on to it for about a block and a half before she let go. She told me that when we got home, I had to account for why I left the dentist's office and "wasted" my money on a silly movie. I tried to explain, but she wouldn't listen to me at that time; we had to hurry to get to the bus terminal on time.

When I got home, I thought I'd get a spanking again, but Mom had cooled down and let me explain why I did what I did. My punishment for my actions was to clean the ashes out of the furnace and mow the lawn. No big deal, and I got to see some of the movie, which I paid for, found my own seat, and enjoyed myself for a while.

The Godfather:

In 1958 my sister graduated from nursing school and in November married Castelletti. A year later, my niece LeeAnn was born, and ML asked me to be her Godfather. I was thrilled but had no idea what it meant in the long term. I held her as holy water was spilled over her head and repeated the necessary words, but I didn't understand that I should also be somewhat of a mentor for her in her later years. I have to apologize to her here and now for failing in that aspect of my duty as her Godfather. Since I've retired, I make it a point to send her and her children birthday and Christmas cards with some money enclosed.

CHAPTER 3:
JUNIOR HIGH SCHOOL

After the sixth grade, students from Riegelsville traveled by bus to the city of Easton. This is the place where Dixie Cup cardboard containers and Crayola Crayons are made. It is also the home of Wolf Junior High School, located on North 4th Street. I was never a natural athlete nor a noted scholar, but I had an attitude that served me well—never give up.

7-U

FOOTBALL

8-P

A Hard Knock:

When I started at Wolf Junior High in 1959, I was in the homeroom of 7U. Seventh grade was not noteworthy, except for the fact that I got a concussion. Riegelsville bordered the Delaware Canal, which during the 1800s and turn of the century was used as a conduit for produce, milk, and meat from the Pennsylvania farmland to the marketing center in Philadelphia. Every winter it froze over, and the people who had ice skates and knew how to skate went there to have fun and play hockey.

I never had ice skates, so I never learned how to skate, but I did want to hang out with the boys. I followed them down to the canal and helped them set up a "rink" to begin their hockey game. They were short one man for an equal-numbered team, so they asked me to be the goalie. I had on leather-soled boots, which weren't very good on ice—in fact, they were slippery as hell. The first time I had to stop a shot on goal, I slipped and fell hard. I landed on my back and hit my head on the ice. From then on, I don't remember anything until I woke up on an X-ray table.

This is what I pieced together from conversations with my friend Brent, my mother, and Frank. Brent said that I hit my head hard enough to crack the ice, so they helped me off the canal and placed me in a sitting position underneath a tree. My mother said that that evening I came home and went upstairs to my bedroom. She called me to come down to supper, but I told her I was very sleepy and had put my pajamas on. I went to bed and slept until the morning. She got me up, I made my bed, and got dressed. I then ate a bit of cereal for breakfast and went to the bus stop. Brent said I got on the bus, sat in my usual seat, and nodded off on the way to school.

Frank said that after homeroom, we went to algebra class. While there, I knocked my pencil off my desk but blamed the boy sitting in front of me, Tim. I told him to pick it up, and he said to pick it up myself. I said I'd make him do it, got up, and began to push him toward the pencil. He hit me. I fell back, hit my head on the rung of the desk next to mine, and got a bloody nose. The algebra teacher, Mr. Uhler, told Frank to take me to the bathroom and clean me up. He did, and while we were standing in front of the mirror, I asked him who that was. He said he told me it was him, Frank, and I said, no, the other guy, meaning me. That got him scared, and rather than go back to class, he took me to the nurse's office.

Mom then told me that after a few tests, the nurse called for an ambulance, called Mom for permission to take me to the hospital, and I was transported to Easton Hospital to be seen by a neurologist. He sent me for X-rays. Mom and Dad came to the hospital. I woke up on the table feeling nauseous but otherwise all right. The doctor told my parents I had a concussion, but there was no fracture. I went home and stayed home for a few days. When I went back to school, I apologized to Tim, the teacher, the class, and Frank. I also thanked him for taking me to the nurse. All was forgotten, I think.

In the eighth and ninth grades, I made the Wolf varsity football team as a center and linebacker. I was on the first string in the ninth grade and also raised my grade average so I could get into the college prep courses in Easton Area High School. What's interesting about junior high school is that the people who were in my various homerooms and with whom I played football remained together throughout our high school years as well. And all the ninth-grade starters on the Wolf Junior High School football team were first string on the Easton Area High School football team.

CHAPTER 4:
LAST YEAR OF JUNIOR HIGH SCHOOL

During my last year of junior high school, my father got a promotion at his work. He began working at the New Jersey Power and Light Company (NJP&L) during the Depression, shoveling coal. It was steady employment and kept his family above water financially. Being a very intelligent and ambitious man, he continued to improve his education. After Hurricane Diane caused the flood that basically destroyed our community, and Dad repaired our home, he went back to school. He enrolled in Lafayette College night school, taking electrical engineering courses.

In 1960 or '61, he got a diploma from the college in electrical engineering and used that to become an electrical dispatcher for NJP&L. Unfortunately, his position was in Milford, New Jersey, a fifteen-mile drive from Rieglesville. So we had a family discussion about looking for another home closer to Milford.

My input was that Mom and Dad asked me whether I would prefer to go to high school in Easton, as they and ML did, or switch to Phillipsburg, New Jersey, Easton's archrival in football. Naturally, I chose Easton, and just before I graduated from Wolf Jr. High, they bought a house at 830 Northampton Street in Easton. We moved in during that summer.

Saying Good-Bye To A Loved One:
Just around the corner from our house lived Frank, so I already had a friend to kind of show me around the neighborhood. Unfortunately, my dad didn't think the city was a good place for our dog, Rex.

We had Rex ever since we moved into the house on Cedar Road in Rieglesville. He was a collie mix, very easygoing, loved to play fetch, football (he was good at tackling me), baseball, or just run and jump around. We got him as a puppy from people living in Belfast, Pennsylvania, near Uncle Earl and Aunt K's home.

My father didn't think city living was good for a dog and decided to find another home for Rex. He said he found a place for him on a farm in Alpha, New Jersey. The men who got Rex came to pick him up just as I got home from school. I saw him being placed in the back of an old Chevy pickup truck. I can still picture his face looking out the back window of that Chevy, with a puzzled expression on his face and his ears pinned back, as shown in the picture. I'm writing this passage as a seventy-plus-year-old retired man, and I still get teary-eyed thinking about him.

A Working Student:

However, life goes on, and we had to settle into a new house, new environment, and new neighbours in the big city of Easton. Like our house in Rieglesville, the one on Northampton Street was heated by a coal-burning furnace. And like one of my chores in Rieglesville, I was required to keep the furnace fire stoked, clean out the ashes, and make sure the coal bin was as clean as possible. But I also wanted to contribute to our coffers like I did in Rieglesville, so I looked around for a job. I found one as a stock boy in Gerstner's Grocery Store on 4th and Northampton Street.

As a stock boy, once a week I was supposed to bring in a side of beef that Mr. Gerstner, a butcher by trade, would cut up into various cuts as ordered by his customers.

Well, the first time I tried to carry one of those suckers into the walk-in freezer, I thought it'd sink me into the ground. I was able to heave it onto my shoulder and, on wobbly legs, carry it into the store, but then there were three steps to get into the freezer area of the store. I found them to be difficult to maneuver the first few times I did that chore, and I needed help to hang it up. But my strength grew, and I was finally able to carry them into the freezer and hang each one on the meat hook.

Mr. Gerstner also had deli meats that were cut by a slicer, so another of my jobs was to clean the slicer.

This was not a difficult job but did take a lot of care and preparation.

The single most important thing to do was to carefully remove the blade and wash that separately before cleaning the rest of the machine.

Once, I tried to cut corners and clean the blade and the rest of the machine without removing the blade. Naturally, I nearly cut my right index finger off.

Driving A Rig:

Mr. Gerstner's son, Jim, and his friend, Ed (Bingy) Wagner, were required to drive their 1945 Ford 40-ton cargo truck down to the Philadelphia Produce Center twice a week and stock up on vegetables, fruit, and dry goods. They would leave at midnight on Sunday, get to the produce center about 3:00 AM just as it opened for business, buy the items on the list, load the truck, and get back to the store around 7:30. They would then unload the purchases, I would bring them into the store and put them where they were supposed to go, and Jim and Bingy would get some sleep; I went to school.

Jim was around 20 and Bingy around 18. He was in his junior year of high school and attended the same school as I. They enjoyed their beer and talked me into going with them to the Philadelphia Produce Center for extra pay. Then Jim asked me if I wanted to learn to drive the truck. I jumped at the chance. The truck was a manual shift that had ten gears. It was a five-gear pattern, and to get to the higher gears, you had to double clutch and pull the gear shift lever up. Then you got to the higher gears by downshifting to second gear and then shifting up normally to tenth gear. Sounds complicated, but after you got the hang of it, it became easy.

Because I didn't have my driver's license yet, they let me drive from Easton into Philly, but we changed drivers before getting to the produce center. Jim would back into the loading dock, grab a trolley, and begin picking up the items on Mr. Gerstner's list. The whole transaction would take around 45 minutes. Jim would pay, Bingy and I would be loading the truck at the same time, and in about an hour and a half, we'd be heading back to Easton. Just outside Philly, I'd take over again. Boy, I thought I was king shit driving this big, old truck around eastern Pennsylvania, especially when we went through Rieglesville.

A Decision:

Now Easton High School football practice started in August with what were called "two-a-days." This meant we'd meet in the morning at 10:00, run, work out, do wind sprints, and then go over different plays until 12:00. In the afternoon, beginning at 1:00, we'd return to the field, put on our practice uniform with full pads, and begin offensive and defensive drills. We'd be finished by 3:00. So my day went like this during the month of August—be at Gerstner's Grocery Store by 7:00, leave at 9:30 to ride my bike to Cottingham Stadium on 25th and Northampton, go to football practice, ride home and get a sandwich and some rest, go to the afternoon football practice, after practice take a shower and return to Gerstner's by 4:00 PM, work until 7:00, and go home for supper and more rest.

In September, the school opened, and my schedule changed drastically. I went to Gerstner's at 7:00, left at 8:30 with Bingy, and went to Easton Area High School. After school, I went to football practice until 6:00. Went home and had supper, then went back to Gerstner's from 7:00 until they closed up at 11:00. Went home and did whatever homework I had to complete and went to bed around 12:30.

However, Sunday and Wednesday nights, I tried to get to sleep earlier, got up at midnight so Jim and Bingy could pick me up outside my house around 12:15. We drove out of the city, and then we switched drivers. I did this from September through October but had to stop because I got exhausted. Plus, I was getting pounded at football practice. You see, the junior varsity team would be the opposing team during the week for the varsity. We would be Bethlehem, then Allentown, then Thomas Jefferson (from Newark, NJ), etc. You get the idea. So I was usually their center, and the nose guard was usually a very big, mean guy. I believe his name was Bob Milkovitz. He would basically run over me, although I tried like hell to stop him. At any rate, I just had to stop driving down to the produce center. I stayed with the store until I cut my finger on the deli meat slicer. That happened around the Thanksgiving holiday, and I wore a large pad on my hand for the Big Turkey-Day Game with Phillipsburg.

The junior varsity team got to suit up for that game, even though most of us would not be playing. That game was always played in the Lafayette College Stadium. It had a seating capacity of 19,000, but for the Easton–P-Burg game, they added bleacher seats that brought the number of people attending to around 22,000. It was always filled. My sophomore year, or JV year, Phillipsburg won by a score of 7–0. For the year, the team had an 8 and 2 record.

I found out that I was going to need more rest and time to work out if I wanted to really compete for a spot on the varsity football team. So I decided to look for a different job—an afternoon job. It took most of the rest of the school term, but I found the ideal job for a teenage boy who wanted time for himself, a decent wage, and an opportunity to, hmmm, play. I was hired to work as an usher for the State Theatre.

Uh Oh:

When I told Mr. Gerstner, Jim, and Ed that I was going to another job, they tried to entice me to stay with them. Mr. Gerstner offered me a raise of $0.25 an hour, and Jim and Ed promised me that as soon as I got my license, they'd let me drive the truck all the way into the produce center. However, I just couldn't continue working those hours with so little sleep. When I told them when my final shift was, the weekend before that day, Jim and Ed took me out to Phillipsburg for a drink.

I always looked older than I was, and they figured they knew a couple of bars there that didn't check to see your age. They told me to just follow their lead and not say too much. So we piled into Ed's 1959 yellow and black Ford Edsel and drove across the Easton–Phillipsburg free bridge, the one my father helped build during the 1920s. We went into a local corner bar, sat at the counter, and they ordered shots of "Cutty" and a beer chaser. Well, I had no idea what "Cutty" was, but I had had a beer or two with my brother-in-law and his twin, so I figured I'd have no problem. Then the bartender placed a shot glass in front of each of us and poured an ounce of Cutty Sark.

Scotch whiskey in it, followed by an eight-ounce draft of Schlitz beer. The guys took the shot glass and threw it into their mouths, swallowed, and then took a sip of their beer. I followed suit and nearly choked to death. It was so damned strong and burned my throat so much that I drank the whole glass of beer immediately after that shot.

Junior Varsity Football

Coach — Mr. Kenneth Hosler

Assistant Coach — Mr. William Pfeffer

They laughed at me but said, "One more time and you'll get used to it." So I tried another shot and a beer. After the third one, I needed to go to the bathroom but had a hard time finding my legs. I staggered into the john, relieved myself, washed my face with cold water, and made it back to the bar. Ed and Jim said it was time to go to another place, so we paid our bill and left.

They took me to a "dance" club. It was a place on Route 22 that had a cowboy motif, a large circular bar with a stage in the middle. There was a band playing in the corner of the place and go-go girls dancing on the corners of the stage. We got a booth, and they ordered another round of shots and beer, but after that one, I told them I didn't want any more Cutty, just beer.

They continued to buy me beers, and I continued to drink them. I didn't realize that I was really getting plastered and became susceptible to different suggestions. Jim began talking about how beautiful the go-go dancers were, and I agreed. Ed suggested that I get up on stage and dance with the one closest to us. So I did. The patrons of the club began cheering me, and the girl I went up to began dancing with me. I thought I was a real cool guy!

Then another guy jumped up on the stage and cut me out. So I moved on to another girl. We began to dance, but another guy cut me out again. So I moved on to a third girl, but she already had a dance partner. I thought the protocol was to just cut each other out and move around. Unfortunately, that wasn't the situation, and that man decided I was NOT going to cut him out and got in front of me. I got in front of him, and then he hip-checked me. I got angry and shoved him off the stage, but when I turned to dance with that pretty go-go dancer, she was gone. Also, one of the bartenders was climbing onto the stage and giving me a real dirty look. Fortunately, Ed and Jim came to the stage and pulled me off. We ran out of the club and into Ed's Edsel. I got in the back seat, and Jim told me to lay down on the floor because the cops were coming. Ed left the parking lot, drove down the road, and made a U-turn to go back to Easton and end our night.

I began to feel sick to my stomach and told Ed I was going to throw up. He told me to open the door and stick my head out of the car. When I did that, I noticed that we were driving over the bridge again, and some of my vomit was going through the spaces between the wooden slats of the bridge. The next thing I knew, Ed pulled up a block from my house and told me to walk home to sober up. I walked home, went up the stairs, and found that the door was locked. So I rang the doorbell, and my sister, who was there with her son and daughter for the night, let me in. She evaluated the situation and took me up to the bathroom. She cleaned me up and put me to bed. The next day, I thought I was going to die and vowed never to drink Scotch again.

Great Job:

The State Theatre has been in business since 1910, when it opened to showcase vaudeville acts. Later it began showing silent films, then talkies, and it continued to screen movies until recently. I worked there from 1962 until 1964. As an usher, I was required to wear a brown uniform, carry a flashlight, show customers to open seats if they asked, clean up the aisles between shows, and ensure that there wasn't any rowdiness.

The balcony was often closed, but employees were permitted to go up there to "watch" the show. As normal teenagers, we often watched with our ears as our eyes were closed, mouths kissing, and hands wandering. A great perk of that job. Plus, I got to rest much, much more than working at Gerstner's Grocery.

A view of the windows I painted from the marquees. Picture will give you an idea of how high I was while painting them. By the way, these are new windows and, although the same shape, are different panes.

We were paid minimum wage, which was $1.15 an hour in 1962. Overtime paid $1.73 an hour, so I tried to get as much overtime as I could. I got that by becoming a "handyman" as well as an usher. As a handyman, I often had to clean up the bathrooms, sometimes turning off the water underneath the sinks and changing the washer in a leaking faucet. My brother-in-law, Robert, showed me how to do that.

However, the hardest and scariest job I did was to scrape and paint the windows above the marquees. The management had a twenty-foot wooden ladder that I brought out onto the roof of the marquee. There was only some hemp-fiber twine to use to secure the ladder onto the building. So I opened the window to Louis dance studio and tied the twine to the radiator underneath the window.

Then I climbed to the third rung from the top, holding onto the rock surface with my left hand, held the scraper in my right hand, and began to clean off the old paint. To get to the far side of the window, I placed my right foot on the middle grille and leaned over to scrape off the old paint. Boy, was I stupid. I never thought about what would happen if my foot slipped off the grille or how hurt I'd get if I fell off the ladder. I only thought about earning $1.73 an hour. I didn't slip off the grille or fall off the ladder, but I did get a wake-up when I looked at the twine after I finished the project. It was frayed and so weak I could break it with just an easy pull. Gees, I was one lucky son of a gun to finish that project in one piece.

That was the beginning of my junior year of high school. This was one of my best years in school. I had one of my better years academically, although I did get a D in Spanish and a D in Chemistry. I had two Cs, two Bs, and an A in Public Speaking. I guess I knew how to spin a tale.

I was in homeroom 319 with my Wolf Junior High buddies: Floyd, Scott, Joe, Alfred, and Tom. The varsity football team let me join, and I got to play in enough games to earn the coveted Varsity E sweater.

Ego Boost Then Realty:

Another very uplifting, ego-boosting, bragging-rights event happened when a beautiful girl in the senior department invited me to be her date to the Senior Christmas Dance. I washed and vacuumed the inside of our 1956 DeSoto that had fluid drive (meaning it was almost an automatic drive car) the day before the dance, dressed in my best suit, and borrowed my dad's overcoat so I'd make a good impression on Wanda.

I bought a corsage to match her dress (my sister's idea) and picked her up right on time. We walked into the gymnasium, and I took her coat and hung it under my overcoat. Then we found a table with her friends, and the evening began. I danced with her as often as she wanted and was also permitted to dance with some of the other girls at the table, mostly because their dates refused to dance to anything but the slow songs.

After the dance, we went to Mizzero's for a cheesesteak and Coke. Then came the big question: "Do you want to go straight home, or go for a ride?" She said, "We'll take our time going home. Have a nice, quiet, dark place we can park?" Again, I was feeling like a king. So we went parking where the Riegelsville Boy Scouts had their permanent camping grounds.

It had begun to snow while we were in Mizzero's, but that didn't stop us. That DeSoto was big, heavy, and made for pushing snow out of the way. When I found a spot where the car would be easy to turn around, I turned off the lights, turned up the heat, and Wanda and I took off our coats. We were going at it hot and heavy when that wrist-breaking, intercourse-preventing piece of clothing got in my way—the panty girdle. This article of clothing kept many people virgins, including me.

After Wanda made it clear to me that that garment was not coming off, we decided to go home. Trouble was, the snow had picked up, and as I was turning the car around, I let it slip into a small ditch. In the spring and summer, that ditch *was* small, but in a snowstorm, it was deadly. So we switched places—Wanda took the wheel, and I got out to push. The wheels spun a lot of debris onto my dad's overcoat, and just as Wanda got the car out of the ditch, I fell headfirst into it. Wanda got a good laugh, but I thought Dad was going to kill me when I told him how I got his best overcoat so dirty.

Turned out that Dad wasn't as upset as I feared. He just had me pay for the dry-cleaning bill and admonished me for being so stupid as to let the car slip into a ditch. Of course, he didn't know the whole truth. I told him we got stuck in a ditch because we went to a party in Forks Township. At that time, Forks Township hadn't yet been built up and had a number of places where one could slide into a shallow ditch.

Conquer"

SUSAN FOSTER
College Preparatory
Psychologist

Some day I will paint the Golden Gate Bridge with you. Love Susi

First Real Crush:

In my senior year of high school, I had my first steady girlfriend, Sue. She was in a few of my classes, but we became a couple after sharing time at a dance and kind of making out on the dance floor. She lived on College Hill, which was known as the ritzy part of Easton, and her family was fairly well off.

One of our more memorable, mmm, adventures was when we were parking in Hackett's Field Park under a tree. It was dark and fairly secluded, so we thought it'd be a nice, quiet place to fool around. As the DeSoto's windows began to fog up, a blue and red flashing light interrupted our exploration. I rolled down the window and got out my wallet to retrieve my driver's license, when Sue asked the police officer what the problem was. He said that the park was not in use after dark and we had to move on. Then he asked why we were there anyway.

Before I could open my mouth, Sue showed the officer her left-hand ring finger, which had a gold band on it, and said we had just gotten married and decided to stop here before heading to the reception.

The cop laughed and said that was a good one but perhaps we should carry on to the reception before we got into trouble. So we thanked the guy for his advice and said we'd do just that. I started the car and followed him out of the park and down to the Circle. We had a great laugh about how we "fooled" the cop, and after driving down the strip and around the Circle a few times, I took her home and went home myself.

Senior year was a busy time. We had to fill out applications for the various colleges and universities we wanted to attend, prepare for the senior prom, take the SATs, and score high enough to convince our choice colleges we were smart enough for them to accept us into their programs. I still worked at the State Theatre most weeknights after football practice, as well as sometimes being asked to stay late to fix a problem or two in the bathrooms or behind the food counter.

My first choice of a career was to be a pharmacist, but our guidance counselor informed me that my grades and SAT scores were not strong enough to get into a university that would prepare me for that kind of job. Not only that, but our family finances would not allow me to get into a private university without some kind of scholarship. I was hoping I'd get good enough as a football player to get one.

Here's a picture of the 1963 football team when I was a junior. We had a record of six wins and two losses. But the worst loss we had was to Phillipsburg on Thanksgiving Day, 9–0. The other loss was to a western Pennsylvania team, Altoona. They killed us, 34–6.

Football in my senior year was disappointing at first. I lost the starting center position to Stan, who was taller and heavier than me. However, I had a better long snap, and when we had to punt or kick an extra point, I replaced Stan. That is until one afternoon in History class. My history teacher was also our head coach, Mr. Rute. He decided to quiz me one day about what the center's assignments were for most of the offensive plays we had in our playbook. I aced the quiz. I knew what to do and how to do it, but I was only 175 pounds and light for a center. As far as being a linebacker, I was behind Chuck, a member of the Pennsylvania State Big 33 All-Star team for two years (he was also Big 33 in wrestling as well), and Steve.

After our second game, a loss to Neshaminy High School near Philadelphia, Mr. Rute told me I'd start the next game against Dieruff High School in Allentown. We won that game, and I remained the starter for the rest of the season. Our next game was against Altoona on their home field. They beat us again 34–6, but I thought I had a good game. Steve got sick, and I replaced him during the second quarter and went both ways for the rest of the game. Back then, it was common for players to play both defense and offense. So I got to live out a fantasy of mine—I mimicked Chuck, playing center and linebacker for my high school football team against one of the best high school teams in the country.

Altoona's fullback was a boy named Mike Reid. Boy, was that guy big and fast. The first time I tried to tackle him, I hit him square on—my left shoulder against his left leg—and I flew backward as he ran over me. I managed to hold onto his leg, but it took a few other guys to bring him down. On another play, I tried to tackle him with my right shoulder and got a sharp pain. I went out of the game and over to our trainer, Mr. Andrews. I told him what happened, and he told me to take off my shirt and shoulder pads. He looked at it and said that it was dislocated. He told me to hold it up as high as I could, then he forced it all the way over my head, put his fingers in my armpit, and slammed the arm down hard. I heard a "pop," and the pain went away. I got dressed again and played the rest of the game.

I'd like to take a little time now to speak about Mike Reid because I'm proud to have played against him. Mike went on to play college football at Penn State, where they moved him from fullback to defensive tackle. He was an All-American and won the Outland Trophy as the best college defensive lineman in his senior year. He then played professional football for the Cincinnati Bengals, where he won the Defensive Rookie of the Year award. He was also selected to the Pro Bowl two years in a row. Then tragedy struck—he got a knee injury and retired from the game in 1974.

But that was not the end of his story. He went on to become a classical pianist, composer, and recording artist. He won a Grammy Award in 1984 for a country song he wrote, "Stranger in My House," which Ronnie recorded. So I tackled one hell of a football player and one hell of an accomplished man. All of Pennsylvania should be proud of him, and I'm proud to have shaken his hand after the game.

Our next game was a tie against Eastern High School from York, Pa. We each scored a touchdown but missed the extra point. Our miss was my fault. We scored our touchdown near the end of the game. Our placekicker, Tony, lined up, and our quarterback, Scott, knelt seven yards behind me. The signal to snap the ball was Scott bringing his right hand from the tee toward me when Tony told him he was ready. I saw Scott's hand move, and I snapped the ball—right over his head and hit Tony directly on his helmet. You talk about being embarrassed. And my dad didn't let me forget it. He razzed my ass for the whole of the following week.

Bethlehem was next on our schedule, and it was a close game. In the second quarter, Chuck got a broken nose, and I replaced him on defense. The score was tied at that point, 6–6. I'll take this time to brag a little bit. I played the rest of the second quarter and the third quarter, going both ways again. I didn't make any mistakes on offense and made the block that allowed our halfback, Dave, to score the winning touchdown in the third quarter. My block was on the right-side linebacker on a 42 trap. Tony made a good kick for the extra point, and we went ahead by seven points, which meant Bethlehem had to make their extra point if they scored another touchdown—and their placekicker was bad.

On defense, I made ten tackles. I know because my cousin, Jimmy, was listening to the game, and every time my name was mentioned in a tackle—either alone or as part of a gang tackle—he made a mark. What I remember best is jumping over Steve, following their halfback trying to round the corner down the right sideline. I then dove at him, got him around his waist, and dragged him down for a loss. After the game, I felt like my hero Chuck must have felt after he knocked Frank of the New York Giants out of their game with a good clean tackle on the left sideline.

We won the game 13–6. Mizzero's Restaurant had a tradition—if Easton won their game on Friday night, the players could get a free cheesesteak and a Coke. So we all went up to the restaurant to get our freebie. I got a lot of pats on the back from Scott, Joe, Stan, and even Chuck that night and was so proud I thought my chest would break all the buttons on my shirt. Then, when I got home, Dad brought me back down to earth when he said, "Jesus, when Chuck got hurt and Coach Rute put you in, I thought the game was lost for sure." That's all he said.

I'll not bore you with the rest of our schedule, except to talk a bit about the Phillipsburg game on Thanksgiving Day. Like I said, this game is *the* game for both teams. The rivalry began in 1905 and has been played every year until 2020. The COVID-19 pandemic forced its cancellation. My dad played in two games—1926, a tie, and 1927, an Easton win, 20–13. I played in two games, 1962 and 1963, both losses. I was a starter in 1963 and played both ways for some of the game. At halftime, the score was tied at 6, and Coach Rute gave us a pep talk. I don't remember all of it, but some of what he said was that we were playing well and he was proud of us. Then our trainer, Andrews, told us that nobody had to be a hero for the game to be ours to win—we just had to do our jobs to the best of our ability.

In the second half of the game, they outscored us 27–0. There are two plays that are permanently etched in my mind. The first one happened in the fourth quarter, and P-Burg had the ball around our 40-yard line. They had about two yards for the first down, and we thought they were going to punt. So our return team, on which I played linebacker, went in. They lined up as if to punt, then switched to an offensive play at the last second. We went into our "prevent defense," where we all lined up between the gaps of the linemen and tried to rush through them. I got lucky and managed to squeeze through the tackle and end. Their running back was going around our left side, and I got a hand on his ankle. He went down for a loss. We got the ball back.

The second memorable play happened after we stopped them on their fourth-down play. It was a pass from Scott to Tim. Tim was covered well, but he jumped as high as I ever saw him jump, even when playing basketball, and caught Scottie's pass over the head of the defender.

Well, that's my high school football career. Not a lot to brag about, but I think I explained that I had a pretty good attitude about never giving up and always trying my best. I'm very happy that I got to share this athletic adventure with some wonderful men. Chuck got a full scholarship to North Carolina State College in football and wrestling. He graduated and went on to become a big-time college football coach with Florida State University and North Carolina State University. Scott became a letter carrier for the U.S. Postal Service. John graduated from Morgan State University, I think. Alfred got a full scholarship to and graduated from Lafayette University. Orlando started his own business in Martin's Creek and recently retired a very rich man. I don't know what happened to most of the other guys, but I'm sure they all did great things with their lives.

The official yearbook picture.

Graduation Decisions And Activities:

After football season, I concentrated on study and work. One of the more astute decisions I made in high school was to take Business Education as an elective. Actually, I took the course because the teacher was very pretty and had a habit of sitting on her desk, swinging her legs. Anyway, I learned a couple of filing systems and how to touch type. I became fairly good at that, typing 90 words a minute by the end of the course. This skill came in very handy after I was drafted and joined the Marine Corps.

I was still dating Sue; we spent a fair amount of time in the balcony of the State Theatre. Unfortunately, after I met her parents, they decided that I was not good enough for their daughter. For one thing, Sue was a member of the Honor Society and a straight "A" student. I got "C"s. Her parents were well off and had white-collar jobs. My father worked for the New Jersey Power and Light Company; we were working class. So, after a few more dates, she told me that we had to break it off. That was just after our Christmas vacation, during which she and her parents went south for a warm vacation. So, I began looking for another girlfriend.

Around March, my cousin Jimmy's girlfriend, LaNor, had a friend who went to Wilson High School and lived very near Mizzero's Restaurant. She persuaded Ursula Tucci to go on a blind date with me — actually, it was a double date with Jimmy and LaNor. You guessed it, we went to Mizzero's first for a cheesesteak, fries, and a Coke. There we decided to go to the drive-in theatre in Bethlehem, which was actually pretty close to where we were. I believe the movie was *Beach Party* with Annette Funicello and Frankie Avalon. Ursula and I were in the back seat of Jimmy's car, and Jim and LaNor were lying down in the front.

Ursula and I got along very well. We left Jim and LaNor alone and walked to the canteen to get some popcorn, candy, and soda. We had planned to share it with Jim and LaNor, but when we returned to the car, the windows were pretty steamed up, so we went back to the canteen and sat on the Adirondack chairs with a table between us, watched the movie, and shared some popcorn. Then Ursula shocked me by saying, "Why should they get all the fun?" So, we returned to the car and knocked on the window to ask permission to get in. Those two laughed at us and told us to come in and get comfortable.

We got into the back seat again and passed the treats up to Jim and LaNor. Then Ursula slid over next to me, I put my arm around her, and we kissed for the first time. Then we began the age-old teenage ritual of heavy petting. Again, Ursula kind of shocked me when, while I was massaging her nipples, she said, "When you do that, it's as if there is a wire that goes straight down there that gives off an electrical charge." So, I felt her down there, but she was wearing a panty girdle. I tried to convince her to go to the bathroom by the canteen and take it off, but she would not hear of going there alone. LaNor said she'd go with her, but when they returned, Ursula still had the girdle on — but no stockings. Wrist pain again!

Anyway, we dated off and on for the rest of the year, and I invited her to our senior prom. But before the prom, Easton held its All-Sports Banquet. I'm not sure exactly when this took place, but I think it was around the end of April after the Easter holiday. All the athletes who earned a Letter Sweater were invited to the banquet, which was held at the Hotel Easton — the classiest place in the city. I wasn't sure I'd be able to go since weekends are the busiest time for a movie theatre, but the manager of the State Theatre gave me that night off and told me to enjoy myself. I think he was told that it was necessary that I be there by someone. I'll never know who or if that was the reason.

I'm glad I went, because I was dumbfounded when Coach Rute began to explain how he was looking for a "pivot man" during the summer practice. Coach DiVietro suggested Stan because he was so much bigger than me, but Mr. Rute knew that Stan didn't understand his blocking assignments on many plays. Then he told the story of talking to me in History class, and I surprised him with my knowledge of the center's blocking assignments. At any rate, I was really surprised when I was awarded the trophy for *Most Improved Player of the Year!*

There were many other awards given out that night, and I'll list them all underneath the picture that was in the *Easton Express* newspaper. It's interesting that five graduates from Wolf Junior High School were presented with awards as well. The five winners from Wolf were: Scott (James V. Nobel Award), Alfred (Offensive Ability), John (Sportsmanship), David (Andrews Memorial Trophy), and me. This was the first time I got my picture in any paper, but not the last. I'm pleased to say that some were for athletic achievements and others for the work I did in my chosen profession. The picture was in the paper.

As proud as I was receiving that award, when I got home, my dad put my pride in perspective again by saying, "You didn't deserve that award."

In retrospect, I wish I had taken part in a number of other activities such as Future Teachers of America, Distributive Education (in which students may hold jobs for credit), Student Council, and perhaps auditioned for the school play. However, I chose to work and used that as my reason for not participating in other activities.

Following the Awards Banquet, we took our final exams, decorated the gym for the prom, and applied for and were fitted with our cap and gown for our graduation ceremony.

The senior prom went well, and my date, Ursula, was beautiful. We got a lot of stares from my classmates, and I was asked all kinds of questions about her.

Everybody was very nice, and Ursula was asked to dance by a number of my buddies. I looked around for Sue to get a dance with her, but I never found her.

I later discovered that she had left school early to go on a European vacation with her parents as her graduation gift. I haven't seen her since and don't know what happened to her. I went to our five-year class reunion, the 25th, 50th, and 60th, but nobody knows anything about her. Such is life.

A Shock:

After the prom, we were invited to a number of parties, but Ursula, being from Wilson, had to get home, so I took her home around midnight. Before doing that, I made arrangements with John (JR #1 to my JR #2), Mac, Scottie, and Joe to meet up at Mizzero's and hit the parties. Since I had to bring my dad's car home, Scottie agreed to pick me up, and I'd go to the parties with him and the other guys.

We were looking forward to going to Elise's party because all the cheerleaders, synchronized swimming team (all girls), and the majorettes were going to be there. We showed up and were greeted by Elise before we all got out of the car. She told us that Joe, Scott, and I were allowed in, but her father wouldn't allow either Mac nor JR in. So we said, "No Mac or JR? That's okay, we'll go find another one." And we did.

That was the first time I experienced any form of racism, but I didn't understand it, nor did I know what to call it. This was 1964, and there had been a fair amount of civil unrest and protest marches around the United States in support of the civil rights movement led by Dr. Martin Luther King. There was a filibuster by southern congressmen about the civil rights bill that Lyndon Johnson's Democratic caucus introduced, and it ended when they invoked cloture. So I assume that Elise's father was afraid we'd bring the civil rights movement into his home.

I forget where we went next, but we eventually met up with a group of graduates at a club in Kitnersville, which is south of Rieglesville on Route 611. This club had a swimming pool that was fed by a natural spring. Although it was June and very warm, the pool was cold. As I recall, most of us went in without a swimsuit. Actually, we were feeling no pain due to the various and copious amounts of alcoholic beverages we consumed. Truth be told, I don't remember how I got home or when I got home. But I'm sure I had a wonderful time.

CHAPTER 5:
COLLEGE - THE FIRST TIME

I went back to my job at the State Theatre. This summer, my big overtime job was to replace the linoleum tiles in the bathrooms. I got to work at 7:00 in the morning, tore up the old tiles, scraped the glue off the floor, and laid new tiles immediately. I only did a small area at a time so that the new glue on the new tiles would be dry enough to withstand the traffic during show times. I was done by 11:30, which was the time the canteen would begin getting set up. I'd go home, shower, eat, put on my usher's uniform, and get back to the theatre by 6:00 PM.

Some of the best movies I got to see again and again and again that summer were *Viva Las Vegas*, *Black Like Me*, *A Shot in the Dark*, *The Unsinkable Molly Brown*, *Good Neighbor Sam*, and *Marnie*. It was during this time that I met Christa Leidy. We met at the theatre, but she was there with her boyfriend. I thought she was BEAUTIFUL and spied on them during the movie they went to see. I guess you'd say I was a bit of a pervert at that time. I still dated Ursula on occasion, but after the prom date, we drifted away from each other.

Christa and her family lived in Bangor, Pa., but moved to Easton after her father was diagnosed with cancer. They sold their house and property in Bangor and moved into an apartment a couple of blocks from our house. While riding around on my bike, I saw her walking on Spring Garden Street and stopped to introduce myself. She was friendly, but obviously very worried about her dad, so I asked her if she wanted to get a snack at a nearby coffee shop and talk about her father. She agreed, and that was the beginning of a two-year relationship.

After I was accepted at West Chester, Kutztown, and East Stroudsburg State Colleges, I chose West Chester because it was the farthest from my home, and my neighbor, Jay, graduated from there in 1963. He was very fond of the college and convinced me that that was the best place to go to become a teacher. He also said the dormitories were fun and the cafeteria food was delicious. So that's where I decided to go.

I talked to my parents about paying the tuition, living in the dormitory, and eating at their cafeteria. I thought I'd have to get a loan from our local bank and Dad would have to co-sign for me, but Mom surprised me — big time! It seems that when I began to earn money and gave it to her for the household, she opened a savings account for me. She was putting half of what I gave her into that account since 1958. So in six years, she had saved up for me nearly $3,500.00. I didn't have to worry about finances — at least for the first year of college.

In August, we took our first drive down to West Chester to visit the campus and put my name in for a dormitory room. I also had a Super 8 movie of some of my better plays in football that Mr. Rute got for me. Actually, he made movies for anyone on his team who wanted to try out for college football. He also wrote an introductory letter for us. I was lucky enough to get a meeting with the West Chester head football coach. He watched the movie, told me that I missed summer practice, but if I was interested, I could "walk on" in the fall.

I thought I was being very early to apply for a dorm room, but I was really too late. Most of the rooms had been distributed at the end of the spring semester, so I was given a room in "off-campus" housing. We located the address and decided to see what the place was like. The owners of the house were Mr. and Mrs. McClintock. Their house was on Walnut Street, within walking distance of the campus. They rented out six rooms, four on the second floor and two in the attic. My room was at the top of the stairs, but there was another room that was occupied by a student who had to take classes in summer school. That man had to walk through my bedroom to get to his, but his room had the fire escape attached to it, and if there was a fire drill, we all had to trudge through his room.

At the end of August, I handed my resignation to the State Theatre manager, packed up a suitcase, and drove down to West Chester with my parents. I moved into the room at the top of the stairs, said good-bye to Mom and Dad, and walked to the campus to register for freshman classes.

Jay told me that the junior class had representatives who would wear a blue sailor's hat. They would greet us and show us around, but we were required to wear the frosh beanie called a "dink." They helped us with the registration process and then began the hazing ritual. They arranged "mixers" for us frosh, which were a combination of silly tasks — like wearing your dink inside out, crawling between the knees of the hazing group while they spanked your butt, dancing with people of their choosing, and doing all kinds of silly things. It was both fun and humiliating.

Jay also told me that he asked a friend of his to meet me and "look after" me. Well, his friend was an attractive girl who I'll call Linda. I do remember that she took me by the arm and led me around the quad, introduced me to other juniors and many freshmen and women. Then she helped me register for my classes and explained about scheduling. All in all, it was a wonderful experience and I felt very special.

Roommates — One Especially!

After the first day's mixer, I went back to my room and met some of the other men who were staying at the McClintocks'. Two were sophomores and the rest of us were freshmen. One sophomore was named Ira, and he played guitar. He introduced me to folk music and to Bob Dylan's protest songs. There was also a man named Walter, who was from Gettysburg, Bill, from Pottstown, and I cannot remember the fourth person's name. But the most interesting man there was Jim. Of course, the guys I met saw me with the junior girl and had all kinds of questions about my "conquest."

Jim was the man who had to go to summer school. I found out the reason for that is he got drunk one weekend and stood out on the roof of McClintock's house, lowered his slacks and underwear, and mooned the president of the college. Well, at least that was the story that was circulated by a couple of his contemporaries. He thought it was just good fun, but the police, his father, and the president of the college did not. Jim had a choice: leave the college immediately, forfeit his grades from the last semester, which he could make up during summer school, or be expelled. He chose summer school.

The first night spent in the McClintocks' home was exciting. I met all these men and listened to Ira play his guitar and sing. There was a refrigerator on the second floor next to the stairs that went to the attic. We filled it with snacks and soda. Around 11:00 PM, we were all fairly tired and began to get ready for bed. I was no different. However, the man who was staying in the room behind mine wasn't back yet, so I decided to stay awake, read the précis of my classes, and write up my class and social schedule and find the practice field so I could "walk on" and try out for the football team.

Around 1:00, Jim came bursting up the stairs and into the room. He walked through my room, never saying anything to me, carrying a shopping bag and a small pizza, which he threw on his bed. He came out of his bedroom again with the bag, walked down the hall, opened the fridge, rattled the bag, and returned to the room. It was then that I think he recognized that there was another person in the room — me. He looked at me and asked, "Want a beer?" No introduction, no "hi," just said, "Want a beer?" Naturally, I said sure, and he tossed one to me and walked back to the fridge and got one for himself. Yep, when I opened it, it made a bit of a mess, but it was cold and tasty. He sat down on my bed and began to tell me about living at the McClintocks'. He said they were a really nice couple and very parent-like. He said they enjoyed their "boys" watching television with them after supper and often made snacks. I really don't remember much more of that conversation, but I can tell you that when Jim begins to talk, you can't get him to shut up. I had another beer, and I begged off to get some sleep. That was how I met my longest-known friend, James. The year was 1964, and we still converse monthly via phone. Sad to say that he is in the first stage of dementia. Hard.

Wrong Size, Slow Learner, And Reward:

Now I was trying to be a walk-on football player and began going to practices in the afternoon. I worked out for a week in jeans and a t-shirt because they said they didn't have any more practice uniforms. I'm a slow learner, but I finally figured out that I was just too small for a college center and linebacker and not fast enough as a running back or defensive back. So I stopped trying out. OK, I gave up. Not pleased with it, but that's what happened. What also happened was that I discovered that college girls weren't that fond of panty girdles. That's all I have to say about that.

About a week after our first meeting, Jim came up with an idea that he shared with me. He suggested that we combine our two separate rooms to make an apartment-like situation. So we moved my bed and wardrobe into Jim's bedroom and his desk, record player, and other amenities into my bedroom and created a makeshift apartment. That was cool, and the other guys thought so as well. We began to have "study" sessions in our apartment, complete with refreshments—beer, that is. So we decided to haul the refrigerator from the hallway into our apartment. Now we had things really together.

Since our bedroom had the fire escape, we used that as another way to get into the house after hours. You see, the McClintocks had a curfew on us so they could lock up safely and go to bed, but Jim and most of the other guys liked to date and party. So abiding by the curfew was, ummm, iffy at best. Often we would be there to watch television with them, then they would lock up and we'd go upstairs. Then we'd leave by the fire escape and pick up our late date or hit the local pub or whatever evil we could get into.

The state college system had a requirement related to a student's grade point average (GPA) that the student had to meet in order to enroll for the next semester. I believe it was only for the first three semesters. The required GPA at the end of the first year was 1.75, the second year was 2.0. I don't remember if this accounting continued or not because, at the end of the fall semester in 1966, I had to quit. Three months later, I received a draft notice.

Partying And Doing Just Enough To Stay In School:

The courses you took were weighted as a 3, 2, or 1 credit course. As well, your mark was weighted on a descending scale beginning with A = 4 points, B = 3, etc. My first semester of my freshman year, I had a 2.0 cumulative average. The end of my second semester, I had a 1.84 cumulative average—good enough to return for the sophomore year. Because of our situation living at the McClintocks', we spent a lot of time partying, drinking, and sowing wild oats.

Jim and I became good friends and shared a lot of adventures. One adventure involved two of his friends who were going to the University of Pennsylvania, an Ivy League university located in Center City, Philadelphia. He took me down there to meet his high school fraternity mates. They both came from very wealthy families and had no problem with rent or tuition or anything else financially. Since neither of us had a car, we had to take a bus to the Philadelphia Port Authority, wait for a city bus, transfer to another bus, and walk a block to their apartment. My first time in their apartment, I saw two refrigerators—one had bottled beer, cold liquor, and snack food. The other had a full keg of beer. I was very impressed.

I saw a poster at West Chester advertising a concert at Penn by Joan Baez and Bob Dylan. When we got to Penn, I asked Jim's friends, Tillman and Bergdoff, if I could get tickets to attend. So they took me to their auditorium, and I paid $2.50 for a ticket to listen to Baez and Dylan. They were fantastic! I went alone because the other guys were "entertaining" girls in their apartment. After the concert, I went back to their apartment but saw no girls in the living room. However, there were three naked lovely ladies in the back rooms. They were feeling no pain and being very friendly. Ahh, college life is great.

Another time, Jim and I went to the Corner Bar to play darts, have a cheesesteak, and a few drafts. We played partner dart baseball against other college guys. We got on a roll and began winning beers. After a while, I got tired and a bit too drunk to continue. So I begged off and left to walk back to the house. Jim became livid and began calling me a bunch of names. While following me home, he pushed me in the back. Well, I was never a pushover. I had a number of fights in junior high and high school, so I challenged Jim to a fight. He took a swing at me, and I swung back. We fought off and on for about four blocks until we were almost back at the house. Jim then said he was going to finish me off. So when we got back into the room, I forced Jim out into the hall and closed the door to our "apartment" and barricaded it with furniture. I then locked the fire escape window, and Jim was forced to sleep someplace else.

The next day, Jim had a swollen lip, black eye, and sore hands. I had a large bite mark on my neck where he bit me; other than that, I was fine. Jim claims he won the fight because I was so afraid of him that I barricaded myself in our room. We shook hands and were the best kind ever since.

Later that year, Jim decided to drop out of West Chester at the end of his sophomore year and join the Army. He was having problems at home with his father, and I guess decided to get away and get some new experiences.

Trouble:

The summer months of 1965 were very eventful for our family. My uncle Ray, who was a nuclear physicist and working at the Atomic Energy plant in Los Alamos, New Mexico, was having personal problems.

My father, the patriarch of our family as the oldest male, decided to take a summer holiday with Mom and drive to New Mexico for a visit with his brother. That left me to fend for myself all summer.

Since I had some extra money and I needed a car to get to work, Dad helped me buy a Renault Dauphene. It was a small car, efficient, easy on gas and registered to me.

Christa and her family moved into the upstairs apartment of our neighbour, Lou Antonocci, and I thought that was really cool. I also had a new job as a replacement driver for the Cook Coffee Company.

This company had many drivers who had their own loyal customers and would visit them every two weeks. They had a basket that had the Cook specials displayed and sold them to their customers, then two weeks later delivered them and got new orders. Most customers had their favourite items, cake mixes, a particular type of coffee, dried fruit, cookies etc. During the summer months, the drivers were given a four-week vacation, to be taken in two week intervals. In order for this to work out, the company hired young men to be their substitute drivers for those particular routes. It was an easy job and paid very well. After the first month, I had earned enough money to pay for the first semester of my sophomore year. Life was good.

Christa's father was getting worse and she was really worried. She was worried about her family's finances and wanted to get a well-paying job. She thought being a stewardess would be the perfect job. After my father and mother left for New Mexico, I went over to help her with supper and make out a bit. After we got supper on the go and a little kissing, hugging and touching, Christa asked me to help her write a letter requesting a job as a stewardess with United Airlines. This was way before the internet and personal computers, so we got the phone book and looked up United Airlines offices at the Allentown, Bethlehem, Easton, ABE, Airport. She called and got the address for their main offices in Philadelphia. She then asked me if I knew how to write that kind of letter. I didn't, but had a couple of English composition books that promised to help. I went to get them.

After getting the most recent book, I returned to the Antonocci's and ran up the stairs two at a time. I made a racket, and Mr. Antonocci got angry and started yelling obscenities at Christa and me. I went down stairs to try and calm him down. I apologized for making so much noise. He then took me by my arm and showed me some plaster on the floor below the stairwell and said that I did that by running up the stairs. I again said I was sorry and promised to repair the hole that weekend. He seemed satisfied, and I thought all was well again.

I went back upstairs and was helping Christa with her letter when Mr. and Mrs. Leidy returned home from Mr. Leidy's doctor's appointment. When they walked in the door, Mr. Antonocci confronted them and vented his anger with me toward them. He called me a whore master, Christa a slut and accused me of wrecking his hallway. I went down and told Mr. Antonocci that if he had a problem with me to take it out on me and let the Leidys go up to their apartment. Antonocci then got real close to me, looked me in the eye and said, "I once thought you were a nice boy, but you a PIG." When he called me a pig, he spit in my face.

I saw red and pushed him away from me, hard. Mrs. Antonocci then grabbed my left arm, and I threw her off. She fell back and onto the radiator. Mr. came back at me and grabbed my throat with both hands, he had strong hands because he used to be a stone mason like my maternal grandfather, and started to choke me. I hit him in the ribs a few times, then hit him in his stomach. He let go of my throat and backed away.

While this was happening, Mrs. Leidy told Christa to call the police, which was done. When I was free from both of them, Mr. Leidy told me to go home and stay there. I did and called my parents in New Mexico to tell them what happened and ask for some advice. They said they couldn't get home to help me for at least a week, but to call a lawyer Dad knew and gave me his phone number. I said I would, but didn't bother to do so then.

About an hour later the police came to the door. I let them in and answered their questions about what had happened. My story, Christa's and the Leidy's were all pretty much the same, with some minor differences, but the Antonocci's story was entirely different. They said that I had broken into their home and caused damage, then attacked Mr. Antonocci. After that, I hit Mrs. Antonocci in the stomach and left in a hurry.

I guess the police believed my story, because if they bought the Antonoccis' story, I'd have been arrested for break and enter and assault. The police left and said that they'd get back to me, but for now to just go on with my normal life. The next morning, I got up, ate and went to work.

The Leidys came over to visit me and see how I was doing. They saw bruises around my neck, and Mrs. Leidy said that I should take pictures of them just to have proof that Mr. Antonocci tried to strangle me. I got my little brownie, and Christa took pictures of my neck. I had them developed and it was a good thing I had that evidence of his attack.

Before my parents got home, the Antonoccis sued me in civil court because the police and Easton's attorney general said there wasn't enough evidence to charge me due to the conflicting statements between them and the Leidys. So they sued me in civil court for damages. After my parents got home, they tried to talk to their neighbours, Mom spoke fluent Italian as did the Antonoccis', but they couldn't get them to stop the procedure.

So I went back to West Chester with that hanging over my head. I thought I'd need to have some extra money for civil court and got a job as a bagger at the local CoOp grocery store. Minimum wage and tips. I was taking 16 credits so I kept busy and cut way down on partying. But I did develop a fondness for harness racing. So did Walter and Ira, and since I had a car, the Renault, we used to go down to the Brandywine Race Track on Saturdays when I wasn't working and make small bets. Sometimes we won enough to pay for the trip down and back. More often we just broke even or lost a few dollars. It was fun. Until…

We piled into my car one Saturday mid-morning and took off toward Brandywine Race Track. About half way there near the Delaware State Line, my breaks became very soft. After stopping at a light, I kept pumping them, but eventually they went to the floor boards and I had NO breaks at all. So we had a decision, turn around and go back to West Chester or go on and enjoy the races. Since my hand brake worked, and since Walter, Ira, Bill and I were pretty big, we decided to use our feet to slow down enough until I could use the parking brake. I continued on, but didn't go any faster than 20 mph. Using the gears to begin slowing down well before a traffic light or congestion, we made it to the race track. Actually won some money and slowly made our way back to the McClintock's.

I took my car to a local service station and the mechanic there told me the brake fluid line probably had a leak in it. He said he could fix it and to leave it with him. I did and walked to work. After work, I walked back to the garage and got my car. Brakes fixed, I paid the mechanic and drove back to the McClintock's.

That October I got a letter that ordered me to be in Civil Court in Easton by a specific date and time. My parents got a copy of that letter and Dad got in touch with his lawyer friend again. We showed up in court with the Leidys' affidavits and the pictures of my neck. The Antonoccis told their story through an Italian interpreter, and it was close to what they told the police the night the incident happened. Then it was my turn and I told my story, showed the magistrate the Leidys' affidavits and the pictures of my neck. I thought I'd have to go back to school and return when the magistrate had made his decision, but he said his decision was clear cut.

He ruled in the Antonoccis' favour even though he did not believe their story. He said that I was 19, they were 59. I was in their home. I admitted to shoving Mrs. Antonocci off my arm and hitting Mr. Antonocci a number of times. Mrs. had bruises on her back and side and Mr. had a broken rib, both confirmed by a doctor's report. He said that although I had been provoked, I was wrong to have struck out. So he ordered me to pay them 1000.00 plus court costs. I had the second semester's tuition money, so paid up.

The Draft: When I got back to West Chester, I found a second part time job to try and save up for the next semester's tuition and board, but found it too difficult to keep up with the classes and both jobs, so I sold my car and decided to take a semester off to save up for the rest of my college education. After the winter semester of 1965, I didn't register for the Spring semester of 1966 and got a job with the Cook Coffee Company again. Back then if you were a United States male citizen, you were required to do two years' military service. It was called The Draft. In May I was sent my draft notice.

Once you get your draft notice, each of the armed forces send you recruitment pamphlets. The Army offered a two years' active duty, 2 years of active reserve in which you have to go to an annual training camp for 2 months as well as weekend meetings and if the Vietnam war escalated, you would be the first group to be recalled, and two years of inactive reserve, during that time you basically are free to do what you want.

The Navy offered three years of active duty, one year of active reserve and two years of inactive reserve.

The Air Force offered three years of active duty, but you could choose the type of job training you preferred, and three years of active reserve.

The Marine Corps offered two years of active duty and four years of inactive reserve. Since the Vietnam war was escalating again, and I was sure I'd be one of the guys sent over there, I wanted to get the best fighting training I could get. I was sure that would be the U. S. Marine Corps, so I enlisted in them, and in May I received orders to report to the bus station in Philadelphia for transport to Paris Island, South Carolina.

CHAPTER 6:
THE U. S. MARINE CORPS

Shock Treatment:

If you've seen the movie *Full Metal Jacket*, and wondered if young men were actually treated like that after they got off the bus in Paris Island, South Carolina, stop wondering. In my experience, the bus ride to Paris Island was fine, but as soon as we went through those gates, all hell broke loose. A large drill instructor, whose name I never learned, got on the bus right after it stopped and shouted that for the next 3 months our asses were his. He gave us 30 seconds to get off the bus, find the yellow feet on the ground and stand in one set of them and the time started right after he stepped off.

We scrambled to get off the damned bus as quickly as we could and looked for the yellow imprints of feet. That was difficult as there was only a few street lights illuminating the staging area and it was around 3:30 in the morning. He told us we were slow as molasses and ordered us to do push-ups until we were marched into the Recruit Receiving Building. In there, we presented our orders to them and then were assigned to a platoon and met our leading drill instructor. I was assigned to First Battalion, Platoon 199 and our Chief DI was M/ Sgt Wood.

From there, M/Sgt Wood led his platoon to the barber shop and all of us got all our hair shaved off. Then we were marched (kind of) to the clothing centre where we were fitted with boots and provided with two utility uniforms skivvies, thick socks and boots. We had to remove our civilian clothes and put on our utility uniforms, including our socks. Our civvies were packed up and we wrote our mailing address on the label.

Our feet were carefully measured for length and width, we put on our socks and then tried on the boots given to us. If they were too big, they were replaced. If they were too small, they were replaced. We had no say in whether they were too big or too small. The marines who issued the boots were skilled at feeling the recruits' feet while sitting and standing and they decided on the proper fit. I must say, my boots were perfect and I used them for years after mustering out of the service. From there we were given a thorough medical examination including an eye exam (and issued appropriate glasses right there on the spot), had X-rays taken, and inoculated for typhoid fever and I don't know what else.

Next came the bucket and rifle issue. In each bucket was your shelter half, mess kit, knapsack, tent poles and stakes. The rifle we were issued was an M14, which was considered the worst military rifle ever used. However, that's what we trained with.

M/Sgt Wood introduced us to S/Sgt Mullins, who would be our senior DI. He was the DI who actually trained us from then on. He had the help of three other DIs: second in command, Sgt Young, DI Shrewsberry, and DI Lowyns. From there, we marched to our barracks and were assigned a bunk and bunkmate. There were footlockers at the end of each bunk bed, which corresponded to which bed you got. Then we were shown how to make our beds "The Marine Corps Way" and told to make up our bunks for inspection.

The Marine Corps Way was how we lived our lives for the next three months. The bottom sheets had to have hospital corners, top and bottom. The top sheet and blanket had to have hospital corners on the bottom as well, but at the head, the top sheet had to be folded over the blanket six inches.

A Break—Sort Of—And Games(?):

We were then given a bathroom break. I had been on a bus from Philadelphia for close to 12 hours—bathroom toilets are all right, but very uncomfortable—taken through the recruitment center, barber shop, given clothing, marched to the barracks, given the bunk assignments, bed making, then, and only then, provided with the opportunity to relieve myself. Think about this: 80 young men had about 30 minutes to get in the bathroom, do their business, and get back in front of the bunk standing at attention waiting for the next order.

The bathrooms were huge. Forty sinks, forty urinals, forty commodes, and forty shower heads in the shower stall. There was no room for any kind of modesty. In comparison, bus toilets were very comfortable.

By the time our bathroom break was over, it was time to begin training for real. Those of us who smoked had to turn in our cigarettes, and no smoking was allowed. We were assembled onto the parade grounds outside the barracks, and our drill instructors had us line up according to height. Then they had us line up four deep and showed us the Marine Corps way to stand at attention—stomach in, chest out, feet at 45-degree angles, thumbs parallel and touching the seam in your trousers. The DIs used to say, "Make that chest touch my hand!" and they held their hand about six inches from your chest.

I'll never forget that session. I used to joke with some girlfriends after I got out of the Marines that I'd teach them how to stand at attention and use the same phrase, "Stomach in, chest out; come on, make that chest touch my hand!" It was a joke, of course, but I got some fun reactions after saying that, and sometimes one would make her chest touch my hand. Hehehehe.

Sgt Young took charge of teaching us the Marine Corps way to march, and the games began. We were marched over to the chow hall and stood at attention until DI Shrewsberry told DI Young how long our wait to get breakfast would be. So DI Young decided that this would be a good time to get started with our exercise routine: bends and thrusts, push-ups, heels off the ground six inches and hold them there, jumping jacks, and finally sit-ups. By the time we had done all of those, we were READY for breakfast—whatever it might be.

We all had heard stories about how bad the food was—powdered eggs, SoS (shit on a shingle), which was chipped beef and white gravy on white toast (actually not bad), raw potatoes, etc.—but I found that the food was very good. Nothing powdered until we were on bivouac and didn't have access to fresh food from the base.

After we lined up, Sgt Young walked alongside us and sized us up, pinching the sides of some of us, and if he got a large enough amount of side fat, he'd order us to the "fat-body" line. I was one of them. Now I was nearly six feet tall and weighed 175 pounds, but I always had, and still have, "love handles," or as my mother-in-law used to call them, "schnabbies." So I was placed in the fat-body line.

The eating rule in the Marines was "take all you want, but eat all you take." That was for the "normal" guys, but we fat-bodies could only have one portion of what was on the menu, i.e., breakfast: one scoop of scrambled eggs, two pieces of bacon, one toast, one milk, one juice, one coffee without sugar or cream. Lunch and dinner always had fruit and cottage cheese, and we were allowed to have two servings of that after our meal. Oddly enough, I wasn't hungry after eating, but I wasn't losing any side body fat either.

After a couple of weeks, S/Sgt Mullins came over to me while I was waiting in the fat-bodies line and asked me what I was doing there. Now, in boot camp, you were not permitted to speak without first asking permission, so I said, "Permission to speak, sir."

S/Sgt Mullins said, "I asked you a fuckin' question, didn't I? So answer the damned question."

I told him that Sgt Young placed me there on our first day. S/Sgt Mullins grabbed me by the arm and hauled me over to the regular food line. So that was that.

The Routine:

So every day went something like this, with variations depending on which point we were in our training.

Reveille at 05:30, the platoon gets out of bed, makes the bed, lines up to shave and go to the bathroom (the three Ss), gets dressed, falls in formation, and stands at attention until the DI gives an order. At 06:15, close order drill begins, sometimes double time, depending on the temperature. At Parris Island, if the temperature got over 90°F, double time was prohibited.

At 06:45, we stood in formation to line up at the mess hall for breakfast. Calisthenics were usually done at that time, always holding your rifle. From 07:30 to 08:30, breakfast was followed by close order drill to whichever classroom your lessons were scheduled for that morning.

From 08:30 until 12:00 were classroom lessons, which consisted of military language (acronyms), various Marine Corps ranks and how they differed from other military branches, how to disassemble, clean, and reassemble a .45 caliber handgun and the M14 rifle, and Marine Corps history.

At 12:00, we marched to lunch and did the same routine as breakfast. After lunch, we marched to our barracks for a short rest. At 2:00, it was back to the parade grounds for close order drill. From 3:00 to 5:00, we trained in hand-to-hand combat, bayonet drills, Physical Readiness Test training, fighting with pugil sticks, the obstacle course, and other activities. Then it was back to close order drill and waiting for supper—same as for all meals.

After supper, there was more close order drill, then back to the barracks for a little rest and what they called "relaxation." During the week, that meant taking showers, cleaning and polishing our boots and brass belt buckles, reading, chatting with platoon mates, and getting ready to sleep. At 10:00, lights out—and welcome bedtime. Of course, there were days when many of us didn't wait that long.

The weekends were a little different. There were no classes, but we still did PE and close order drill on Saturdays, as well as polished our brass and boots. Sundays were completely a day of rest. Church services were offered but not required, and we wrote letters home and received our mail.

After we'd been in training for three weeks, that Sunday, DI Young said something like this: "You swinging dicks who want to smoke again, the smoking lamp is lit. Get your bucket and line up out back." Many of us did—around 50 men or so. We were placed in a circle, and the DI sent every fifth man to fill his bucket with sand and place it in front of him. Then two men on each side formed a smaller circle.

The DI handed out cigarettes and lighters to each five-man team and told us we'd be smoking "by the numbers." We were ordered to remain at attention and light up. On 1, we placed the cigarette in our mouths. On 2, we drew in. On 3, we inhaled. On 4, we exhaled. He practiced the numbers with us— "1, 2, 3, 4. Got it?" Easy enough. Oh, did the nicotine taste good.

Then he began again: "1, 2, 3... 4. 1, 2, 3... 4. 1, 2, 3... 4." You get the idea. By the third round, men started coughing, vomiting, getting dizzy, falling out of attention, and generally stopping. I was determined not to stop, to beat the DI at his game. I'm sorry to say that I did. I would have been much better off if I had gotten sick and quit that habit when I was 19. I didn't—and I've been suffering from COPD since I turned 50.

Variations To The Routine:

Also during the third week of basic training, we began conditioning marches. These were anywhere from five to ten miles after breakfast, a break from classroom sessions. Really, the classroom sessions became fewer and fewer as conditioning and combat training began to take over.

We spent days practicing tent pitching, hand-to-hand combat, fighting with bayonets (using pugil sticks to actually hit each other), close order drill, and doing calisthenics to build strength and endurance.

June began with our platoon doing double time conditioning marches and preparing for the bivouac at Elliot's Beach. For this phase of training, we packed all our gear into and on our knapsacks. We then went on a long conditioning hike that lasted about six hours.

When we got to Elliot's Beach, we paired off with our bunkmates and pitched our tents. That was done by buttoning our half tents together, overlapping the top to fend off any rain that might come. Then we assembled the tent poles we were given upon arrival, tied our guy ropes to the poles, and used our spades as hammers to drive in the tent pegs. Success—that was where we'd be sleeping for the next two nights.

We had to disassemble and reassemble our rifles blindfolded, practice first aid as if our fellow Marines were wounded in combat, learn how to dig foxholes properly—umm, I mean "the Marine Corps way"—prepare and eat K-rations, and go through the Confidence Course.

This was an obstacle course beefed up to king size. We had to climb up a 20-foot log ladder where each rung was about 3.5 feet apart, then descend on the opposite side. There was another kind of ladder made of logs that were about five feet apart but only had three rungs. You jumped up to the first rung, threw your leg over, and somehow got to stand up so you could jump to the next. Once you reached the top, you had to roll over, hold on, and drop 15 feet to the ground.

Next came a similar climb, but this time using a rope to get to the first rung. You climbed up three more rungs spaced about three feet apart, then up a ladder that started wide and narrowed to about a foot at the top. You had to lay over the top rung after climbing, grab another rope, and slide down to the ground. Two of the most difficult obstacles were saved for the end. One was a simple looking inclined climb of about 20 feet in height. This time the rungs were made of steel bars and were about 4 feet apart. The first thing you did was pretty easy, climb to the top with the incline facing toward you. Then you had to swing over and climb down with the incline facing away from you. That is more difficult that it seems when describing it, believe me.

The last one was the most difficult obstacle and began with another rope climb, hand over hand until you got to the top of a 60-foot structure, then go the other side and slide down a rope that traversed a pond from 60 feet up to 4 feet on the other side of that pond. You were required to begin sliding down the rope head first, until you reached a knot on the rope. Then you changed position by rolling under the rope and continue head first, but backward. Then you had to change your hand hold by twisting your wrists and arms, let go of your feet and hang down facing the opposite shore. Swing your feet back onto the rope and continue to the next knot on the rope where you were to let go of your foot hold and finish the traverse hand over hand to drop to the ground.

Rifle Training And Birthday Joy? Oh No:

The third week of June, we went to the rifle range. Now, my birthday is July 1st, and I wrote to Mom after our Elliot's Beach training that for my birthday present I'd really like to have 86 Polar Bars, one for each member of the platoon. Mom complied but had to send them in two separate batches.

After supper on July 1, 1966, the DI on duty that day, I think it was Sgt Young, called my name to the front of the barracks. He said something like, "So today's your birthday, hmm? Well here's your present," and he handed me a package my mother sent. I opened it, and there were 48 Polar Bars—not enough for everyone.

Sgt Young then told me to get my canteen and empty the GI can, a huge garbage can, and bring it into the barracks. When I returned, he told me to fill up my canteen with water. I did. He then told me to turn the GI can upside down and get underneath with my canteen. I did. Then he took all the candy and slid it under the GI can and ordered me to eat it all because, since there wasn't enough for everybody, I must be a selfish pig. "If you're a pig," he said, "then you can eat all of it yourself," or something close to that. I don't remember the exact words.

Then he continued with mail call. I ate a couple of bars and drank a bit of water, then heard one of the guys slap the floor. I figured that the DI must have left the barracks and returned to his office, so I picked up the side of the GI can nearest the bunks and began to throw the candy out. I heard scrambling and one of the guys said, "Keep it going. We'll return the wrappers for you to show Sgt Young."

So that's how that first delivery of the candy was taken care of. I was under the GI can for about two hours and was dying to take a piss, but I couldn't leave without the DI's permission. I asked one of the men to see if he could get the DI to come back and check on my progress, which was good—I didn't have any bars left, only a bunch of wrappers.

Sgt Shrewsberry came into the barracks and told me to get up and present the wrappers. I did, and he said, "OK, clean up your mess." I asked permission to speak and was given permission, so I asked him if I could "hit the head ASAP?" He smiled and said, "After I police the area." I was very fast in cleaning up the mess. Got in the head and promptly pissed, then threw up.

The next day, Saturday—thankfully—S/Sgt Mullins was on duty when the other package arrived. When he presented it to me, he said, "Didn't you get a package yesterday?" I said I had. He then asked, "Why are you getting another today?" I explained that my mother must have sent them separately due to the size and weight. He then told me to get my bayonet, cut them in half, and share them with the platoon. All I can say about S/Sgt Mullins is that he was really tough but reasonable. Unlike Sgt Young, who I believe was sadistic.

The two weeks spent at the rifle range were very important. We learned the various shooting positions and practiced getting into them with our rifles—but without bullets. We also did rifle calisthenics and, sometimes, rifle punishment.

The M14 weighed 11 pounds, and as punishment, we were required to hold them out straight, elbows locked. It didn't matter how strong you were; your shoulders could only hold that position for a few minutes before gravity took over. Believe me, we had some very strong men in our platoon. One guy did 75 push-ups in one minute, and another man could bench-press different men of various weights 20 or more times. He once tried out for the Pittsburgh Steelers and benched 250 pounds 26 times in one minute. So they were as strong as oxen—but gravity still forced their arms to fall.

The shooting positions were kneeling, sitting, prone and standing. For me, the most difficult position to get into and remain there was the sitting position. In this position one sat on your foot, the right foot if you were right handed, left foot if left handed. Your opposite leg was bent at the knee and you braced your opposite elbow against that knee. Your rifle strap was wound around the shooting arm to help stabilize your aim. From this position, you were supposed to fire rapidly. The recoil of the rifle would rock you back a little, then you'd return to the original position and fire sitting position again. If you were seated correctly and the aim was good the first time, the rest of the shots would follow suite. That was the theory, anyway. It didn't work for me.

The next very difficult position for me was kneeling. This was very similar to the sitting position, except you didn't sit on your foot, you knelt back on the heel of your boot. The opposite position and elbow placement was the same and, again, you were supposed to be able to shoot rapidly. I was better at this position, but still not great.

The easiest position was the prone position, but from this position you fired at the target from the longest distances; 500 yards and then 300 yards. The standing position was just that. You stood side on to the target, wrapped the strap of your rifle around the shooting arm, rested your elbow on the stomach, and held your trigger arm high, aimed and fired.

What is stated underneath this picture of the standing firing position is a kind of prayer about your rifle. The first paragraph says, "This is MY RIFLE. There are many like it, but this one is mine. My rifle is my best friend. It is my life. I must master it as I master my life."

As you can see by the first paragraph above, being qualified as a marksman in the Marine Corps was extremely important. To qualify, a recruit was required to get a score of at least 170 points. You could qualify as an Expert shot with a score between 200 and 250, which was a perfect score. A Sharpshooter classification meant a score between 190 and 200.

To score points, you fired at the target from 200, 300, and 500 yards. You had to hit the bullseye to score 5 points. If you missed the bullseye, which was a black circle 10 inches in diameter when shooting in the prone position from 500 yards away, your score decreased depending on how far you missed the bullseye. If you missed the target altogether, you got 0 points. Every time you fired a shot, the man in the butt detail for your range placed a white circle on the bullet hole, and the DI keeping your score marked the amount it was worth on your score sheet.

You had two targets at 300 yards and were required to shoot 5 rounds sitting and kneeling, slow fire, which meant a shot fired every 10 to 15 seconds, then 10 rounds of rapid fire in the kneeling position. At 200 yards, you fired 10 rounds of standing slow fire and 10 rounds of rapid fire in a sitting position. Rapid fire targets were different from slow fire targets in that they were shaped like the top half of a human and were generally larger. Hitting the black meant 5 points, with fewer points awarded the farther away you were from the black.

To graduate from boot camp, every recruit had to qualify at least as a Marksman. Those who didn't were sent to remedial rifle training and remained there until they achieved the required score—or returned to day one of basic training.

An interesting aspect of being at the rifle range was that from that point until graduation, physical training (PT) was done with the rifle. Climbing the rope—30 feet up, ring a bell, and descend—now included the additional 11 pounds of your rifle. Going through the obstacle course also included carrying the M14. These exercises were designed to build strength and stamina to pass the Marine Corps Physical Readiness Test (PRT). Every recruit had to pass both the PRT and rifle qualification to graduate from boot camp. We were also taught and repeatedly practiced the manual of arms.

Kitchen Patrol Duty And Extra Training:

Another part of rifle range life was Kitchen Patrol, or K-P duty. That meant cracking eggs for breakfast, peeling potatoes, dicing onions, peeling and cutting vegetables, and cleaning up after meals. During K-P, you ate first—and fast. Cleaning up after meals meant washing trays and silverware, but most importantly, sanitizing GI cans with hot, soapy water, then blasting the insides with a steam hose. In the summer heat of South Carolina that meant getting hot and sweaty in record time.

When 20 men from your platoon had K-P duty, the other 60 got additional weapons training with the .45 caliber handgun and the 7.65 machine gun. We didn't just learn to shoot them—we learned to field strip, clean, and reassemble them.

When firing the .45 handgun, you were told to grab your wrist with your opposite hand and hold tight. The reason was the kickback. We had one guy who thought he was strong enough to shoot one-handed—yep, the same pro-football tryout guy. He ended up with a bloody lip for that effort and some harsh teasing from both the DIs and the rest of us.

After the weeks spent at the rifle range, we marched back to our main base and prepared for final tests and inspection. Now, the preparation was more competitive—not against each other, but against other platoons.

The most fun competition was called the Field Meet. There were races of all kinds. Push-up competitions matched you with a recruit from another platoon to see how many repetitions you could do in one minute. To count as one push-up, your counterpart lay on the ground in front of you with his fist under your chest as you got into position. He started the stopwatch and counted out loud the number of times your chest hit his hand. No touch, no score.

Tent-pitching competitions tested which team could pitch their tent the fastest, starting from the time the tent and gear were packed in the knapsack until it was fully up and standing on its own.

Then there were the relay runs. One was the standard baton relay—carry a baton, run 400 yards, pass it to the next man, and so on until a mile was completed. The team who crosses the finish line first wins. In the very difficult one, your partner, usually one who weighed the same as you, laid on the ground 50 yards away. At the sound of the starting pistol, you ran to your partner, picked him up and hoisted him into a fireman's carry and ran back to the starting line.

Another relay, was where the members of your team one after the other, run 25 yards to a baseball bat laying in a circle. You pick up the bat, place your forehead on the handle and run in a circle three times before returning to the starting line and passing off to the next in line. Believe me, you did get disorientated with the circular movement and were running on wobbly legs back to your teammates.

Graduation Prep:

Although these competitions were fun, we didn't realize that our placing would be counted toward awards the platoons could win, mostly for our Drill Instructors and their superiors. During the last week of our boot camp, we had to prepare for three very important tests: The Physical Readiness Test, Close Order Drill, and Final Inspection. The PRT consisted of five exercises. All of these had to be done with a full pack and rifle, so we were carrying an additional 20 pounds while doing them. I don't remember the exact order in which we completed the exercises, except that the 3-mile run was last.

#1 – The Sprint:

It was a 100-yard sprint, but it wasn't done in a straight line. You had to zigzag as if on a battlefield, drop to the ground and roll over when the referee blew his whistle, then get up and continue. We had 30 seconds to complete this test, which might sound like plenty of time, but with the extra 20 pounds, the zigzag running, and the drop-and-rolls, I really struggled to make it. A few of my platoon members had to redo this part of the test.

#2 – The Rope Climb:

You had 36 seconds to climb up a 30-foot rope, ring the bell, and return to the ground. This one wasn't very difficult because the ropes had knots tied in them that you could use as footholds. Nobody failed this test.

#3 – Step-Ups:

On a concrete block approximately three feet high, you had to complete 60 step-ups in 45 seconds. It sounded easy, but near the end, it took real effort to keep the pace.

#4 – The Buddy Carry:

As described earlier, your buddy was 50 yards downfield, lying on the ground with his rifle next to him. At the whistle, you got up from the prone position, ran in a zigzag pattern carrying your rifle to your buddy, picked him up in a fireman's carry, grabbed both rifles, and ran back to the starting line. We had one full minute to complete this, and most of us needed at least 55 seconds. This one was very difficult, especially since it usually came right before the final test.

#5 – The 3-Mile Run (In Formation):

The platoon had 36 minutes to complete the run. It sounds like a lot of time, but since this was the last exercise and everyone was exhausted, we usually needed the full 36 minutes. The time started with the referee's whistle and ended when the last member of the platoon crossed the finish line. We all made it. The platoon with the lowest total time in the 3-mile run was the winner of that contest.

Close Order Drill:

Close order drill was another competition, and it was the one our Senior Drill Instructor, S/Sgt Mullins, cared about most. That's why we marched everywhere—to every class and activity. Even when we were running double time, he insisted we stay in step and in perfect line. Let me tell you, if those lines didn't stay straight, the whole platoon stopped. The recruit who fell behind or moved too fast was singled out, and everyone did bends and thrusts for however long the DI decided. Sometimes it was five minutes, sometimes less—you never knew.

The judging for this competition was purely subjective and done by the four Battalion Commanders. Platoon 199 was in the First Battalion, and our Commander was Lt. Col. Perrich. I don't know the names of the other three Battalion Commanders, but they were all on the parade grounds during the competition. The winning platoon in close order drill was awarded the Bronze Boots. We won! We also won the trophy for the most victories in the Field Day competition.

Final Inspection:

Final inspection was held the day before graduation. It was done by Lt. Col. Perrich and Capt. Mossey, the Company Commanding Officer. Getting ready for it was something else. Our rifles had to be spotless and gleaming, our shoes spit-shined, and our brass polished until it sparkled. One final detail—our ties had to be tied in a full Windsor knot and perfectly centered under the collar. The DIs made sure of it.

We were all perfect—except for one man. Zills couldn't keep his tie centered no matter how hard he tried. The CO actually straightened it for him during the inspection. We all passed!

Drill Instructors

The picture is our official platoon picture. You can see the bronze boots to the left of S/Sgt Mullins and the PRT trophy to his right.

After the final inspection, you officially became a U. S. Marine. Then it was family day.

During this time, there was a review parade, awarding of promotions for the best of each platoon; they graduated as Private First Class or PFC. All of us others were Privates or Pvt and remained at that rank until we got to our duty station.

My parents came down to Paris Island for my graduation from Boot Camp and took a couple of pictures. We were not permitted to go off base as yet, but our parents could share time with us in the camp. They got to watch our review parade and witness the award ceremony.

My father took some pictures of the Review Parade, and after we were dismissed, I took them on a bit of a tour of the facility: the museum, the statue of the raising of the US Flag on Iwo Jima, and the barracks area.

Platoon 199 marching in the review and a picture of me and my bunk mate, Billie Rogers, in front of the Iwo Jima statue.

Learning How To Kill - In Many Ways:

Although the 13 weeks of boot camp at Paris Island was over, our training was still incomplete. Next stop was to Camp Lejeune in North Carolina for the Infantry Training Regiment (ITR). This was another 8 weeks of training, specifically training to fight as an infantry man.

The training here was similar to that at Paris Island with one major exception, there was "live fire" experience. The classroom instruction was fairly limited, we were taught hand signals that were used in the field of battle, how to care for and make simple repairs to your field phone, and various battle positions.

The hands on instruction continued with hand to hand combat, but with a twist, on patrols, other Marines would ambush you and you were supposed to fight them off and 'kill' them. One Marine asked the DI, "What do you do if a Viet Cong drops down on you from a tree?" The answer, "Turn your head and bite the prick's thigh or his cock if you can get to it. He'll get off you pretty damn quick!" That was the first time we were taught that in war, hand to hand combat is "no holds barred." Bite, scratch, poke eyes, pull off ears, pry open nostrils, all of that is what you do to stay alive. Some interesting facts came out of these experiences. It only takes 7 pounds of pressure to pull off an ear, 5 pounds of pressure to put your thumb into a eye socket and pop the eye out. If you get a throat hold, with 15 pounds of pull, your enemy's larynx can be removed. Yep, they really tried to turn you into a killing machine.

Some of the training was really harsh. We got to wear gas masks, first to try them on and learned how to make them fit properly. Then we wore them in barn like structure and the DI in charge set off a tear gas capsule. We learned that they kept your eyes, nose and taste buds in good shape. Then after the barn was cleared of the gas, we went back in without our gas masks on. We carried them in our hands. When the DI set off the tear gas capsule, we had to clear the mask by blowing into it as hard as possible, then place it on our face, adjust it and only then were we allowed to leave the barn. Let me tell you, tear gas if awful. You feel as if your eyes would swell shut, your nostrils burned like hell and there was a taste left in your mouth that was like nothing I can describe. It was terrible!

Another aspect of ITR was to learn about hand grenades. You know how in the movies the military hero pulls the hand grenade pin with his teeth and throws it like a pitcher directly into the pill box?

That's maybe not impossible, but extremely difficult; actually, you'd probably lose a tooth. Also they're heavier than you think, which is why they are heaved toward the object with a stiff elbow. Accuracy isn't really necessary because of all the shrapnel that's built in and surrounds the explosive. Also, after you pull the pin, there is a small handle that you keep closed, if that is released, you have 10 seconds to get it away from you.

We learned how to throw them by being in a hole surrounded by sand bags. You pulled the pin with the opposite hand from which you'd throw it over the sand bags toward a shell of a vehicle. After you pull the pin, you stand and throw it. The handle will detach itself just over the bags, and you duck down, because the shrapnel will fly in a 365-degree circle, coming back toward you as well. After the explosion, which is LOUD, you count to 15 then get up to see how far the damned thing went. Most of us got it about 20 feet away.

During these 8 weeks of this intense training on how to fight an enemy and care for your fellow Marines, we were tested to see in what job we might best serve the Corps. We were asked if we had any special skill, and I wrote that I knew how to touch type. So at one point during ITR, those of us who said we had a skill were removed from the platoon and questioned about our skill. I was given a typing test to see if I was lying or not. They found that I could type at 65 words a minute and noted that. (In high schooolmI was at 90 WPM). Here I am after ITR, taken at the Camp LeJeune statue of Iwo Jima. Turns out that all the Marine Corps training bases have a version of this statute.

So after these intense 8 weeks, we had another graduation ceremony. My parents didn't come down for this one, which was too bad because after this training we got a furlough, two weeks of vacation. Naturally I took the bus to Easton, my family and Christa.

Above is our graduating picture from Camp Pendleton. I'm in the 3rd row, 5th from the left. Herman is not in the picture, wonder why.

A Holiday And On To The Next Training:

However, before going to my permanent duty station, I was given another furlough—three weeks this time. So at the end of October, I flew back home for another holiday. This time I brought a couple of souvenirs from Disneyland for my nieces and nephew, and a gift for my sister, whose birthday is October 30. The vacation wasn't very eventful, and soon I was getting ready to return to Camp Pendleton for my flight to Hawaii. This time, I had to pay for my own transportation to and from Pennsylvania. Fortunately, I still had some money saved from the tuition work I'd done earlier, as well as from barely spending much of the $96 monthly pay I earned as a Private.

Hawaiian Experiences:

I remained at Camp Pendleton for a few weeks, working as a clerk/typist in the unclassified office there until my MOS was required in a company that was part of the 1st Marine Brigade. My orders came through in mid-December 1966, and I boarded a Marine Corps C-130 transport plane with about a hundred other Marines. We spent the next four hours flying over the Pacific Ocean toward Hawaii. It was thrilling. We landed at Hickam Field, Joint Air Base, Pearl Harbor. After deplaning and collecting our baggage—basically a single duffle bag big enough to hold all our Marine Corps uniforms—we climbed aboard a bus headed for Kaneohe Bay.

I was to be one of the 14,000 Marines sent to Vietnam, and I'll admit, I was scared. Still, I was ready to accept my orders. Besides, as a personnel clerk, I figured I'd likely be sitting behind a desk surrounded by filing cabinets rather than out in the field with an infantry unit. It was around December 20 or 21—can't say for sure which. We reported to the CO, were assigned our barracks and bunks, and then… nothing. For the next few days, we just waited. Finally, our CO told us we could have the next few days off to see the sights if we wanted to. He warned us, though, that Hawaii was an expensive place to visit. Since it was Christmas weekend, I got my pass, changed into civvies, and packed a few essentials—shorts, a swimsuit, underwear, and flip-flops—into my knapsack. Then I headed for Waikiki Beach in Honolulu. I was a 20-year-old, horny young Marine who wanted to see the beautiful women in bikinis that everyone said crowded the beach. This time, there was no military bus to drop me off, so I walked off base and hitchhiked. I got a ride pretty quickly, which took me to the Pali Lookout. All I can say is that Hawaii has the most lush, breathtaking greenery I've ever seen.

From there, a couple who had rented a car offered me a lift all the way into Honolulu, to the hotel where they were staying. They were kind people, and once we arrived, I figured I'd check how much a room would cost for a few nights so I could celebrate Christmas there — my first Christmas away from home, and in warm weather no less. It turned out to be far above my pay grade, so I thanked them for the ride and went off to stroll around the beach. Before walking onto the sand, I took off my dog tags and tucked them into my knapsack for safekeeping — and to keep anyone from knowing I was in the military.

It was getting to be nightfall, so I found a little bar called the Queen Surf, got a beer and a hamburger, used the facilities, and went back to the beach to ogle all the girls. I needed a place to sleep and wandered around looking for a safe spot to curl up for a nap.

I found a Banyan Tree that looked promising. It was near Waikiki, near a couple of bars and perfect for me. The picture is one that looked similar to the one I slept in. They are very easy to climb, have a lot of leaves for cover and to help keep out the street lights. I slept soundly until the sun came up, around 05:00.

I Make A Lifelong Friend:

I was a bit stiff and still wanted to rest up, so I made my way down to the beach near the Queen Surf Bar, found a secluded place to change into my swimsuit and flip-flops, found a large shrub, and proceeded to lay down for another nap. I used my knapsack as a pillow and fell back asleep. The laughter, talking, and splashing woke me around 10:00.

I decided to try the Hawaiian ocean water, buried my knapsack under the sand beneath the shrub, and walked into the lagoon that was part of the Queen Surf Bar's attractions. The water was extremely warm. I swam around for about an hour and decided to dry off, put on my clothes, and get a beer and burger at the Queen Surf.

It was the day before Christmas Eve, and I was feeling a bit down and lonely. Anyway, after getting my Miller Lite and a "Nui" burger, I sat down at a table and looked around at all the happy people. Sitting at a table near the wall separating the beach from the dining area was a young couple. The girl had long brown hair, and the guy had long blond hair and a beard. They were playing cards and sharing a pitcher of beer. Periodically, other young people would stop by, sit down, have a beer and a laugh, then move on. Some of their friends walked up from the lagoon to have a drink and chat. I was envious, for sure, of that couple who seemed to have so many friends.

After the third or fourth visit, the guy looked over my way and waved for me to come over. I turned around to see who he was calling to, and he said, "Hey sir, you with the Miller, want to join us?" Dumbfounded, I pointed to my chest and said, "Me?" He responded, "Sure, come on over." So I did.

The next thing I knew, he took my half bottle of Miller Lite and my glass of beer, poured them into their pitcher, and said, "The first thing I have to do is teach you how to drink Primo Beer. It's local, good, and the cheapest." Then he filled my glass from his pitcher and said, "Hi, I'm Steve, this is Marcia. Who are you, and which branch of the service are you in?" I introduced myself and asked how he knew I was in the service since I wasn't wearing my dog tags. He laughed and said, "Look in the mirror — head shaved bald, very white skin, but tanned arms. It's obvious." I told him I was in the Marines, and he said they had a roommate who had been in the Marines — "Big Steve." He added that Big Steve was now a professional surfer. I didn't know surfing could be professional, but I pretended that was normal information.

He asked if I knew how to play Pedro, a kind of bidding card game. I didn't, so he and Marcia began to teach me. Around that time, another fellow stopped by — Spencer Malecka. He lived in the basement apartment of the house that Steve and Marcia shared with Big Steve. Spencer asked if they were going to Moira's party that night. Steve said they were and asked if they could bring me along, then introduced me to Spencer. Spencer said, "Sure, no problem, so long as he's not obnoxious." I assured him I was not obnoxious, though I really had no idea what that word meant. Either way, I had just been invited to a Christmas party in Hawaii. Life was great.

I bought another pitcher of Primo Beer, and we continued to play Pedro while chatting with more of their friends. They started introducing me as "Marine John," their other Marine friend. When that pitcher was finished, Marcia said we should go home and get ready for Moira's party. I asked where I should meet them, and Steve said, "Just come home with us. We'll grab a bite to eat on the way, and you can take a shower if you want."

So we bummed a ride to their house on St. Louis Heights. As I remember it, Steve, Marcia, and Big Steve lived in the two-bedroom upstairs apartment, while Spencer lived in the basement apartment. Steve and Roger tell me I'm wrong, and I'll correct this later. The house I remember — 1468 St. Louis Heights — was about halfway up an inactive volcano and had a garage at the bottom of a steep driveway. The place was better than any college apartment I'd ever been in. It had a large living room, kitchen, and two bedrooms, if my recollection is correct.

It turned out that Steve, Marcia, and Spencer were university students. Spencer was a genetics major and pioneered aquaculture in the islands, and Marcia was an English major. Big Steve worked on cars, lived off his parents' money, and spent most of his time surfing. Steve told me to make myself at home — there was beer and wine in the fridge — but not to touch the large bottle of white wine, as that was for the party. They had a TV, so I turned it on to look for NCAA bowl games and helped myself to another Primo Beer. Steve and Marcia went off to their bedroom, and about an hour later, Marcia came out wearing a towel and went into the bathroom for her shower. Steve came out in a lavalava, grabbed a beer, and sat down to watch the game with me.

After Marcia came out of the bathroom, Steve went in. Marcia came out partially dressed, carrying a towel for me, and asked me to pour her a glass of wine. I did and asked her what her major was. She told me she was majoring in English and planned to become a librarian. We chatted for a bit until Steve came out of the bathroom. Marcia went into the bedroom to finish getting dressed, and I went into a very steamy bathroom.

After we all got cleaned up and dressed, Steve made a phone call and Spencer came upstairs. Big Steve came home and changed clothes, then Steve said we were waiting for his friend Richard, after which we'd all drive over to Moira's house party.

Richard Akutagawa, who was engaged to Moira's sister Sharon, arrived, and we all piled into Jack McCarthy's Chevy. Steve and Marcia were in the front seat; Richard, Big Steve, Spencer, and I were in the back. Since I was the new guy, I got the middle spot. Spencer said we didn't really need to bring the wine, but it was a nice gesture. He also said there'd be all kinds of food and drinks there and to just have a good time.

Christmas Party – Hawaiian Style And A Big Laugh:

Then Steve said, "Marine John, when you get to the party, tell everyone you're a mahoo. Mahoo means newcomer, and they'll all treat you very nicely." Marcia started to say, "That's not what it means," but Steve told her to hush. I was so green, I didn't think anything of it, nor did I question why Richard and Big Steve were grinning when I repeated the word "mahoo."

Jack parked the car on the street, and we all walked up to a large ranch-style house where Spencer opened the door for us. We walked into a nice-sized living room with oak hardwood floors and large pillows scattered around. There were about fifteen people already there when a petite, ebony-haired young woman greeted Spencer with a kiss. Spencer introduced me as "Marine John" to Moira Hata, the hostess and his fiancée. I told her my last name was Reade — "spelled just like read a book with an E" — which made her smile. She introduced me to the rest of her guests, though I can't remember any of their names now.

She then took us to another room where two long tables were set up on opposite walls. One table had a keg of beer in a No. 9 tub filled with ice, along with several kinds of wine and just about every liquor you could imagine, including warm sake. The opposite table had hors d'oeuvres — or as they say in Hawaii, pupus. There were dinner plates, and several metal trays filled with water and lit with canned candles underneath. Moira explained they'd be serving a traditional American Christmas dinner along with a number of traditional Japanese dishes. I was impressed.

Then an older gentleman came out of a back room, and Moira introduced him as her father. I later learned that Mr. Nisei was the owner of a large import/export firm and was very wealthy. Steve, Marcia, Big Steve, and Richard already had their drinks and were in the living room chatting. I slipped quietly into a corner, feeling awkward. Here I was — a small-town boy, fresh out of boot camp — "socializing" with a group of sophisticated twenty-somethings who were friends of a well-to-do, third-generation Japanese-Hawaiian family.

I guess my attempt to blend in made me stand out, because a blonde woman approached me and started a conversation. She turned out to be a stewardess for United Airlines and a high school classmate of Moira's. I told her about Christa and her dream of becoming a stewardess, and we talked about her training. I learned they had to be certified in Red Cross first aid and renew it every two years. I told her about Easton and Riegelsville and was beginning to explain my draft story when Mr. Nisei called for everyone's attention.

He announced that dinner was ready and that it would be served buffet-style, with turkey, dressing, candied yams, and all the trimmings of a traditional American Christmas — but with one rule: we all had to use chopsticks. As we got in line, I asked the stewardess if she knew how to use them. She said she did. Then I said, "Would you please teach me how to use them? I'm a mahoo and never used them before."

The whole place burst out laughing. One man in front of us turned and asked who I came with. I said, "Steve," and pointed across the room. The man laughed harder and explained that "mahoo" didn't mean newcomer — it was Hawaiian slang for transvestite. So here I was, trying to charm a pretty stewardess while proudly telling her I was a transvestite. Really smooth, right?

She laughed and kindly showed me how to use chopsticks anyway, and I picked it up fast enough to finish my dinner. There wasn't a dining table big enough for everyone, so I knelt by a coffee table with a few others to eat.

Later that night, Mr. Nisei learned it was my first Christmas away from home. When I told him I was from a small town in Pennsylvania, he kindly offered to let me call home. I reversed the charges and called my parents. It was 10:00 p.m. Christmas Eve in Hawaii but 5:00 a.m. in Pennsylvania. Dad answered, thinking it was NJPL calling about an outage. It had been snowing all night, a record-breaking storm, but thankfully no power issues. We talked for a few minutes, and then Mom got on the phone. I told her everything that had happened since I left Camp Pendleton. She laughed but also worried about me being so adventurous.

After that call, I was in high spirits and ready to really party—and we all did. I have no idea when we left the Nisei residence or how we got back to St. Louis Heights, but the next day, we were all hungover. I had to get back to Kaneohe Bay the day after Christmas, so I told Steve and Marcia I'd like a ride to the Pali Highway later on so I could hitch a ride back to the base. Marcia asked when I needed to be there, and I told her by 12:00 on December 26th. Steve told me not to worry—just give him some gas money and they'd drive me back. I agreed, and that's exactly what happened.

Another Serendipitous Event:

I honestly don't remember what happened on Christmas Day or when I told them that I was forming with the First Marine Brigade and was probably going to Vietnam. That's when Big Steve asked me what my MOS was. I told him, and then he asked if I wanted to go to Vietnam. I said I sure did *not* want to go, but what could I do about it? He told me about the MOS board that most bases had. He said the board listed all the bases that needed a specific MOS and that I should look for a base that needed personnel clerks. He suggested that I find the board at Kaneohe Bay and, when I found bases needing my MOS, officially apply to be stationed there.

After I got back to Kaneohe Bay and checked in, I did exactly what Steve told me to do. I found out that my MOS was fairly popular—there were quite a few bases that needed personnel clerks. I applied to Guam, Germany, and Aiea, Hawaii. I got very lucky and was transferred to Camp H. M. Smith, Aiea, Oahu, Hawaii.

I checked in there in January of 1967 and was assigned to the unclassified files of the Commanding General Fleet Marine Force Pacific (CGFMFPac). The office I shared with four other Marines was responsible for creating responses to the requests the CGFMFPac received from parents, doctors, congressmen and women, senators, and other Marine officers. These responses were reviewed by the Major, then sent to the General for final approval or corrections.

Changing The Marine Corps Way:

I was paired with another private, Carlos Montalvo, and we were tasked with filing the correspondence appropriately using the Marine Corps method. We also had to locate various letters from parents or doctors for a particular Marine serving within the Pacific Fleet. That was the hard part. I've already described that system, and that's exactly what caused the backup of files and paper on everyone's desk. I immediately thought of the system I was taught in high school and told the NCOIC of the office, S/Sgt Ramirez, about how a color-coded filing system would make our work more efficient. He responded with the same line my instructor at MOS school had used.

Montalvo and I, being the low men on the totem pole, were also taught how to make the coffee—the Marine Corps Way. We had to take turns making coffee for that section of the building. The coffee pot was huge, used by at least three other offices, and held about 50 cups. It had to be filled three times a day: morning, noon, and afternoon. The Marine Corps way to make coffee included the use of eggshells, so either Carlos or I had to go to the Mess Hall every morning and collect a bunch of shells.

We crushed them and kept them in a box. Fortunately, the cooks knew the shells were important and didn't throw them away — they kept them in a separate container for us.

I was making coffee during my second or third month at the duty station when a Master Gunnery Sergeant came by to fill his mug. He noticed I was new to the base and asked my name. I told him, and he asked how I liked my job. I said the job was fine, but the filing system could be improved. I explained the process, just as I've described it here. The Marines were using something called the Ellis-Dran Filing System. I told him the frustrating part was how often Marines' names were misfiled — either alphabetically or under the wrong subclassification.

The Gunny asked how I thought the system could be improved, and, never being shy about something I knew, I told him about the color-coded filing system I'd learned in high school. He asked me to come with him and introduced me to the Major in charge of unclassified files. I explained the color-coded system to the Major, who said it sounded promising and that he'd run it by the CG's office manager.

Well, I was gone a long time from the office for what was supposed to be a five-minute task. I was gone nearly an hour. When I got back, S/Sgt Ramirez was furious and chewed me out. I told him I had been speaking with the MGySgt, who had taken me to see the Major. When I started to explain why, he cut me off and told me to get back to work. I did, but I knew right then that things were going to be rough between us — and they were. It got worse when I met his daughter at the PX and asked her out on a date. Suffice to say, I planned to get off base as often as possible.

I have no proof that I was responsible for changing the filing system for the Marine Corps at FMFPac, but I do know that from 1967 onward, they used a color-coded system. I was also promoted, meritoriously, to Lance Corporal (L/Cpl), or E-3 pay grade. That meant I got a raise — from $96.00 to $128.70 a month.

I Get Into Trouble With The Corps – The First Time:

Montalvo got promoted at the end of 1967 after we completed an arduous task: transferring seven years of old files onto microfiche. Once that was done, we had to empty the filing cabinets currently in use and move those files into storage, then refill the cabinets with the newly processed ones. It was a long, tedious job. We started in October and finished just before Christmas. That's when I got into big trouble. I'll elaborate on that later.

The first time I got into trouble was because I wanted to fit in more with the university students I'd met through Steve and Marcia. So I decided to grow a moustache. After a week of not shaving under my nose, I had one, and I thought it looked pretty good. However, S/Sgt Ramirez didn't think so. He asked to see my Marine Corps ID. The photo had been taken in boot camp — no moustache — so he ordered me to be clean-shaven when I reported to work the next day. I found out that the only way to have a moustache in the Marines was to have it on your ID card.

So I came up with a plan. To get a new ID, you had to lose the one you had. I shaved off my moustache and reported that I had lost my ID. Then I started growing it back. I thought I was clever — until the Provost Marshal called me the next day with a replacement ID, using another boot camp photo. Damn! So I took that one and, the next week, reported that my ID had been stolen. This time, the Provost Marshal called me in to take a new photo. By then, I had my moustache grown again, so I finally got an ID with it showing. Ha! Take that, S/Sgt Ramirez!

There was nothing he could do to me now, except make my life miserable. And he did. For the next month, the Company Duty Sergeant gave me the hardest cleaning assignments every morning. I had to get back to base early because the clean-up brigade had to finish before reporting to our regular duty. After a month of that, the NCOs stopped harassing me. I even made a few friends among them by bringing pre-rolled joints. It seemed like every Marine I knew smoked weed—especially those who had returned from Vietnam.

I Get A Job That Pays Well And I Learn A Skill:

Most of us would take the city bus that stopped about a hundred feet outside the base entrance, head down to Waikiki Beach, and spend the afternoon swimming. Some would rent surfboards, others would hit a few clubs, and the rest would find a restaurant later on. But those were usually the Marines whose parents were well-off and sent them money each month. On $128.70, I didn't have much spending cash. So I started looking for a job I could do after office hours.

I also began hanging out again at the Blue Goose, a college bar on University Avenue that Steve and Marcia had taken me to once. That's where I found out their phone number and address. Steve later told me that he and Marcia didn't live together at 1468 St. Louis Heights, where I reconnected with them, but my recollection is that every time I was at the house, Marcia was there. There were so many people either living there or crashing there that it's all a bit fuzzy now. Anyway, I knew I couldn't really enjoy Hawaii on Marine pay alone, so I looked for work.

One afternoon, while walking down Kalakaua Avenue, I saw a sign in the window of the Heidelberg Restaurant looking for a dishwasher. I went in and applied. I told them I was in the Marines and could only work after 5:00, and they said that was perfect because they needed help with the supper crowd. I was hired on the spot.

The top chef was named Joachim, and he drank a couple of pitchers of beer during supper hours. The pastry chef's name was either Helmut or Helmuth, and at first, he was a bit snarky toward me because I was a Marine. But over time, we became drinking buddies after our shifts.

This was the perfect job. I earned double the money I was making in the Marines and got paid weekly, the Marines paid on a monthly basis.

The chef and cooks were very nice and most were from Germany as was 90% of the waitresses. They wore uniforms that looked like this.

So I would get off work at the Base, change into my civvies, take the bus downtown and laze around for an hour or so. Then I'd begin working as a dishwasher from 6:00 to 12:00. The serving of food would stop at 9:30, but I had to wait until all the diners finished eating and the waitresses cleared their area. Then after washing all the dishes, silverware, and glasses, I had to clean up my work area, including the dishwasher. This had to be taken apart, the insides had to be washed down with a disinfectant and then that had to be washed off.

After I got done, I'd go out to the bar and have a few cold beers. Most nights Joachim and Helmut would be there with the preparation cook, a man from the Philippines, Pete. After a while, I found out that the cost of the beer Joachim drank during his shifts was deducted from his salary. I thought I could save him money if I were to buy his beer at the PX and bring it to him. He'd save money and I'd score some brownie points; worked too.

Of course carrying 2 dozen beer on a bus and walking to the restaurant was more work than I wanted to do, so I looked around for some other form of transportation. I found a used Suzuki, 125 cc dirt bike that was in my price range and bought it. That solved the transportation problem, not only for working at the Heidleburg Restaurant, but for enjoying weekends with Steve and Marcia at the house on St. Louis Heights.

I was a dishwasher for about 2 months when Joachim asked me if I'd like to learn the cooking trade. I said sure, what do I have to do? So Joachim told me to come to work Saturday morning at 9:00 and report to Pete in the prep kitchen. I did and learned a lot about peeling onions, carrots, and potatoes as well as chopping them into various sizes, depending on what the specialized dish was. Pete was quick and steady with a knife.

I was being taught how to prepare veal for rouladen, a delicious meat dish. The veal is cut into triangular pieces and filled with a piece of bacon, finely chopped onions, mustard and a pickle. The veal is then rolled into a croissant shape and fastened with a toothpick. Pete then would place the finished prep pieces on a baking sheet and place in the walk-in refrigerator. When Joachim cooked them, he first braised them, then placed them in a roasting pan. He then made a gravy out of the left overs from the braising and poured the gravy over the veal. Then they were baked for 45 minutes, taken out of the roasting pan and placed on the steam line. They were served with potato dumplings, sweet red cabbage and asparagus.

Pete really impressed me one day with his ability to wield a knife. As he was preparing the veal for rouladen, a large cockroach began climbing up the wall in front of the cutting block. Without missing a beat, Pete cut that cockroach in half then

continued slicing the veal. It sounded like, swish, swish, swish - SLAP - swish, swish, swish. That roach fell to the floor in two pieces and the veal continued to be shaped.

So I would wash dishes 4 days a week, do prep work on Saturdays and party the rest of my time off base. I also developed friendly relations with a number of University of Hawaii students through Steve and Marcia.

Scary Transportation:

I had been stationed at Camp Smith for about 7 months when I was up for a long furlough. My old girlfriend, Christa, had moved to Costa Mesa, California, which is very near Camp Pendleton. So I decided to take my furlough there and made arrangements to stay with her for a week. I then got permission to ride on the same C-130 transport airplane that brought me to Hawaii. Christa was going to meet me at the Camp Pendleton Air Base at a specific time, but I don't remember when that was now.

Before I left, I asked one of the waitresses, Gisela, for a date at a going away party we were having at the house on St. Louis Heights. She accepted and after work that Saturday, we left together on my Suzuki 125 motorcycle. Gisela and I got to St. Louis Heights with some beer. I had already packed my knapsack for the trip and brought it with me. Steve, and a couple of other friends, whose names I don't recall now, went to Hanauma Bay in Steve's Chrysler convertible named Esmeralda. We swam, drank, fooled around for a few hours, then made our way back to the house via the Blue Goose. Gisela, I seem to recall had never been there before and thought it was very untidy, but fun. By the way, on the beach, in our bathing suits, I discovered that German, women do not shave their under arms or anywhere else.

The C-130 was supposed to leave at some unGodly hour and I had to report to the base by 03:30. So Steve, Marcia (I think), Roger, and Gisela dropped me off at the front gate of the base and I made my way to the holding area. There were quite a few of us taking advantage of free transportation to California, and we were all half drunk and tired. We were ready to get on the plane and settle in for a nap, but were informed that takeoff would be delayed until they completed a repair on one of the engines. About 30 minutes later we were told to walk to the tarmac and climb aboard. I did and settled in a seat, locked my seat belt tightly and began to get comfortable for a nice nap.

The big, old plane rumbled down the runway and took off, heading into the sun. I closed the window shade and then my eyes. I was nearly asleep when the captain announced that they were having trouble with one the the four engines, but there was no need to worry because if they had to feather down that engine, we could still get to California on the other three since we were safely in the air. OKAY! I found it a little more difficult to get back to my nap, so I opened the window shade and looked at the two engines on my side of the plane. They seemed to be purring along nicely. Good!

About an hour later, the captain got on the intercom again to inform us that the number three engine and number two engines were going to be feathered down and we were returning to Hickam Field. He turned the plane around and headed back to Hawaii. Only one more problem, the plane had too much fuel and, consequently, was too heavy to land safely. That meant we had to circle the field until enough fuel was burned up and/or dumped into the ocean to land.

By now it was mid-morning and I decided that I was not going to stay on this old C-130 anymore. After we landed, I called a taxi and two other service men and I shared the cost of going to the Honolulu Air Port for a commercial flight. I was lucky enough to get a United Airline flight to the Los Angeles airport almost immediately. As I was waiting to board the flight, I was called to the gate where I was informed by a very attractive stewardess that my economy ticket had be bumped to first class so another service man could join the flight. I could not believe my luck. I boarded the plane before most of the other passengers, got a huge seat in front of the fuselage, was given free champaign, a prime rib dinner on real plates with silverware, fluffy pillows and a blanket. I finally got to take a nap.

Upon landing at LAX, I called Christa to let her know what happened and to apologize for her wasted trip to Camp Pendleton Air base. She was understanding and picked me up. It was early evening, warm, clear, and just very comfortable. The next five days spent with Christa were uneventful. She went to work during the day and I relaxed by the pool in her apartment complex. Met a number of her neighbours, and planned dinner for us when Christa got home. I had learned how to cook a couple of German dishes as well as regular American cuisine - hamburgers, french fries, steak, beans etc. Christa was pleased, but not impressed enough to share a bed with me. Oh well, there was always Gisela when I got back to Hawaii. Five days later Christa took me to LAX, kissed me good-by and that was the end of my weeks' vacation in Costa Mesa, California.

After returning to Camp Smith, I fell back into my normal routine of work in the office, work at the restaurant, dating Gisela, sleeping at the house on St. Louis Heights and riding my little Suzuki, 125 cc motorcycle. Fun times for sure.

Over a number of beers at the Blue Goose, I learned about the background of the

Vietnam conflict. I also remembered a couple of interviews President Kennedy gave to Walter Cronkite and Edward R. Murrow. In both of them, he was clear that Vietnam was a civil war and the USA, under his leadership, would only provide South Vietnam with military advisors and not actual troops. President Kennedy, "In the final analysis, it is their (Vietnam people) war. They are the ones who have to win it or lose it. We can help them, we can give them equipment, we can send our men out there as advisers, but they have to win it - the people of Viet-Nam (sic) - against Communists."

Unfortunately, after his assassination in 1963, Lyndon B. Johnson became president and escalated the US military efforts. It was obvious to the university students, many of whom came from Asian families, that President Johnson was influenced by the military/industrial complex. In 1968, LBJ announced that he would not run for reelection after ending the Vietnam War.

From watching the Rachel Maddow Show, I found out the reason why he decided not to run, and it was because he failed to broker an end to the conflict via a meeting between Ho Chi Minh, the leader North Vietnam and Ngo Dinh Diem, leader of South

Vietnam in Paris. That meeting didn't happen because of some dirty business by Richard Nixon and a Chinese woman of influence, Anna Cheunnault. It is a complicated story that I cannot fully recall to repeat in this memoir. However, it confirms that Richard Nixon was not only a crook, but a traitor to the nation.

So I began to join the student marches against the Vietnam war. Once I even wore my uniform. That, I'm sure was partly responsible for the following story. The one I alluded to earlier.

I Get Into Trouble With The Corps - The Second Time:

At the end of each year, the files that were 7 years old had to be placed on microfiche so those filing cabinets could be emptied to hold the files from the current year. In September, Montalvo and I were ordered to begin putting the files from 1959 on microfiche, shred them, and prepare the empty filing cabinet to house the 1967 files. We worked our butts off daily down in the storage room, but occasionally, we had to return to the office to type reply letters, file current letters or find letters of interest for the

CGFMFPac.

The day before we were to get our extra-long Christmas furlough, Montalvo and I had only one and a half drawers to finish putting on microfiche and moving the 1967 files down to the empty drawers. So we decided to return to the office after supper and finish the job. We got back to the work after 18:00 hours and began to work as fast as we could. This type of work is slow going and by the time we were half way through the last drawer, it was after 01:00. We had to decide whether to stop and get some sleep before reveille or continue on and complete the job. Then we'd have the whole Christmas holidays free and be finished setting up the new filing cabinets with the colour coded system that had been approved by the Major in charge of unclassified files for CGFMFPac.

Montalvo reminded me that since I was the acting non-commissioned officer in charge (NCOIC), I could write up "sleep-in" chits for us so we could sleep through reveille. That's the reason we decided to work until the job was done. Around 03:30 we moved the last drawer downstairs to the storage room, returned to the barracks where I got the sleep-in chits from the Duty Sergeant. I filled in the form, signed one for Montalvo and the other for me. We then went to our bunks, but mine was filled. It seems that my immediate boss in our office, Corporal Reynolds, knew that I was staying off base most nights and decided to use my rack for his rest so he didn't have to bother making his own bed every morning.

After attaching the sleep-in chit to the foot of my bed, I, literally, threw him out of my bunk. He was pissed, but didn't want to make too much out of it and went to his own room. I got in bed and fell to sleep immediately. At 05:00 reveille was called and the Duty Sergeant honoured Montalvo's sleep-in chit, but ordered me to get up. I told him to Fuck Off!

About 07:30 the 1st/Sgt of the company grabbed my mattress and threw it on the floor, with me still in it. He said, "You have 5 minutes to report to the CO in the UD! Move it!" Translation: I had 5 minutes to dress in the uniform of the day and see the commanding officer of the company. So I got up, made my bed, and walked to the CO's office. Now in boot camp when you reported to the DI's office, you stood at attention parallel to the door and pounded the wall with an open hand three times, step into the doorway and say, "Pvt Reade reporting as ordered sir." However, after you become a "real" marine, that practice stopped. Being as pissed as I was about my sleep-in chit not being honoured and finding out that Corporal Ryan had been sleeping in my bunk and making my area messy, I reported to the CO as if I was still in boot camp and in my skivvies, not the UD.

When I stood in the doorway and said, "L/Cpl Reade reporting as ordered, sir."

The CO looked up from his desk and said, "What is your problem, Boy?" I answered,

"Your Fucking Marine Corps, Sir!" He said, "Get the hell out of here."

So I left his office, walked across the hallway to the Duty Sergeant and asked for my leave pass. He gave it to me, I dressed in my civvies and left the base. I rode my Suzuki 125 down to 1428 St. Louis Heights with the intention of deserting the Marines. Yes, I was immature then, for sure.

Fortunately for me, Steve was there and calmed me down. How? Well, we smoked a couple of joints, drank a few beers and talked. What I mostly remember is Steve asking me what I wanted to be after I got out of the Marines. I told him I wanted to teach. He asked me if I thought I could get a job as a teacher if I deserted the armed services of the United States anywhere in the US? So I said something like, hell, I'll fly up to Canada like the draft dodgers and draft card burners. Then he asked me if I really identified with them. I honestly could not say that I did.

Being raised in small town in Pennsylvania I always knew I was meant to serve in the forces, just like many of my older neighbours did. I knew men and women who were in World War I, World War II, and the Korean War and respected them all. I admit that I wanted to be respected like that as well. So I decided to return to the base, on time, to face my punishment.

I Am Not A Mechanic - Pain:

It was during this time, I seem to recall, that I again hurt myself badly. I took my motorcycle down the hill to get something to eat. On the way down, my rear brakes broke and I had to use the front brakes only. I bought the food and returned to the house, taking the cycle into the garage. After eating, I went to see why my rear brakes weren't working. Simply put, the brakes used a wire that went through a hole in the middle of a metal cylinder and had a type of screw that adjusted the tension on the wire. The metal cylinder was broken and the wire slipped out.

To get out to Chinaman's Hat, we had to swim up the shoreline well past the island, then turn toward it and follow the current at an angle to get to it. Then we would swim around and around the island. Sometimes we'd swim up to the rocks and climb out of the water for a rest before we returned to the girls.

Chinaman's Hat

Once, Steve spotted an oxygen tank and a weight belt. They were about 15 to 20 feet under the surface. It took me a couple of tries to get all the way down to them, but we both got there and grabbed the whole thing. As we pulled the tank out of the sand, we discovered there was a regulator and hose attached as well.

Let me tell you, it was HEAVY, but we managed to get them back to shore. I'm sure Steve did the yeoman's job with it because he was a much stronger swimmer than I. We thought we'd pick up a couple of hundred bucks for it back in the city, but after Spencer checked it out, he said that the belt was fine, but the rest was junk. There went our windfall.

Second Near Death Experience in Hawaii:

Steve and I began to swim out to Chinaman's Hat when he pointed out a school of Butterfly or Parrot fish, not sure which ones now. We made a big mistake because we stopped swimming to gawk at them. We actually followed them for a couple of strokes, which was enough of a distance to get us caught in the current we knew was there, was dangerous, and avoided it until that day.

We tried to get out of it immediately, but couldn't. The good thing was that on that day neither of us had the Hawaiian Sling. The bad thing was that we had to go with the flow. So we angled our bodies toward the shore and slowly kicked along with the current. Where we went in to swim to Chinaman's Hat was about 5 miles from Hanauma Bay. Hanauma Bay is where the iconic opening scene for the television show, Hawaii 5 - 0 is shot. It's also a very popular surfing spot, with big, long lasting waves that the top surfers can catch and ride right into the shore.

I don't remember if the girls saw us get caught in the current, or if they actually called the Coast Guard for us, but I'm sure that if they did watch us swim out to the open ocean, they'd be worried and would have probably contacted them. I only remember that the current carried us beyond Hanauma Bay. Then our efforts came to fruition, and we began heading directly toward a mountain on the shore. We were then able to turn toward Hanauma Bay and slowly make our way to shore.

Once we got into the bay itself, Steve began to body surf the waves in, but I was not that skilled. Although I tried, I wound up being tossed under the waves and tumbling around underwater for what seemed like 10 minutes.

When I broke the surface, I forgot to clear the snorkel and took a mouthful of water down my lungs. I spit out the snorkel and coughed up the worst tasting water in the world. I was definitely in big trouble, trying to stay afloat while clearing my lungs.

Serendipity met me again. There was a surfer nearby and he paddled over to me. He asked if I was all right, and I shook my head 'no' as I coughed up sea water. He then hauled me onto his board and took me close enough to the shoreline that I could easily swim the rest of the way. I do not know who that good Samaritan was, but I thanked him profusely then, and I do it again here and now. Without his help, I probably would have drowned, just like in 1958 and the flood in Riegelsville.

All in all, Steve and I were in the water for over 4 hours and went about 5 miles from where we entered. I don't know about Steve, but I was exhausted and had leg and arm cramps that night.

Guard Duty:

Also in February, I was taken off duty at the office and assigned to guard duty at Hickam Air Base. I was there for 6 days, stationed in a private room away from the barracks. That was the first time I experienced what it might be like making the Marines a career. I had privacy, easy access to the PX, and NCO club.

Part of the attraction of being in the US military services is that everything you want you can purchase at the PX and it is very inexpensive. I remember that a carton of cigarettes was $2.75 and two dozen local beers, $1.25, everything you wanted to buy was cheaper because there was no tax placed on the items. I was part of a contingent of soldiers guarding a B-52 aircraft. There were always 2 of us and we were charged with walking around the plane for 4 hours straight. We carried water in our canteen, but were not permitted to leave the area until relieved of our duties. We then had 8 hours off, then 4 hours on, 8 hours off, etc. During the 8 hours off, we could sleep or hit the NCO club.

A B-52 is huge! When it wasn't carrying fuel for its missions, the wings were so far off the ground that I could walk underneath them without any problem. However, the wings have wheels attached to their tips because when it's filled with fuel, the wings were on the ground. When it was taking off, the wings created lift and the wheels dropped off onto the tarmac.

While off duty one day, I went to the PX for some smokes and met a pretty, young newly married woman. Her husband was in the Navy and just deployed to Vietnam. She was studying to be a teacher, as was I, so we had a lot to talk about. I told her where I was stationed and my schedule. She invited me to her residence for supper the next night when I was on my 8-hour rest, and I agreed. I have no idea what she made for us to eat, but, suffice to say, I found out that newlyweds were horny women.

Mustered Out of the Marines:

After my tour of guard duty, my next big deal was to re-qualify at the rifle range, which I did, then do the PRT. I passed that test as well. All this happened between January and March, court martial, swim trouble, guard duty, re-qualifying with the rifle and the PRT. Then in April I got orders to report to Treasure Island, San Francisco, California for release of duty. I must say, I was never given a lecture to re-up. Nope, the company and office NCOs were happy to see me leave the Marines.

On the plane ride to Treasure Island, I met a man I went to boot camp with, I believe his name is Ronald Nicol. He was with me as we were forming with the First Marine Division in Kaneohe, Hawaii. He remained with them as an infantry gunner and was stationed at Quang Tin. He told me that there were many nights where he was on guard duty and would light up a joint, smoke it slowly and sit down on sand bags. He said a few times a Vietnamese would join him and share the joint, not saying a word, just being mellow. Now I don't know if the person who joined him was from North Vietnam or not, but he swore the story was true and that kind of thing happened many times, not only with him, but with other Marines on duty. For some reason, I believed him.

We got to Treasure Island in the first week of May, and I immediately called Moira Hata, who was nursing in the University of California San Francisco, UCSF, Medical Centre in the Castro area of San Francisco. She was pleased to hear from me and invited me to her apartment for a dinner when I could get away. I promised I wouldn't miss it for the world.

To get to Treasure Island, one had to drive on the Oakland Bay Bridge. This is a bridge that has 5 lanes going east from San Francisco and 5 lanes above going west from Oakland. About half way across the bridge there is a turn off that goes to a small island called the Yerba Bueno Island, then another bridge onto the Naval Base at Treasure Island. There you travel to the Marine Corps Barracks and begin waiting for your discharge papers. I was worried that I might not get an Honourable Discharge because of my court martial, but those worries were unfounded.

Marine Corps Barracks at Treasure Island was just that, a home for those of us who were being let out of the service. But true to Marine Corps tradition, we were still lowly Privates or, in my case, Lance Corporals and had to fulfil specific duties, specifically, cleaning up the whole place. The first job I was given was to pick up all the cigarettes that weren't field stripped. There were a lot. Once our 8 hours of clean-up duty was finished, we got our leave passes and could go into San Francisco or Oakland. I called Moira to see when I could come over for a visit, and she said that she had three days off, beginning on Friday. Since that was Thursday, I requested a three-day leave for the weekend and share that time with Moira. My duty that day was to clean the GI cans around the base with disinfectant, hot soapy water and steam.

That night, Moira called me to say that she'd pick me up the next day around 11:00 AM and that she had her spare room fixed up with a cot for me. I cannot emphasize how thrilled I was to be able to get off the base and into civilian life again.

San Francisco is an amazing city.

It was then and when I was there in 2001, it was still an amazing place to visit. But as Mark Twain said, "The coldest winter I ever spent was a summer's day in San Francisco." This might be true, but I can say for certain that summer mornings at the University of San Francisco can be very cold, especially if it's foggy.

Moira's apartment was near the University of San Francisco because, as I said before, she was nursing there.

When we got to her apartment, I phoned my parents and told them that I'd be released from the Marines on the 30th of May. Mom and Dad decided to make plans to meet me at Uncle Ray's new home in Davenport, Iowa in June when Dad had vacation time. They had wanted to see Uncle Ray again anyway since he left the Atomic Energy Commission in Los Alamos and had his divorce finalized. So we made plans to meet as soon as I could get there.

Making Money and My Future Was Predicted:

After my phone call, Moira asked me what I'd like to eat for supper. I told her that I'd like to cook something for her, perhaps a steak and all the trimmings. She agreed and took me to a grocery store. While looking around, I saw a kind of cross between a newsletter and small newspaper called the Berkeley Barb.

I bought a copy and read it while I cooked. It was very anti-Vietnam war, supportive of voting rights, the Black Panther movement, of which I had never heard, higher education and just about everything I was interested in, including the legalization of marijuana.

I called the number on the editor's page and asked if I might get involved. I was told I could sell them if I wanted. So I did.

Again I was making more money selling the Barb on street corners of San Francisco than I earned as a Marine.

One evening I was on a corner of Market and Eighteenth Street, when this attractive, older woman approached me and asked me what I was doing. I told her I was waiting to get out of the Marine Corps and selling Berkeley Barbs to make some extra cash. She asked to see my left palm so she could read my future.

She said that I was destined to do something much better with my life than what I was doing at that time.

I thanked her and put that prediction out of my mind for a number of years.

Moira gave me a key to her apartment so that I could leave the base daily, which I did.

This was fine with the CO as long as I returned in time to fulfil my last month's duties. Again, all the other Marines at Treasure Island got a reenlistment lecture, except me.

I also called Christa and made plans to meet her at her apartment in Costa Mesa on May 31st. May 30 finally came and I was discharged from the Marines with a nice check for $650.00. That was the severance pay and the air fare from San Francisco International Airport to Philadelphia International Airport. I was RICH!

I said farewell to Moira and thanked her for her wonderful hospitality, then asked her if she'd mind taking me to the on ramp to the Coast Highway so I could hitchhike down to Costa Mesa. She didn't mind, so I cashed my check, packed my belongings in the duffle bag and set out to see Christa again.

Christa met me just outside of Los Angeles and took me to her apartment on June 1st. First thing I did was to take a shower and get dressed in my new, just bought civvies. Then we went out to dinner. She was talking a lot about her new job and the great restaurants in the area. So for the next time we went out, we made reservations at a restaurant

What you see when you enter la Cave called la Cave. This place was in the basement of an office building. You'd take the elevator to the basement floor, and when the doors opened, the decor was just like that of a cave. The maitre d would greet you and show you to your table.

The Dave Trio was the entertainment that night, and they were fantastic. Our waiter asked us for our drink order, and when he returned with them, he brought a cart with him. On the cart were plastic replicas of their daily entrees, vegetables, and the wine they suggested one drink with each entree. No menu, no prices, just the replicas. Anyway, we each had a surf and turf entree and a bottle of Chablis. The dessert tray was the same, but I couldn't eat any dessert, Christa had a piece of chocolate cake. I had Drambuie and coffee. When we got the bill, it was over 300 dollars in 1968. I nearly shit a brick. Half the money I had in the world went to pay for one meal, but it was worth it, now that I'm looking back. Also, this restaurant was a favourite of many celebrities in 1968, I read where John Wayne would often eat there.

A Dangerous Adventure To Help A Stranger:

I stayed with Christa for 4 days. When she was at work, I swam in the pool, swam in the ocean, lay on the beach, and prepared supper. Then it was time to hitchhike to Davenport. Christa dropped me off in Santa Monica where the famous Route 66 begins its long, sprawling journey across the USA.

Almost as soon as she dropped me off, I got a ride to Needles, California, which is the last community in California in the Mohave Desert. I remained there for a long, long time. Finally, around midnight, a 1954 green, 4 door Chevy coupe stopped. The driver told me to throw my duffle bag in the back seat and get in.

He asked me where I was headed, and I told him. I then asked him how far he was going, and he said he wasn't sure. Maybe all the way to Oklahoma City, it just depends. I asked him what it depended on, and he said, "Depends on where I find my wife."

Turns out his wife was having an affair with the Southwest Regional manager of the Best Western Hotel chain, and she took off with him and their daughter. Joe thought the daughter was his, but she claimed the little girl belonged to the manager. Joe didn't care. He raised her for the first three years of her life, and he wasn't going to let his wife take her from her brother and sisters.

Turns out Joe was a truck driver living in Bakersfield, California. When he got home from one of his jobs, she was gone and left the other children in the care of Joe's mother. So he did what any cowboy would do, he went after her. So he got in his car, gassed up, and left Bakersfield to follow the path of all the Best Western Hotels in the Southwest. He had been driving from early morning and asked me if I knew how to drive a standard. I assured him I did. Then he asked me if I'd take over driving for a while so he could get a nap. He said just stay on Route 66. So I took over, and he napped.

We were headed to the hotel in Flagstaff, Arizona, so I just settled down and drove to the nearest gas station and filled up the tank. Since he was driving me a fair distance, the gas was on me. He liked that a lot. I drove us into Flagstaff and found the Best Western there. He woke up quickly and went to the front desk. He came out and told me they had been there, but left for Albuquerque, New Mexico. So we paid for a room, got something to eat, showered, and then he took over driving.

I'm a terrible passenger, but since I needed some sleep, I curled up in the passenger seat and listened to country western music on the radio and tried to sleep. I must have dozed off for a few hours, because when I awoke, we were in New Mexico and Joe was gassing up again. I guess it took us about 5 or 6 hours to get to Albuquerque, and after a pit stop, we headed into the city proper. We found the Best Western Hotel around mid-morning, but had missed the couple again. This time we had to get to Lubbock, Texas.

Joe continued to drive, but a couple of hours later, he asked me to take over. I had had a nap and felt pretty good, so we changed seats, and I began to drive to Lubbock. I drove for a few hours, noticed that the gas needle was nearing empty again, and decided to stop at the next station to get fuel for the car and me. When we stopped, Joe woke up, but I told him not to worry, just getting some snacks and gas. He went back to sleep after we got back on the road.

Now I don't know if you've ever driven across a desert, but it is f l a t, and driving on roads that have very little scenery is mesmerizing, especially in the dark. New Mexico and Texas are huge states. I got us into Texas around midnight and looked for signs pointing to Lubbock. All of a sudden, for some reason, the car started to bounce around and became hard to steer. I had fallen asleep, the car veered onto the shoulder, and woke us up. I got the car under control and just missed plowing into an abutment of a bridge. I crossed the structure, pulled over, and Joe took over.

Well, we found the Best Western Hotel in Lubbock around 5:00 and discovered that the couple left for Oklahoma City the day before. From there, they were planning a return trip. Joe had to make a decision, wait for them to return to Lubbock or try to get them at Oklahoma City. Joe decided to ambush them in Oklahoma City the next morning. Since it was about a 6-hour drive, he decided that we'd get a good meal, have a drink or two, and get a long nap in a bed. So we shared the cost of a room with two beds, ate, and left a wakeup call for 11:00 PM. That was a good decision, and the rest was perfect.

We got up, showered, shaved, and got back on the road. Joe drove all the way and made good time. We pulled up to the Best Western Hotel in Oklahoma City around 5:30. Joe developed a plan. He'd case the joint and see what the best way to find their room would be. So he walked up to the front desk, only to see the three of them in the restaurant eating breakfast. He walked back to the car and decided that the best plan was for him to hide behind me as I walked through the restaurant to their table. He'd snatch his daughter from her high chair and run back to the car. My job would be to keep the manager from stopping him.

Okie Dokie, I was game. Actually I was pretty stupid to go along with him, but I felt obligated to help him get his daughter back. So I put on my Marine Corps overcoat and walked through the restaurant toward them. Joe's wife saw him about 3 fourths of the way to their table and began to yell something like, "You're not taking her from me." The guy started to stand up and grabbed a steak knife off the table, and I played hero by grabbing his hand holding the knife and forced him back into his seat with my other hand. Yep, I'm cool. Nope, I'm dumb, but because Joe got his daughter out of the high chair while his wife held onto her arm. There was a bit of a struggle, but Joe got her away from his wife and ran out the door.

And there was Johnny Reade, holding the Regional Manager of the Best Western Hotels in his seat. Not for too long, because I thought it'd be a good idea to run after Joe. My stuff was still in his car which was parked around the corner from the hotel. As soon as I let go of him, the manager picked up the knife and ran after Joe, I was slow and followed the two of them out the door.

In the meantime, Joe had already made it to his car and sped away. So there I was, on one of the main streets in Oklahoma City, alone after assaulting the regional manager of the Best Western Hotels. What did I do. I turned around and walked swiftly away from him and his girlfriend, who was crying and still hollering at Joe for taking her daughter. If the police had come at that time, I probably would have been arrested for aiding and abetting a kidnapping, assaulting a citizen, and being a hippie marine. Oklahoma was and remains a very conservative, red necked, cowboy state.

But I was lucky. Joe drove around the block and was actually waiting for me at the intersection at the direction I was walking toward. I saw the hood of this car and began running toward it. I got in, and he took off away from that hotel. He asked me to hold his daughter, who was crying and shaking and smelled terrible. Her dress was stained, her hair was matted, and her face was dirty. Joe drove around a bit until he saw a drug store. He went in, bought a baby bottle, formula, pampers, baby lotion, clean clothes, a hair brush, baby shampoo and soap.

Then he found a motel, and we got a room. I asked him what he would have done if the manager had been able to get up and get near him. He told me to look in the glove department. I did. There was a pistol there. I didn't know it at the time, but he had the damned thing in his pants the whole time we entered the hotel and was prepared to use it if necessary. What a scene that would have been. What a mess I would have been in. Boy, I was lucky as sin. Thanks again serendipity.

When we got in the room, Joe got a bath ready for his daughter, whom I call Jill. He then undressed her, and I decided that I had done the right thing by putting myself at risk. Her diaper was filled with dried shit, her bum was red, her vagina was red, and her knees were bruised. Joe gently put her in the bath and cleansed her slowly and carefully. Then he asked me if I knew how to dress a toddler, I told him I had had plenty of experience with my nieces and could take care of her. Joe called the Best Western Hotel and spoke with his wife. I don't remember the conversation, but he asked me to make the formula and feed his daughter while he went to speak with her.

When he returned, he asked me if I wanted to stay with him and his daughter while he drove back to Bakersfield or get back on the road. I chose to get on my way and put as many miles between Joe, me, and Oklahoma City as fast as I could. Joe gave me 20 dollars for babysitting, while he spoke with his wife, then took me to the entrance of the interstate highway I 35. It was around noon by then, beautiful blue sky, but hot and dusty.

One Crazy Navy Officer:

I was nervous that a state trooper might see me trying to hitch a ride, stop, and question me about what happened at the Best Western. Instead, the third or fourth car that entered the freeway stopped. Wow, a silver Cadillac, with an older driver. He told me to store my gear in the trunk and hop in. I did. After we got started on the highway, he asked me where I was headed, and I told him to Davenport, Iowa. He said he was on his way to Ann Arbor, Michigan, so he'd take me right there. Wow. Luck hit me again.

He said he was a Captain in the Navy and was injured in Vietnam. I told him I just got out of the Marines and was on my way to meet my parents at my uncle's house in Iowa. I also told him that I'd help drive if he needed it. He laughed at me and said no dumb jarhead was going to drive his baby.

Then he floored it, and we began accelerating, and the odometer showed the speed going up to 60, 70, 80. When we hit one hundred MPH, I began to worry. He noticed that I tightened my seat belt and laughed again and called me a scared pussy leatherneck. Then his face contorted in pain. He took his foot off the gas, turned to the back seat, and opened a briefcase. He brought out a fifth of Old Grandad bourbon and a bottle of pills. Opening the pill bottle, he popped two into his mouth, opened the bourbon, and swallowed the pills with a long pull of the bottle. He let the car slow down, 90, 80, 60, 50, 40, 30, all the while remaining in the passing lane. Cars pulled up behind us and passed us on the right, blowing their horn at us. He didn't give a shit. He just stared ahead until the pills worked their magic and his pain subsided. Then he hit the accelerator again and kept it up until we were passing all those idiots who passed us just a few minutes ago.

His story was that he was hit with shrapnel in his back and lost a kidney. That was enough to get him out of the Navy, but he really didn't want to leave. The only way he could stay in the service was to get a clearance from a specialist doctor at the Veterans Hospital in Battle Creek, Michigan. So that's where he was headed. He also said that he left the hospital in Houston without permission, but he was getting his job secured no matter what it took. He was officially AWOL.

So I was stuck in a car with basically an injured, hurting, pill popping, drunk of a Navy Lifer Wannabe, who kept driving like a maniac, swallowing pills with bourbon, and talking nonstop. When we got to the outskirts of Wichita, Kansas, he said he was hungry and needed gas, so we stopped at a truck stop. He said he'd buy me a nice steak with all the fixins as he drove to a tank. I told him that I had had enough of this drive, thanked him for the offer of a steak dinner, and said I'd try to get a ride with a trucker. As I was getting my duffle bag out of his trunk, he came around and was really angry at me for deserting him and to stay out of the trunk of his baby. I just opened the trunk, got my duffle bag, and walked away.

I got to the truck stop exit and sat on my bag hoping for a decent ride. It was getting dark now, and I was hungry, but more interested in getting away from that jerk. I don't know how long I had to wait, but I was picked up by a couple of women who were on their way to work at a halfway house for teenage girls in Kansas City. I got in the back seat and chilled while one of them drove sensibly for about 2 hours into Kansas City and dropped me off at the side of the facility. I got out and made my way to a secluded spot where I could wrap up in my overcoat and get a nap before I got back on the road.

The next morning, I found a restaurant near the place I was dropped off, went in, ordered a breakfast, used the restroom to wash up a little, and saw that I had grown a fairly nice beard while on the road and my hair was looking a bit more hip, at least that's what I thought. After eating, I got back on the highway and was lucky enough to get a ride all the way to Des Moines, Iowa. I was let off at another truck stop and made it to a phone booth. I called my uncle's number and let my parents know where I was and that I'd be in Davenport later that day if I got a good ride.

A Heated Conversation and I Buy My Old Man A Beer:

Uncle Ray said they could be in Des Moines in a couple of hours and told me to get to the on ramp of Route 80 and wait for them. I said that sounds like a good idea, and that's exactly what I did. I picked up a couple of snacks and soda and walked to that on ramp. To be honest, I was grateful to just get to a place where I could drop the duffle bag and rest. That damned bag got heavy after a while carrying it on my shoulder.

About a half hour after I got to the on ramp, my uncle and parents drove up in my Dad's new car, a 1958 green and black Dodge 4 door sedan, and asked me if I wanted a ride. Boy, was it ever good to see them.

Naturally, my Mom was really worried about me hitchhiking all that way and then extremely angry at my appearance. She didn't like my beard, hair, moustache, clothing, or anything but me, her "Johnny." I put the duffle bag in the trunk and got in the back seat. I have to say, it was a very large, comfortable car, almost as comfortable as the Cadillac that crazy Navy guy had.

That's my Dad in the driver's seat in the picture.

We stayed at Uncle Ray's for a couple of days, long enough for me to get cleaned up to please my mother. We had a decent few days, but one conversation we had become very contentious. I'm not sure exactly how it started, but we began talking about religion, specifically the Roman Catholic religion. Dad remained silent throughout the discussion. Mom spoke about how the church always helped her out when she felt depressed. She loved being a member of the RC church. I reminded her that the church at the top our street, St. Anthony's, wouldn't let her become a parishioner because her last name was Reade and told her that the Irish Catholic church in Wilson would be a better place for her.

Mom remembered, but also said that when she explained that she was baptized in that church, the rector allowed her to join. But my point was that the church is elitist and hypocritical. Well, Uncle Ray got involved in the discussion then. For some reason he didn't like that I used the word "hypocritical" when talking about the Catholic religion. So I said most religions are hypocritical, especially the Christian churches. When I was asked how, I told them that the first commandment said that thou shalt not worship any idol or other God before me, and the first thing Catholics do is to kneel in front of a statue of a man hanging on a cross. It seems to me that's worshiping an idol.

Both Uncle Ray and Mom said that was not a statue but an image of God's son, Jesus, who died to take away our sins. However, Jesus was from the middle east, Jewish and was probably a dark skinned, dark haired man. But the man on all the crosses I've seen is a white, long haired hippie kind of man. Whoops, big mistake. Again Uncle Ray and Mom began berating and yelling at me, so at that time, I just laughed and stopped trying to argue. It was also the time Dad decided to speak up. He said that this discussion was getting out of hand and to give it up. Of course, Mom began crying and Uncle Ray was red in the face, so I definitely agreed with Dad.

We only stayed with Uncle Ray for another day. My father's vacation time was limited, and he wanted to see the Soo Locks in Sault Ste. Marie, Michigan.

He planned to see the locks, then take the International Bridge into Ontario and make our way to Niagara Falls. Then we'd cross back into the USA and drive down from Niagara Falls, through New York State and into Easton.

Although I had my driver's license for six years, Dad refused to let me drive his "new" car. He was really proud of it. It had an automatic transmission with push button gears in the dash board. He liked the idea of that. So we took off from Davenport, Iowa, north on Route 151.

The plan was to drive as far as we could, then find a motel for an overnight, then continue into the city to explore the lock system and drive across the International Bridge into Sault Ste Marie, Ontario.

From there, we planned to stop in Sudbury, Ontario for the night and continue to Niagara Falls.

To me, the most significant part of this trip was that I got to buy my Dad a beer in Madison, Wisconsin, which is where we got a motel for the night. Mom went shopping for gifts for my sister's family, and Dad and I went into a local bar in the shopping district. I had to talk him into it, but he finally gave in.

I must say, we had a great conversation, with me doing most of the talking. I told him of my experiences in the Marines and my friendship with the guys and gals at St. Louis Heights, Hawaii.

He was most interested in my plans for the future. I assured him that I was already accepted back into West Chester State College for the fall semester and planned to graduate on time.

This trip took place in June of 1968. Four months later, Dad died of a massive heart attack while driving to Martin's Creek, Pennsylvania to take my sister to work.

I had returned to West Chester State College to continue on my quest for a degree in education.

I also got a job with the Pennsylvania Liquor Control Board.

I began working for them in a store in Easton, but was permitted to transfer to the store in West Chester so I could continue my education.

Dad Dies Which Forces Me To Develop My Theory Of Death:

In late October, I had a date with a coed who was in my Children's Literature class. It was not our first date, but was our first time being together in bed. While we were there, my phone rang. I ignored it and continued with our love making. Then it rang again, then again, then once more, and I finally decided the distraction was too much.

On the other end of the line was my brother in law, who had the task of telling me about Dad. Well, I quickly got dressed, drove my date back to her dorm, and began the drive home to my grieving family.

I really can't describe exactly how I felt, it was a combination of anger, loss, emptiness, pride, but no tears. For some bizarre reason, I just couldn't get the tears to flow. I got emotional at different movies, when my sister graduated from nursing school, when Mom and Dad danced at her wedding, but I just could not cry for Dad that day. I guess it was the shock of the whole situation. By ignoring the phone call at first to continue having sex, I was feeling guilty, until my cousin, Jimmy, pointed out that I had no idea who was calling or why, and that being guilty for continuing my activity was really all right, but not necessary.

I remember my sister asking me, "What do we do now?" She's nine years older than me, a nurse, married, mother of four children, and she asked me what we were going to do now. At that time, I wasn't mature enough or had developed enough empathy to understand how guilty she felt. It was her that he was going to take to work. It was her children that he was going to bring home until Robert, their father, would pick them up. But I only thought about why she would ask me such a dumb question. I didn't say that to her, what I did say was, "I guess we just go on living as best as we can."

Life is so ironic. Dad had had high blood pressure due to being overweight and a lack of exercise. While I was in the Marines, Dad changed his life style and began exercising and cutting down of his food portions. A couple of days before he died, his doctor gave him a clean bill of health. Then a massive heart attack. Go figure.

The single most shocking thing about Dad's death was how well Mom was coping. She got down to business and made arrangements for a funeral home to pick him up from the hospital. Then she went searching for the insurance documents and his last will and testament. Finally, she called the lawyer who represented me with my situation with the Antonoccis to advise her as to the rest of plans she had to make.

The funeral arrangements were made, but Dad's brother, Earl, who became a catholic just before he married Aunt K, decided that my father, a lifelong atheist, had to be baptized post mortem and buried with the blessing of the church. Mom, herself a practicing catholic all her life, agreed, and the deed was done.

I hated the everything about my father's death, that it happened while he was doing a good deed, that he never got to retire and have free time all for himself, thank he was cleared of having high blood pressure then died of a heart attack, that I preferred to have sex rather than answer that phone call, that Mom had to make all the decisions about his burial, that Uncle Earl took over some of the funeral arrangements and had Dad baptized, that my sister was at her wits end, that after the burial, Mom changed from a decisive, competent "alpha" woman to one who couldn't decide who to vote for in the upcoming election. Most of all, I hated that there might be a God who thought all of this was necessary.

From the time Dad was buried, I began thinking about the existence of a God. In all honesty, my understanding of death took quite a few years until I developed this theory. This is the result of my thought process, and how my explanation mirrors different religions, I developed this philosophy on my own.

I believe that the idea of God and religions are separate entities. Religions exist to control people, God existed to explain various phenomena such as thunder and lightning. From what I remembered from the various times I was sitting in with the summer time "classes" of the three religious parishes in Rieglesville, if one did not believe in the Bible as interpreted by the Lutherans, United Church of Christ, or the Roman Catholic Church, you were going to hell. When my friend, Sheldon, was studying for his Bar Mitzvah, if you believed the Messiah came to earth in the form of Jesus Christ, you were going to hell. So my logic told me there had to be something else.

The night my father was buried, through my tears, alone in the woods of Rieglesville, I looked up at the stars and saw light beams heading directly to my eyes. That caused me to think of energy, the purest form of energy had to be light. Physics class taught me that energy never dies, it may change form or direction, but it continues on infinitely. So light energy continues on indefinitely as well, right. Sure it does. So what do people who have had a near death experience say. They saw themselves heading to a bright light. That makes sense to me, their life energy is turning into light itself.

Then I wondered about the human brain. What is it made of. When I first asked this question, the answer was grey matter, today it is made up of grey and white matter. And what is matter. It is the substance of which any physical object consists. So the brain is made of a substance that creates electrical energy, which explains how it is possible to measure brain waves. The brain has been studied for years by the best medical minds in the world. They've determine what different sections of the brain control muscle activity, thought, hearing, sight, touch, and how to interpret these senses. How it controls them is by electrical impulses, synapse. How these impulses are made is still unclear, even though the synapse have be measured and classified into 5 main types. What brain tissue is made of is still unclear. We do know that the brain is also the home of a person's mind or thought processes.

From biology classes, I learned that when a sperm cell fertilizes an egg cell in a human the first thing that is formed is a zygote. This is composed of the brain, brain stem, spinal cord, nervous system all the way to the liver. In other words, the first part of a mammal to form is its brain and spinal cord. We already learned that the brain is made of matter that makes electrical energy to communicate with the parts of the body, but it also makes the human mind. What is the biggest difference between humans. The way they think. What allows a person to think. One's mind. I believe that the brain not only makes energy, but collects energy as well.

Now when a person dies, the body quickly decomposes and becomes part of the evolution of the earth. That person's brain releases the energy it has collected as well as the energy it created. This energy goes back into the evolution of the universe. To my mind, that explains such phenomena as deja vu and how a new born can resemble a person who is not a relative, but was a good friend or acquaintance. So in my mind, there is no such thing as heaven or hell, and God is the energy that exists within the universe.

Anyway, that's the theory I developed to ease the pain of my father's death. It still works for me, so that's how I live my life, without formal religion.

My mother changed a lot after burying Dad. They were married for over 25 years, had the numerous ups and downs like all couples and went through tragedy and triumph. Some of the stories Mom shared with me after Dad's burial I'll share here.

Their Deciding Date That Lead To Marriage:

Mom's maiden name is Schettino. Her parents came from the Po River area of Italy in 1908, the year Mom was born. She was the first of her family to be an American, I'll have more about that later on. Dad's family had ties to the US for a long time. My great, great, great grandfather was one of 6 men who signed both the Declaration of Independence and the U. S. Constitution, George W. Read, who was a lawyer from the state of Delaware. So their family's dynamic was very different. Mom's family was a strict patriarchy, whereas, Dad's family was more of a matriarchy.

Their first date ended in a conflict with my mother's father. Dad picked Mom up around 6:30 to get a Jimmy's hot dog and go to a movie. While they were in the movie theatre, it began to rain very hard. With the snow melt and the heavy rain, the Lehigh and Delaware Rivers swelled and flooded the bridges that lead from the South side of Easton to the central city, where Mom's family lived.

When Dad tried to drive Mom home, they discovered that the bridges were washed out, so the only way for them to get home was to drive 12 miles into Bethlehem to another bridge that crossed the Lehigh River and hope that that bridge wasn't washed out. They were fortunate, and were able to cross over the river and drive back into Easton. They walked up the stairs to the Schettino apartment, Mom saw her sister, Philomina, sitting in the rocking chair wringing her handkerchief and knew her father was very angry. She said to Dad, "George, I think you should just leave me here. I don't want you to get in trouble with my father."

Dad told her not to worry, and he'd explain the situation. Now you have to understand that my mother's father was a stone mason, and stood well over six feet tall. Dad was very strong, but was only 5'9". So when they knocked on the door of the apartment, Nunie, Italian for Grandfather, opened it and in a very angry voice said, "I thought you said you gonna bring her home before 11:00."

Dad looked up at him, pointed his finger at his face, and replied, "I said no such thing. Here she is, safe and sound. We're a bit late because of the damned flood, no other reason." According to Mom, nobody had ever talked back to Nunie like that before, and especially no one my father's size. She thought there'd be a fight, but Nunie just motioned for Mom to get in the apartment, nodded to Dad and that was it. After Dad left, however, she was reprimanded and spanked for being late. The next day, when they talked, Dad asked her if she wanted to get married, and she accepted.

Dad's Cool Wedding Vow:

The next story she shared was of their marriage. Mom's family thought they were getting married so quickly because Mom was pregnant, not true. Dad's family thought the same thing and that Dad was being cajoled into marrying the diego, not true. Anyway, because Dad was not a Roman Catholic, they were not permitted to be married in the church itself. So the ceremony was performed in the rectory, witnessed by only the best man and maid of honour. During the ring exchange, Dad tried to place the ring on Mom's middle finger, not the ring finger. When she pointed it out to him, Dad exclaimed, "Well shit, I never got married before. How the hell am I supposed to know which finger the damned ring goes on."

After the ceremony was done, the priest blessed everyone except Dad and said, "Good luck Mary. You'll need it." The snub never bothered Dad, and they were married for over 25 years, as I said before.

Mom depended a lot on Dad for many things, but she was a strong woman and had a mind of her own. I don't recall them fighting very much, but when they did, Mom was the loud one, while Dad was fairly quiet but adamant in his arguments. He usually one the argument due to his logical thought process. When Mom acknowledged that he was right, she never wavered from her support of the decision that they made.

Financially, we were never "rich," but we were never hungry or without a roof over our heads. When Dad died, Mom had a hard decision to make, try to keep our house in Easton, or sell it and move into an apartment located above my sister and brother in law's garage. She sold the house. I'm not completely sure how much she was asking for the house, but I know she didn't get what she thought it was worth. She sold it to a couple who had immigrated from Lebanon, and ever since that time, she thought Lebanese people were cheats. That didn't help my relationship with my wife or her family, but that's for a later time in this story.

After selling the house and moving into that two-bedroom apartment with my sister, Mom's independent thinking changed. It took her a long time to adjust to living without Dad, selling off her house and most of her possessions, and deciding on who to vote for in various elections. 1968 was a big election federally. Dad was an Eisenhower Republican, and they both voted Republican for as long as I remember. But for this election, my mother asked me who to vote for. I was dumbfounded. I told her the background of the candidates and told her to decide for herself. As you might recall, that was the election between Richard Nixon and Hubert Humphrey. When I told Mom that Nixon was Eisenhower's vice president, she knew who she'd be voting for. So my vote countered hers, but it was not enough, Nixon won by a landslide.

CHAPTER 7:
COLLEGE - THE SECOND TIME

After Dad was buried, I returned to college and my job. Both the professors and my supervisor at the Liquor Store were very sympathetic. The routine of work and school helped me acquiesce to the fact my father was dead and gone. All these years later, I still miss him and can see his smile when dancing or playing the ukelele. My sex life suffered after the phone call experience, but, fortunately, there were a number of girls willing to help me overcome that trauma.

Accident Proves I'm A Hard Head:

After I returned, I had a near death experience, again. One of my professors was a man for whom I used to buy alcohol at the liquor store in 1964 when I was a freshman. I always looked older than I was, so I never was asked for ID when I went into a bar or the liquor store. So I started a kind of business. Upper class men and women wanted booze and wine, but were not old enough to buy it, one had to be 21 back then. So I would get a list of the items they wanted, get their items, and charged them an extra $0.25 for each bottle. It wasn't a lot of money, but I got my alcohol for nothing that way. Ron Jenkins graduated in '65 and became an associate professor of education later that year. He married his high school sweetheart, had two children, and bought a house on Price Street.

When I first attended his class, he asked me if I'd stay after class was over so he could talk to me. I said sure. It seems he remembered me from my alcohol purchases and wanted to reminisce about his time as a student back then. We talked for a while, then I had to get to my next class. He asked if I'd like to meet his wife and children and have a drink for old time's sake, he'd provide the refreshments, ha ha. So I showed up to his home around 4 and met his family. Ron's wife asked if I wanted to eat supper with them, but I declined because I had a date with a woman who lived in an apartment next to mine. I was going to cook supper for her and me, and later we'd do something else.

Ron was drinking scotch and soda, but I wanted nothing to do with that foul whiskey and drank bourbon instead. The kids had their supper around 5, but Ron and I just kept talking. After eating, Ron's son joined us in the living room, so we tuned down our recollections and stories. Anyway, I was enjoying myself drinking, talking about the Marines, and playing with his 4-year-old son so much that I forgot about my date. Ron's supper was ready at 6:30, and his wife reminded me that I had a date.

I was late, so left his home in a hurry, climbed into my 58 Volkswagen bug, and drove to a pizza joint. It took so much time to order and get my pizza that it began to get dark. I put the pizza on the front seat of my VW and began the 15-minute drive to Downingtown. I forgot to put my headlights on.

The road from West Chester to Downingtown is very winding, hilly, and surrounded by trees. So the drive home was on a very dark road, but I was too drunk to notice. I had driven that road for so long that I knew all the twists and turns by heart. Unfortunately, the car coming opposite to me didn't, and he had on his high beam headlights. As we approached a mutual curve, he was over the dividing line, his lights blinded me, I panicked and pulled my steering wheel hard to the right. I went up a hill, stopped, and the VW flipped on its back, then rolled back onto the road. The car was totalled, but I was alive.

I tried to open my door, but there was something very wrong. Moving to my right so I could smash my shoulder onto the door was really hard. I took off my seatbelt, and the clasp side fell onto the door. I couldn't figure out what the hell was wrong when the passenger door was opened by an older man.

He was standing on the side of the VW and holding the door open. He asked if I was all right and if I could move around to give him my hand. I wondered why he wanted my hand, why he was standing on the car, why he was holding the damned door opened, and what the hell happened.

I gave him my hand, and he pulled me out of the driver's seat and had me stand on the driver's door. Then he told me to pull myself out of the car. It seems that the car was laying on the driver's side, which was why I couldn't open the door. Also there was the stench of gasoline that was leaking from the tank and the heater. After I got out of the car, he asked me if I was feeling okay and if I had a headache. I said I was feeling no pain, meaning I was drunk, but he showed me why he was asking. The VW's roof was now concave except where my head was. At that spot there was a noticeable convex shape in the roof. I suppose what had happened was when the car flipped backwards, my head, protected by the felt and insulation of the inside roof, kept that part from collapsing.

Another Farmer Helps Me Out Again:

That man was a farmer and kept me from being arrested that night for drunk driving. His wife had called the state troopers about the accident, which was good for me because they were farther away than the local police. She then put flares on the road to warn other cars about my VW being in the middle of the road. Then they helped me to their kitchen and poured strong coffee for me to drink, which I did. Then they gave me a tooth brush and paste and told me to clean my breath before the cops got there. I did.

When the State Troopers arrived, I was sober enough to pass their street sobriety test, thankfully this was before the breathalizer. The Trooper who gave me the test threw some coins on the floor and told me to pick up a certain amount. I did that correctly. He then added some more coins and asked me to pick up a smaller amount. I passed that as well. Then he asked me some questions about my home address, my work, who the president of the US was, where I was at that time. Then he took me out to the farmers walk way and told me to take 10 steps, placing my left heel against my right toe and repeating the procedure. I was wobbly, but passed that as well.

After my car was removed from the road, they actually drove me to my apartment building in Downingtown. My date for that night never spoke to me again, for some reason. The only mark I had from that accident was a scratch on my left wrist where my father's watch was sitting. So I again escaped death. This time because of my hard head.

Roomie Returns:

I completed the Fall Semester of 1968 with a 1.59 accumulative average, which was better than I could have wished for. You see, that semester I was taking the course "Physical Disabilities of Children" in night school, and the night of the mid-term exam was the night I had my date and my father died. Fortunately, the professor didn't know about me deciding to skip the exam for the date, but was very supportive when I told him I missed the exam because Dad died.

However, I had no good excuse for missing the final exam. The afternoon of the exam, I was holed up in my apartment cramming for that test when my former roommate, Jim, called from the Corner Bar. He just got out of the Army and wanted to get together for a beer. How could I say no. So I drove to the bar and met Jim. We had a few beers and began swapping service stories. He suggested that we get a case of half quarts of Schaffer Beer, go back to my apartment, and order a pizza just like old times. To be honest, I completely forgot about my final. That was the only college or university course I flunked. Looking back now, it was worth it. I made up the credits during summer school, so it really was no big deal.

CHAPTER 8:
THE HIPPIE

1969 saw me take a different job from the Liquor Store. I was letting my hair and beard grow, and they had a dress code, which included all male employees being clean shaved, wear a tie and slacks. No jeans, "T" shirts, sandals, etc., etc. So I got a job with a local construction company. The owners were very laid back and didn't care how one looked, just if you could work hard. I could and did. The owner was the oldest of us, who lived above the Corner Bar and had us all meet him there at 6:30 every weekday morning. What was really unique about him was that each and every morning he'd ask the bartender for his "orange juice," and he'd get a beer glass of gin and orange juice. As he sipped his morning juice, he'd tell us our job site and what we had to do.

Almost Made It To Woodstock:

I learned how to do many useful things that helped me later in life after buying my one and only house. I learned how to put a new roof on a house, clean and repair toilets, install a commode, put siding on a house and last, but very significant, how to drain, clean, sanitize, paint and enclose a cesspool.

That summer I was dating a beautiful, local girl named Irene. She was a blond haired hippie chick who loved to paint, drink, smoke joints and read. She read about a large concert that was going to happen in upper New York State and thought we should go. It was to be a three-day love in from August 15th, 16th and 17th. She cut out a form to send to the organizers for tickets and gave it to me to fill in and get us tickets for all three days. It would have cost me $36.00 for two tickets for all three days, and I was hesitant about spending all that money. In '69 that was a lot of cash, especially when a minimum wage job paid $1.30/hour, and I thought it might actually be a scam. However, I later learned that not only was it the real deal, but that Joan Baez and Bob Dylan were going to be the opening act, so I bought the money order necessary to add to the ticket request and mailed it off.

Irene was really happy when the tickets arrived, but she later became really angry when I discovered that I would have to work that weekend. But she asked me if she could have the tickets so she and her girlfriend could go. Her girlfriend's name was Bonnie and had promised to pay me for her tickets. So I got half of my money back, and they hitchhiked up to Bethel, New York. I went with the crew to a farm house and into a cesspool. Yep, while Irene and Bonnie were partying and doing everything you could imagine while sharing three days with 400,000 other people during a rain storm and heavy duty rock concert known as Woodstock, I was helping to drain the cesspool, scrub it down with hot water mixed with Lye, repair the concrete, paint the concrete and rebuild the cover for it. Ahh, what a great Hippie life I was leading.

When Irene returned to West Chester, she dumped me for the guy she had latched on to during her stay at Woodstock. Bonnie was a little taken back with Irene's coldness to me, and we developed a friendship. It was also during this time that I met Bev.

I Make A Friend Who Is A Girl And The Best Car I Ever Had:

Bonnie and Bev were roommates sharing an apartment on North High Street. Bonnie and I had been dating since she returned from Woodstock, and after school opened in September, she asked me if I had ever been with a virgin. I said I had not, then she told me about her roommate, Bev, who lamented to her that she didn't want to remain a virgin and asked Bonnie to find a man who would make her a woman. So she asked me if I'd do the honours. I agreed. Then she told me that Bev's problem with finding a lover was her size, she was obese, but had a cute face and great personality. Honestly, I didn't care, I was just so pleased that Bonnie would ask me to do Bev that I asked when I should do her. She said, why don't you take me home and come up to meet her tonight. So I did.

That meeting was the first time I met the woman who would stay in my life for the next six years. Bev graduated from West Chester after 4 years and began a very successful teaching career in the Chester, Philadelphia area for 30 odd years. It was also when I began to let my hair and beard grow out and began to really feel like a hippie. This was especially true after I participated in the West Chester Anti-Vietnam War protests. We gathered in the Quad, set up a stage and sound system, then read the names of all the soldiers who had died since the conflict began. It took all night.

In the spring semester of 1969, I took 15 credits, had Cs in all of the courses and brought my accumulative average up from 1.59 to 1.89. Thus I could stay in the college and take more courses. That summer I took the make-up course for Physical Disabilities of Children and three other courses. My efforts brought my accumulative average up to 1.94, so I was nearly eligible for my senior year. To begin the final year at West Chester one needed to have a minimum accumulative average of 2.0.

Since I totalled my VW, I needed another car and found one for $25.00. It was a 1953 Chevy Bel Air. It was licensed for 1969 and only had one problem, no starting motor. But since it was a standard transmission, it was easy to kick start. All you had to do was get it to move around 5 MPH, put it in second gear and pop the clutch. My apartment at that time was on Oakburn Road, which was narrow but had a slight incline. I always parked in the last spot near the intersection, so I only had to give it a small push and pop the clutch. That car got me through two semesters and was a conversation piece for the various girls I dated.

In June of 1969, I was driving home to Martin's Creek when the oil light came on. I stopped in a gas station and checked the oil, but the dipstick showed that there was plenty of oil in the engine, so I asked the mechanic on duty what would cause the light to come on. He said that with a car this old, it was probably the oil pump. Well, I didn't have the money or the time to buy an oil pump and pay the mechanic to install it, so I just drove off. At each stop light, I put the gear in neutral, kept the engine running fast, then when the light changed, I'd put it in second and move on to the next stop. The car was smoking like mad, and I was worried I'd be stopped by the police, but luckily they missed me. I did this until I got to my sister's house. Then I parked the car on the street and listened to it sizzle, creak, and shake until it stopped. It actually stopped completely with a frozen block. That car was toast.

My brother in law, Robert, looked at it and said we can forget about it. He then hooked up a tow bar to his truck, and we towed it to the nearest junk yard. The owner paid us $70.00 for it. We split the money even steven. So to this day, I say the best car I ever owned was that 1953 Chevy Bel Air because it cost me $25.00, took me through two semesters, and when it died, I put $35.00 back into my pocket.

Since Bev and I were going together steadily and she had her own automobile, I didn't bother to buy another car. After Robert and I sold the Chevy, I called Bev and asked her to drive up to Martin's Creek and get me. She was home with her parents at that time and told them she was going on a vacation in the Pocono Mountains with her friend. She got there in the middle of the week and bunked down with me in Mom's apartment. We didn't want her to actually lie to her parents, so we drove to Mount Airy Lodge in Mt. Pocono for a couple of days. It's a beautiful location and had top notch entertainment, people like comedian Buddy Hackett, impressionist Frank Gorshin, and musician Count Basie. We saw them all that weekend.

A Friend In Need:

After our weekend there, we returned to West Chester and found an apartment together. Actually, there were three of us sharing the place, Bonnie also moved in and shared the expenses. All I can say is it was one great Fall semester for me, in more ways than one. I only took two 3 credit courses and got B's in each one. Jim graduated with his BEd and married his girlfriend, Sam. Jim and Sam moved into an apartment in Pottstown.

An adventure I had with them was after a bad winter storm hit our area the winter of 1969. I got a phone call from Jim late afternoon saying their apartment was flooding and they needed help to save their furniture.

I told them I'd be there ASAP.

Unfortunately, there was no car for me to use, so I hitchhiked from West Chester to their apartment in Pottstown. By car, it was only a half hour drive, but hitchhiking in a freezing rain storm took quite a bit longer. I got to their place about 2 hours after Jim's call.

Their place was a mess. It took us working nonstop all night, but we managed to save their new furniture. After the rain abated, it didn't take too long to finish getting all the water out, cleaning, and drying the rooms. Sam had a bottle of Gordon's Vodka, and we celebrated by having a party with vodka and orange juice and a meal of hot dogs and french fries.

Jim's First Date With His Future Wife (Kinda):

Funny story about Jim, Sam, and me, I had Jim's first date with Sam. Yep, I had a date with Bonnie, and we were going to double date with Jim and Sam. Sam was living with her father in King of Prussia, Pennsylvania, which is a suburb of Philadelphia, and was teaching in an elementary school in nearby Paoli. Jim had dated Sam when they were both in West Chester State College and had met her father. He didn't like him because he thought Sam's father hated him. So Jim convinced me to pick her up at her father's house and meet Bonnie and him at the Denny's Restaurant on Pike. So I did; however, Jim didn't show up. He also didn't pick Bonnie up or call her to let her know the change in plans. Rather, Jim made it to the Corner Bar and proceeded to drink a few cold ones.

Sam ordered a plate of french fries and two cokes while we waited for Jim and Bonnie to meet us there. Then she did something that few people do; she poured mustard on her plate and dipped the fries in it. Well, I was a bit flabbergasted, but Sam persuaded me to try it. Ya know, it's pretty tasty. I still prefer ketchup, but mustard is not a bad substitute. So we waited and talked about her college days, teaching career, Jim's silly habits and fears, and everything under the sun for over an hour.

After the fries were finished, I paid the bill and took her home. Then I went to the Corner Bar and reamed Jim out for not showing up or getting Bonnie. And that's exactly what happened. Bonnie was pissed off at me, but after I explained what happened, she cooled down, and life continued on.

Seeing The Usa – The Hard Way:

In the Fall Semester, I only took two courses, both 3 credits, and I got B's in them to pull my accumulative average up to 2.00 and be eligible for my senior year. I also became flustered by my mother and began feeling as if I could do nothing to get her back to her normal feisty self. So I decided to leave college again and hitchhike back to California. Steve was living in Oakland and going to Hastings College of Law in San Francisco. He was also buying a house, living with a beautiful blond woman, and working as a claims adjuster for Aetna Life and Casualty Insurance Company.

I left in February to a sedate send off from Bev, Bonnie, and some of the cast of characters that the three of us associated with. At that time, the song "Hitchin' A Ride" by Vanity Fair was popular, and Bev made sure that song played over and over again. She drove me to U.S. Route 1 where I began my trip south. I planned to get to Hollywood, Florida, and stay a few days with Hilda, a friend from Rieglesville. Hilda's mother was our Kindergarten teacher and my first crush — Hilda, not her mother — well, her mother was pretty as well.

I was doing very well and got all the way into Virginia the first day's hitchhiking. I was picked up by a family whose father was a doctor in the military stationed in the medical center in Richmond. They dropped me off near a Holiday Inn, but I didn't want to spend any money on a room there, and got something to eat, then found an all-night laundromat to crash in.

Jail Time:

I got back on Route 1 early in the morning and got a ride into North Carolina with a truck driver. Not a big tractor trailer trucker, but a guy in a pickup truck carrying fencing in his bed. I threw my backpack in the back on top of the stuff and got into the front seat of a nice warm Ford. He dropped me off in a town called Mocksville.

I remember that name because of what happened there. I began walking down the road back onto Route 1 when I spotted a sign that said, "NO HITCHHIKING." So I got some cardboard out of a garbage can and bought a black marker and some adhesive tape. I figured that if I got injured, the adhesive tape would be better than scotch tape (smart huh?). I then taped a sign that said FLORIDA on my backpack and began walking down Route 1.

I walked for maybe an hour when a police car pulled over and an officer got out and approached me. He asked me where I was going, and I told him to Hollywood, Florida. He wondered if I was going to walk all the way there, and I said that I was hoping a good samaritan might stop and offer me a ride. He then asked for identification. I showed him my Pennsylvania driver's license and the pink discharge ID from the Marines. He took them and told me to get in the back seat of his car. I asked him why and was told there was a no hitchhiking law in North Carolina. When I tried to tell him that I wasn't hitchhiking, he started to get angry.

Well, the last thing a long haired, hippie freak wearing a Marine Corps top coat and military boots wanted was to argue with an angry cop. So I took off my backpack and got into the back seat of his Ford Police Vehicle. He closed the door, and I noticed that there wasn't any handle for me to use, so I was arrested for walking alongside a road with a sign on my back. I got worried.

I was taken to a Justice of the Peace in Mocksville, who looked at my ID, listened to the Sheriff's explanation of why I was in his office, looked at my backpack sign and asked if I had my thumb up when the sheriff stopped. He said I didn't, and the Justice of the Peace said that by just walking on the road was not breaking the law. Then he asked me where I was going, and I told him that I was going to see an old girlfriend in Hollywood, Florida. Where was I coming from, was the next question. I told him from West Chester, Pennsylvania. Then how much money did I have. I told him about $250.00. I thought I was getting away free of charge, but that old codger said I was a vagrant in his county and needed to spend 24 hours in jail and pay a fine of $25.00. I was flabbergasted. I began to complain, when he asked me if I preferred to spend more time in their facility. I shut up. See, I did learn from my court martial.

So I spent the night in a cell that was 6 paces long and 4 wide. It had a bed that was fastened to the floor, no pillow or sheets, just a blanket. It had a small sink that probably hadn't been cleaned in a year and a drain with running water. The jail keeper said that was for me to piss in, and if I needed to shit, I had to call him and he'd take me to a toilet, in handcuffs. Since it was a little after noon, he brought me a hot dog in a bun and some sweet tea in a metal cup. Then I was on my own until around six, I think. A new jailer came in to get the cup and ask me if I wanted supper. I said that I did and was given a plate with another hot dog, some beans, some kind of greens, and another cup of sweet tea. The food wasn't really that bad tasting, but I would have liked to have had some ketchup or mustard for the hot dog.

The next afternoon, I was given a choice by the sheriff. He'd take me to the next county or to the bus station. I chose the bus station and bought a ticket back to Philadelphia. I stood at the on ramp of the Schuylkill Expressway heading west and hoped I'd get a good ride out of the area. I sure as hell didn't want to go back to West Chester and face Bev and Bonnie as a failed traveller. I was lucky enough to get a ride all the way to York, Pa. There I set up my pup tent in a deserted field, slept for a few hours, and got back on the road early.

Boston:

A group of young people who were going to Boston stopped and offered me a ride. I thought, never been to Boston, might be a fun trip, and I could look up a girlfriend from Rieglesville with whom I kept in touch, Lisa. She was going to Boston College and had an apartment near the school. So I hopped in and went to Boston. When they dropped me off, I looked up Lisa's number in a phone booth (remember them?) and called her. She welcomed me warmly and said that I could camp out in the boiler room of her apartment building. So I did. Then she showed me around the campus and some of the city. Four days later I got back on the road going west.

Another Run In With Uncle Ray:

The rest of my journey was uneventful until I made it to Davenport, Iowa. I decided to drop in on Uncle Ray and see if I could spend a day or two resting up. He was not very receptive, for sure. He did feed me and allowed me to set up my tent in his back yard. I used the bathroom and showered, then he invited me to have a drink with him. He was drinking scotch, which I hate, but I decided to share a glass with him to be polite. I sipped the damned stuff, but Uncle Ray drank quickly. He told me that the reason he didn't want me to sleep in the house was because he thought I would be a bad influence on his daughter, my cousin Jaimie. Okay, I guess it was because of the argument we had when Mom and Dad picked me up back in '68.

Then we started talking politics. I told him how I protested against the Vietnam War, and he called me a communist sympathizer. He asked me what I thought of Nixon's overwhelming win to the presidency, and I told him I thought Nixon was a creep and a crook. That was such a bad answer that he told me to finish my drink and get the hell out of his house. I did. The next morning, he let me in to get some breakfast and wash up, but that was all I was permitted to do. He was kind enough to take me to Route 50 so I could continue hitchhiking west. That was the last time I saw Uncle Ray until he visited my mother one summer after I was married.

Picked Up By A Psychedelically Painted Vw Van:

From Iowa, I decided to go south and take Route 61. I had planned to get to Route 66 again and go into southern California. It didn't happen that way. A VW van full of hippies stopped and picked me up. They asked where I was headed, and I told them Oakland, California. They said they were going to LA and to hop on.

There were 3 girls and 2 guys, so I thought I had it made. They got on Route 80 West, and we were on our way. After driving for a couple of hours, the driver said that they needed to get gas and stopped soon after that in a Mobile Gas Station. The trick was to collect money from each of us to pay for it. Unfortunately, there were only 2 of us that had any kind of money, I still had around $200.00, and one of the girls, Susan, had about $75.00. The others had just a few bucks, maybe totalling 30 or 40 dollars. So I said I'd pay for this fill up and got some snack food for all of us.

When we got back on the road, I was asked if I wanted to drive because I got the gas. Well, since I do enjoy driving, I agreed. One of the guys rolled a joint, and one of the girls took out her guitar and began playing folk songs. I thought life on the road with these people would be great. I'd get to California, be high for most of the trip, and enjoy some kindred spirits. I drove us into Nebraska and let another guy take over. He got us nearly into Utah when we had to fill up again. This time I took a collection from each one of my fellow travelers, I wasn't sucker enough to pay for all the gas on our trip, then we decided it was time to take a break from the van and walk around.

When we got back to the van, we all arranged ourselves as comfortably as possible and slept. The sun awoke us fairly early in the morning, and after we all relieved ourselves, I got us back on the road. We were nearly near the Great Salt Lake in Utah when we changed up again. This time Susan was driving, and she decided we needed to fill up again. We did, and she got us to a park right on the Great Salt Lake. Again we decided to spend the night. In the morning two people were missing, and so was most of our money. I had $35.00 in the pocket of the jeans I slept in, but the rest of my money was gone, as was Susan's and the couple who owned the van. That wasn't going to be enough to get us to LA, that's for sure. We debated about looking for them, or looking for a job, or just driving into Las Vegas and take a chance on gambling.

My vote was to look for the crooks, but I was alone in that. The other three thought it'd be an adventure to hit Las Vegas, and that's what we did. Big mistake, in my opinion, but that's life on the road. We took off for the bright lights and casinos of Las Vegas in the hope of winning enough money to carry us into Los Angeles.

On My Own Again, Chess In Los Angeles:

The only experience I had had with gambling was playing hearts, cribbage, and other card games against friends for hamburgers or beer. So I decided I'd leave my hippie friends to try their luck, and I'd continue to hitch hike on to Oakland. Their plan was to do some busking for gambling money, but since we were sharing, I bought us some fast food, and we ate our last meal together. I then made my way to Route 15, an interstate highway that went to California.

I was there for about an hour or so when a couple in an Oldsmobile convertible stopped and picked me up. They said they were on their way home from a weekend vacation to the Strip. They said that they lived in Los Angeles in a two-bedroom apartment, and I was welcome to spend the night with them if I wanted. Well, I was dirty, without money or a change of clothes, hungry, and welcomed the offer. I told them my story about being picked up by the hippies and the decision we made in Las Vegas. The man, who was driving, said I probably made the right decision and not to worry, they'd help me out. I thanked my lucky stars and asked them what I might be able to do to pay them back. The woman asked if I knew how to play chess. I told them I did, but wasn't very good. She said that doesn't matter and to just entertain them while one or the other was working.

So I spent three days with them in their apartment. The first thing I did when we got settled in their place was to ask to take a shower and wash my clothes. After the shower, they were talking about getting some food on the go, and I offered to cook them dinner. They preferred to order in Chinese food and then set up their chess board. So I spent most of my time with them playing chess with one or the other. Fortunately, they never asked me for any money and were the sweetest hosts one could have had. When you're down and out and meet people like these two, you really learn to appreciate the gift of sharing. Since then, I have tried to do the same when I could.

They took me to an on ramp to Highway 100N and wished me good luck. I thought my luck was pretty darned good since I met them and thanked them profusely. I now had a full belly and clean clothes. But, most important, I still had $5.00 in my pocket and was in California, heading to my friend Steve's house in Oakland. I had forgotten how far LA is from Oakland, but learned quickly that it was an all day and all night trip. The rides I got were many and unmemorable. I spent most of my $5.00 on food and water, so when I walked up to 2032 86th Avenue early Saturday morning with, literally, $0.02 in my pocket, rang the doorbell. Steve let me in and told me to make myself comfortable in the back porch for a few hours while he and Karen slept for a while longer. That's what I did, and had no trouble quickly falling asleep. I have no idea what time it was when I awoke, but Steve and Karen were in the kitchen talking about making something to eat. I got up, used the bathroom, and joined them in the kitchen. We made small talk for a short time, then I told them my story about hitch hiking across the USA. When I shared the story about my ride with the hippies, Karen was not the least bit surprised.

Then I told them that I made it to their doorstep with only $0.02 in my pocket and the clothes that were on my back and in my backpack. Steve assured me that there were plenty of good jobs in Oakland and that I'd be able to get one quickly. He then gave me the Oakland Tribune to look for jobs. I found a couple Steve in 1970, that I thought I'd be able to do and called a few to see if I might get an interview on Monday. Obviously I didn't have a suit and tie to wear for a job interview and Steve's clothes were too small for me. I thought I might borrow some money from him and purchase something suitable from K-Mart.

Steve's House. 86 Ave Oakland Ca

Being A Minority:

After looking around their kitchen cupboards and fridge, I got out some frozen chicken, pasta, tomato sauce, onions, celery, and spices. I made my version of chicken parmesan. While I was cooking, one of their neighbors dropped by. His name was Chilli. Oh, I forgot to mention that Steve and Karen were the only white people in a 4 or 5 block radius, and Chilli was African American. He commented on the smell from the kitchen, which is when Steve introduced me to him as his new cook. We talked for a while, and I told him a short version of my trip across the country.

Chilli was the regional manager of the Safeway Grocery Chain in East Oakland and married to a gorgeous Norwegian woman named Ingrid. When I met her, she had just returned from the grocery store and was angry as hell at "all" men. She was livid because one of the bags of groceries she had, and was trying to place in the trunk of their car, ripped. Although there were a few men around, no one offered to help her and, in fact, ogled her as she bent over to pick up the items that fell. To be honest, I understood why the men were gawking at her; she was a knock-out.

Steve had two other neighborhood friends. Chilli lived a couple of doors down 86 Avenue, but Al lived to our left and Louis on the right. Louis had a couple of dogs that were friends of Steve's dogs. There was a large fence between the houses that the dogs would run around, bark, and generally play together. Al was a man about my size, and when we met, Steve told him my need for a suit and tie to wear for a job interview, and Al said he had so many that he didn't mind lending me one. So I borrowed one from him to wear job hunting.

I Get Fired From My First Job:

I had lined up three interviews on Monday and got to all three of them. I chose to become the manager of an A&W Root Beer Stand at East 11th Street and 2nd Avenue. This was back when A&W had waitresses who used roller skates to deliver food ordered by radio to cars parked in their lot. The owner of this particular A&W also owned two other franchises and was a devout Mormon. He paid 10% of his profits to the church, so he was very keen about the amount of profit he earned from his restaurants. This would prove to be my downfall after six months of managing this A&W.

The staff were very nice and worked hard, especially the waitresses. There was one older cook who made the tuna and egg salad mixtures, recipes that I use to this day. His secret ingredient for the tuna mixture was dill seed, and in the egg mixture he used tarragon. The other cook we had was about my age, and we became buddies.

He took me to an after-hours bar in San Francisco where he knew the manager. Actually, she was his aunt. When we walked in, she asked us to sit at a particular table so we could watch her car and let her know if anyone went near it. She was worried that the three drunks she threw out of the bar just before we walked in would retaliate by damaging it, either with a key or by breaking a window. She told us our first few drinks would be on the house for doing this.

We sat down, but almost immediately saw three men walk across the street toward her car, so rather than call out to her (she was behind the bar), we decided to run down and confront them. That's what we did, and they seemed to walk away from the car. We watched them walk down the street for a bit, then turned around to return to the bar.

Right in the middle of the street we were crossing, someone kicked me in my back and knocked me down. The cook was shoved onto a car that was parked on the opposite side of the street by two of the cowards and threatened with a knife. I managed to get back up to confront the coward that kicked me, and he hit me in the face. I hit him back and shoved him backward toward another parked car. I got him on the ground and began to hit him in his face over and over again, but one of the men that was threatening the cook saw what was happening and came over to help his compatriot by kicking me in the ribs.

I managed to grab his leg and pulled him down as well, but in the meantime, the cook had given his attacker some money and told him to get his friends off me, although I was doing OK in this fight. He and his attacker came over to my side of the street and pulled me off the man who kicked me in the back and got the both of them to run away. I was livid, a madman, the Irish and Italian mix in my DNA was working overtime. Fortunately, I seem to have this ability to be extremely angry one minute and be over it the next. I calmed down enough to get back to the bar and get my free drinks.

The only thing that had happened to me, beside a couple of bruises, was my new K-Mart plaid, polyester pants got a hole in the knee. Of course, my knee was cut as well from falling down onto the street. Cookie's aunt offered to sew them up, and I allowed her to do that. So here I was, back in San Francisco, sitting in an after-hours bar without any pants on, drinking free beer. Wasn't life just grand?

How did I get fired from the A&W job? Well, I'll tell ya. Behind the restaurant were a number of apartment buildings. Also around this neighborhood were an outdoor basketball court and a playground.

Most of the families living in these apartments were very poor and lived on social assistance. I'd notice some Native American children hanging around the dumpster behind the restaurant's kitchen.

Curious as to what they were doing, I saw one boy be lifted into the garbage container and throw out some bags of orders that were uneaten. They proceeded to open the bags and eat what was left over. I went over and asked them what was up and was told that their mother worked as a cleaner, and they didn't have enough food to eat while she was gone. Later that night, I saw a woman enter their apartment and went over to meet her. She was nice, and we had a great chat. I asked her if there was anything I could do to help her out, and she said they were getting along all right, but often ran out of food between her paychecks. I said that I'd see what I could do to help out.

I thought that rather than throw out unused vegetables, fries, and thawed hamburgers, I'd collect them, save them in a part of the fridge that was hardly ever used, and give them to the kids after I closed up. The cooks noticed what I was doing and decided to help out as well, so often after their shift was over, rather than eat their dinner or lunch that was part of their salary, they'd make a sandwich or two and pack them with the other leftovers I saved. This was all right, but then I became "creative" by taking the five or six frozen burgers left in the box and adding them to the kids' groceries. That cut into the owner's bottom line, not by a lot, but enough that he asked me why the profit margin was declining. I told him what I had been doing and offered to pay the difference. Unfortunately, he just saw my behavior as stealing from him and gave me two weeks' notice. I stopped the handouts and looked for another job. This happened in the fall of 1970.

I Meet A World War Ii Refugee And Move Into A Warehouse:

One of the waitresses was dating a tall, long-haired guy named Clem M., who was friends with an older man named K. M. Klaus had led a very interesting life. He was originally from Austria and was Jewish. In 1938, Klaus was two years old when the Nazis killed his father, and his mother decided to run away south. She carried him over the Pyrenees Mountains into Spain and continued to Gibraltar, where she got a boat into Morocco. From there, she managed to get onto a container ship going to Argentina. From Argentina, she made her way north until she finally got into Florida.

This trip took three years, and WWII was raging. She applied for and was given asylum. After the war, she and Klaus became naturalized U.S. citizens. Mrs. M. was a good cook and got a job working in a Miami restaurant noted for its German cuisine. As a teenager, Klaus quit school and started working in the same restaurant as his mother. By the time he was in his twenties, his mother and he opened their own place and eventually wound up with a number of restaurants along the southern U.S. border. Then Klaus got married.

When I met him, he had been divorced, and as part of the settlement, his wife got the restaurants in Florida and Alabama. Klaus got the ones in Mississippi and Texas. He promptly sold these and moved to the Los Angeles area. There he opened another restaurant, and after it became a success, he sold that and moved to Oakland. It was at that time that I met him.

Klaus and Clem were planning to rent a warehouse with an option to buy and renovate it into living quarters for hippies. Klaus drew a picture of what he thought this place would look like, and they asked me if I would like to join in their endeavor. I considered that if I shared in the plan with Klaus and Clem, I would have an equity stake in that residential venture, and it would be an adventure.

Finally, I thought that since I was recently hired as a stock boy with Newberry's Department Store and the warehouse was much closer to the store than Steve's house, I'd move on. Of course, also in making my decision was the fact that while I was tripping on acid, I had tried to get into bed with Karen. Karen was really pissed with me and said she could no longer trust me to be in the same house with her. Sooo, I had to move out.

The Barter System And Hallucinogenics:

I had purchased an old Nash Rambler station wagon while working at the A&W and filled the back up with a mattress, blankets, a pillow, and my clothes. That's where I lived until the deal was made with the owners of the Western Transformer Company to rent to buy the warehouse on East 11th Street. Actually, since there was so much work that had to be done in that space, I remained in that car for around three months before the warehouse was livable.

This picture is a very good likeness of the actual car I was living in. The color was more of a green than blue, but it's the same year, 1957, as my car. Having the hood up is accurate as well, I learned a lot about fixing a flat head six engine as well as changing the exhaust manifold, muffler, brakes, and reinforcing the tail pipe. So in the fall of 1970 I moved in with Clem and Klaus.

We didn't have much money to buy the needed materials to renovate this old place, so Klaus struck up a deal with a demolition, construction company. They were tearing down an old home in Berkeley, and for every 3 pieces of lumber that we cleaned, we could keep one for ourselves. We also made the same deal for the bricks that formed the huge wall that surrounded the house as well. Klaus had a 1934 Ford pickup truck that had extra heavy duty springs, which we used to haul our take to the warehouse.

I would get to work at 7:30 in the morning to log, stack, and organize the items that were delivered to the department store, clean up any messes that the customers made on the store floor itself, and get off work at 4:30. From there I'd drive to the warehouse, take a nap until Clem and Klaus got home from the site. We'd eat something, unload the truck, drop some acid or peyote, and make it back to Berkeley to load up the truck again. We usually finished around midnight and went back to the warehouse. Unloaded the truck again, then went to bed or continued to party until the high wore off.

We didn't have any hot running water, so our shower consisted of a hose hung up outside the back of the warehouse. We confiscated a palate, which we used as a shower floor, and I took a cold shower every morning before going to the department store.

One Friday, we went to the site and began taking down a brick wall. After we had Klaus' truck half loaded, Clem suggested we take a weekend off and go up to Geyserville and spend the rest of the weekend at the hot springs and geyser, spa. So we went back to the warehouse, parked the truck, and piled into my Nash Rambler. We had each taken a hit of peyote, and I was beginning to really feel it. Although I knew I shouldn't, I got into the driver's seat, and we took off for the Golden Gate Bridge.

I paid the toll and began to squeeze through the entrance onto the bridge. I hit the backdoor on the driver's side of the car going into the space and the passenger side back panel coming out the other side. Clem and Klaus both shouted that we should change drivers as soon as we got to Sausalito. I agreed and took the first turn off into the storied town. Klaus took over, Clem got shotgun, and I laid down in the back seat and let my mind wonder.

We were about an hour out of Geyserville when we all had to make a pit stop. So Klaus pulled off the road, and the three of us went looking for a "pee" tree. I moved much slower than the other two, and they got back to the car before me. Klaus began to honk the horn, and I tried to hurry up. I got back to the road, and as I approached the car, Klaus pulled away, not far, just enough for me to keep walking. I decided to run up to it, but he took off faster, then stopped again. I said to myself, "Fuck this shit, John. Take a hike up this hill and see where it goes." So I did. Klaus and Clem got out of the car and yelled at me to come on, but I just kept climbing. They decided to move on, and I was left on my own.

My Spirit Animal:

I stripped off my clothes and began walking around the hill and between the trees naked as a bear. As a matter of fact, that's what I decided to be, a brown bear. I walked around on all fours for a while, ate some blueberries, scratched my back on a tree, and found a nice, soft spot for a nap. When dawn broke, I awoke, found my clothes, and put them on. I felt refreshed and very peaceful, but now I had to find out where I was and how to get back to Oakland by hitchhiking.

Deciding that up was better than down, I climbed to the top of the hill and found myself in some kind of a military looking encampment. I walked down the road to a small town and stuck out my thumb when I heard a car at my back. Surprisingly, the driver stopped and asked if I needed help. I asked if he could point me toward Route 100 so I could get back to Oakland. He said that he'd do better than that after he took his packages home to his family and asked me to help him with them. I agreed and got into his car.

Arrested Again:

He was a practicing Jehovah's Witness and began asking me about life and the afterlife. I told him of my theory and how I developed it, but that just added sparks to the fire. Fortunately, we weren't too far from his farm, and I helped him carry his packages into his house. His wife asked me if I'd like some coffee, I agreed, and then asked to use their bathroom to clean up. In there, I stripped down again and washed off the grass and dirt I had all over my body from running around the woods naked. I didn't lock the bathroom door, and their daughter walked in on me as I was drying off. She was shocked and ran downstairs to her mother and told her there was a naked man in the bathroom. Mom became angry, I guess she thought I was some kind of a pervert, and told her husband that I had to leave their home and property immediately.

So after putting my clothes back on, got into his car, and he drove me near the on ramp to Route 100. After insisting that I take his bible with me for solace, he dropped me off next to a wooden and barbed wire fence and near a concrete bridge that lead to one of the on ramps to the highway.

After he left, I climbed the fence and walked to an apple tree a few feet from the road. I blindly opened the bible to the Book of John, used the tree as a chair back, and began reading about John the Baptist. I was nearly asleep when a state trooper called out to me. I never heard the car come up or anything, so I guess I must have fallen asleep again, or perhaps began another mind trip, don't know.

The trooper told me I had to get out of the field because the owner of the farm didn't want anybody to trespass. He had a large breeding bull that he wanted to let out into the field to graze and was worried he might charge me. I walked back to the fence and began to climb it, but the trooper stopped me and said that the farmer had just electrified the barbed wire to keep his cows and bull within the field. He told me to go down to the bridge and climb over there. I did.

Then he wanted to know what I was doing out there at such an early hour. I told him that I had been partying with some friends when they left me passed out in another field. I also explained that I had been dropped off there by another area farmer who gave me his bible. Then I told him that I was just reading about myself. The trooper asked me to tell him all about it, but opened the back door of his cruiser and told me to get in while I talked to him. I asked him if he'd drop me off on the on ramp to 100 South, and he said, "Sure."

The next thing I knew I was locked up again and being taken to the Santa Rosa jail until I could see a judge Monday morning. So I spent the rest of Saturday reading the bible in a jail cell with six other young guys. This jail was pretty nice. It had 12 bunkbeds, 4 commodes, and a games area. I had missed lunch and was getting pretty hungry, luckily there was one prisoner that had a large bag of sunflower seeds, and he shared them with me. To this day, I love sunflower seeds.

I got to use the phone and thought it would be best to call my boss at Newberry's Department store, and I tell him that I'd probably not be making it to work on Monday and told him why. I promised to make it up by working for free on Saturday, but he just laughed that off and told me to get back as soon as feasible.

Monday arrived, and we were taken to the Santa Rosa court house. When it was my turn to speak to the judge, he asked me why I was there. I told him about partying and being left behind, etc., etc. He thought it was funny that I had been arrested for being "incoherent and talking to God." The judge told me to get a bus ticket back to Oakland and be careful with whom I party with in the future.

I was taken to the bus station, but decided to hitchhike instead. Walking to the on ramp, my old, blue Nash Rambler drove by. Klaus and Clem decided to look around for me rather than just driving back to the city. How we connected can only be described as serendipity, like so much of my life. Klaus got us back to the warehouse, and we smoked a couple of joints while I told them about my experiences.

Real Cool Chicks:

They told me about the women they met at the spa and said that they had dates lined up for next weekend. So, the next Saturday, we rolled some joints and took off for Healdsburg to meet up with the girls they had met. We drove through the town of Sebastopol and onto a long dirt road that had grape vines on each side. The women lived on a winery and were in charge of growing the grapes that were used to make the Sebastopol Boutique Winery's various white and red wines. The most important part of their job, they said, was to make sure the grapes were picked when they were ripest. By doing this, they lived in the house for free and got paid enough to buy the necessary things "Hippie Women" needed. Which, really, wasn't very much.

So we all piled into my Nash Rambler and were off to the Geyserville Spa, for my first ever visit. When we got there, we all got out and stripped naked and walked into a large building that had a very distinct smell, sulphur. Inside the building were 4 different, shallow pools. They were differing degrees of heat. One was icy, the other like a warm bath, the third a hot bath, and the fourth was a hot tub. One of the women, I think her name was Rose, jumped into the cold pool first and stayed there for a few minutes, well actually long enough for her nipples to become rigid. I joined her and allowed my little don doolie and scrotum shrivel up to nearly nothing. We didn't stay there too long. After soaking in the other two pools, we finally found our way into the hot pool and began to talk about everything under the sun.

I was fascinated about her description of timing the grapes and carefully looking at their colour as well as the thickness of the skin. After some time, we all made it to the mud baths. Again there were different temperatures of mud and, surprisingly, laying in warm mud was very relaxing, intoxicating, and exotic.

Of course, the joints that we shared had a little bit of an influence on us as well, but the greatest feeling was from the mud. When it began to get dark, we showered off, got dressed, and drove back to Rose's house. Klaus made a tasty meal for us all, and the girls broke out a couple of bottles of wine for us to consume. At that time, I didn't realize how stupid I was about women and their desires. Rose and the other women helped me learn.

Another thing that happened on that trip was that my brakes started to get soft. We made it back to Oakland, and on Wednesday night, I decided to join Steve and some other friends at 86th Avenue for a game of Hearts. One of the regulars there was a man named Jake.

The Hippie Mechanic:

Jake had a unique business. He renovated a 1940 Chevrolet panel van into sleeping quarters and a workshop. You see, Jake was and remains a master mechanic. However, Jake liked his independence and working while stoned. He was just not suited to work in a garage with a boss and other mechanics. So he drove around Northern California, fixing vehicles, getting paid in cash, food, booze, and or marijuana. I told Jake about my Nash's brakes. He said he'd take a look and see if the brake lines needed to be replaced. Thursday I brought my car to Steve's backyard where Jake checked it out. He said the lines were fine, but the shoes and rotors should be replaced. I had no idea what that meant, but asked Jake to get what was needed and I'd reimburse him and pay him what he wanted to fix the problem.

That weekend, we drove back to Sebastopol to party with the girls again, but as we neared their house, the brakes almost didn't work at all. So we left the Nash and used the girls' truck to get to Geyserville for another day at the spa. When we got back to the house, I called Steve to see if Jake was still there. He was there, and I talked him into getting the necessary parts and drive up to Healdsburg. He arrived on Sunday, and we set to work fixing my brakes. Jake showed me what to do as he replaced the brakes of the rear wheels on the driver's side. I replaced the front brakes on the driver's side while Jake supervised me. Then he ate some peyote, and we smoked a couple of joints. The girls decided that Jake needed to relax at the spa, and they took off for Geyserville while I fixed the other brakes.

My Next Best Vehicle, Arwen:

I decided to sell that car when I found a 1948 Chevy pick-up truck that was for sale in the Geyserville area. I asked Jake to take a look at it to see if it was worth the $250.00 the owners wanted. He said it was in good shape and worth the cash. So I sold the Nash for a couple hundred, added the necessary money, and bought the truck. I drove that beauty to work the next day.

Another Love of My Life:

That Monday, I met a young woman at Newberry's who had set up a photograph display. She would get parents of young children to let her pose the kids and take their picture. If the parents liked what they saw, she talked them into getting more poses and to buy a package of all of the pictures. Letty Robinson was from Washington State, and her family had an apple tree farm. She wanted to see more of the country, so she took a photography course with the company she worked for and began to work her way through various department stores down to California.

Letty had a VW van which she had set up as a camper, complete with fridge, stove, and mini shower. That was where she lived as she travelled around the North Western states taking pictures of cute children and sometimes recent high school graduates. To my eyes, she had a Marilyn Monroe shape. She was about 5'4 and 120 pounds. To my eyes she was a perfect specimen of womanhood, full breasts, childbearing hips, shapely legs, brown hair, blue eyes, and a very pleasing personality. We hit it off immediately. I met her while setting up a display near her workspace. We chatted about her job, and I asked her if she'd like to have lunch with me. So around noon, I went down to her spot and waited until she finished with a customer. Actually, she had a couple of people waiting, so she and I did not have lunch together, rather I ate my lunch while I watched her work. Actually, I was guilty of Ingrid's complaint, I ogled.

She finished work at 5:00, I was done before her, washed up in our staff bathroom, and waited for her. She had to pack up her camera, money, and credit card papers, I helped her and carried her things to her VW. Then she followed me to the warehouse.

By this time, we had completed our bathroom area, 3 separate rooms, one with an old fashioned 4 legged bathtub and shower, another for the commode, and the third that housed a sink and mirrored cabinet. Our kitchen was nearly done, we had a propane stove, sink, cupboards, and I made 2 counter tops out of old 2 by 4s that I split in half, then used dowels to splice together, sent them through a planer, sanded them down, and used polyurethane to finish them off. They were strong, useful, and pretty.

Letty followed me to the warehouse from Newberry's, parked just outside the place, and came inside. My bedroom was on the first floor in what used to be the Western Transformer Company's show room and office. It had a large picture window under which I built a platform bed. I also glued tinfoil on a set of drapes so that I could sleep without the street lights and later the sun interrupting my slumber. Letty saw what I had done, was kind of impressed, but said she'd make something nicer for me. We made love that first day we met and continued to do so every opportunity we got. I thought I had met my future wife. She and I talked about many things, one of which was how beneficial it is to have your own business. So I decided to quit my job at Newberry's and set up my own business with my new truck.

My Best Friend And Partner:

We were in the final stage of completing Klaus' dark room when I met Letty. It was also around this time that I met a fluffy, black puppy that began to follow me around the warehouse. I picked him up and carried him around the neighbourhood to see if he had a family. I never found one, so I fed him and he began to become a fixture around the warehouse. Because he had a habit of disappearing and reappearing at will, I named him Mandrake. From 1971 until he died in Newfoundland 16 years later, he shared my life experiences.

After the Christmas holidays, I again contacted Jake and asked him if he thought the truck could be used for light hauling. He advised me that to do that, I should add heavy duty springs and shocks. So we did that, I mean I bought the equipment and helped Jake. Then I got a part time job with our next door neighbour, as did Clem.

Our next door neighbour was a chemical company that had a 'help wanted' sign on the door. So we stopped in to see what kind of help they needed. Well, the owner was General Dwight Gustafson US Army (ret), and would use his connections with the Army bases around the Bay Area to purchase various chemicals in large quantities at a, shall we say, very reasonable rate. He'd then package them in smaller containers and resell them back to one of the military bases at a profit. One job we did was when he bought Hydrochloric Acid in 50 gallon containers. We then filled 5 ounce bottles with the acid, labelled it, sealed it to specifications, packaged them in boxes that held 12 bottles, labeled those boxes and then packed those boxes into a larger box to transport back to the base. He hired his son to cut and make the cardboard boxes and many of his son's friends to do the packaging. He made a tidy profit by doing this.

Shape Products building.

That's Conal standing in front of the door. The sign that says, "Shape Products" I made out of left over plywood. I made it with Dwight's materials on my own time. He liked it enough to put it on his business. So Clem and I got a job there with the other young, lazy people. Mr. Gustafson one told me that he liked to hire 'lazy' people because they would find the quickest, easiest way to get the job done, then he'd save money on their hourly wage. Our job was to move the chemicals to smaller containers, pack then in boxes then pack those boxes into bigger boxes and load them on the truck that was delivering them to the nearby military bases.

I told him about my truck and light hauling business, and he hired me to deliver his goods. So I got paid the minimum wage for working in the factory with all the other hippies and another $15.00 per delivery.

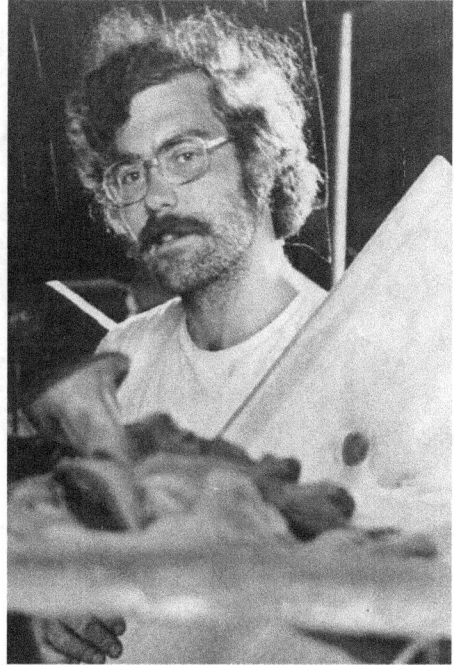

Shape Products - Motley looking crew at a Christmas party.

Of course, Clem, Klaus, and I continued to renovate the warehouse. And Letty would drive to the warehouse after she finished taking pictures at one or another department store. It was a great life for me in Oakland at that time. Then Letty left Oakland to work in San Jose, and I decided I'd ask her to marry me. So I wrote a letter to my mother telling her about my plan to marry Letty and requested the Reade family heirloom wedding ring.

Sign says "No Hippies Allowed"
1971

With the letter requesting the family ring, I sent the picture as a Christmas gift. I think that picture might have influenced Mom's hesitancy to immediately send the ring.

I thought I looked like a fine working hippie, which is exactly what I was. Although I had just quit the job at the department store, I did have another job, a truck, a light hauling business, a girlfriend, friendly roommates, and was feeling pretty good about myself. Obviously, Mom thought differently. She was worried that I didn't look like her "Johnny" anymore. So she made plans to come and visit me in Oakland, California, to meet this Letty girl. I didn't think Mom would like to stay in the warehouse, so I asked Steve if she could stay in his guest room. Naturally, he said yes, and the arrangements were made.

Sign Language:

Prior to all of these happenings, serendipity again played a part in my future. As all the things described above were happening to me, I had enrolled in Laney Junior College. I took two courses, the first was a carpentry course in which I used their tools to make our counters in the warehouse. The second was a philosophy course where the professor challenged us to find a way to communicate non-verbally. My first thought about this was to use sign language, like I remembered Tonto and The Lone Ranger using when I was a kid. However, what I found about signed language was very different than that.

I learned that there was a "Signed Language" course being taught in the Oakland Adult Public Education system. It was a night course, once a week for 10 weeks. My instructor was a Deaf woman, who used the first book published by the National Association of the Deaf about sign language. *A Basic Course In Manual Communication* was published in September of 1970 and merely had pictures of the hands and face of people signing English words. There were 45 lessons and sentences for us students to sign to our teacher. Amazingly enough, I caught on very quickly, but when I watched my teacher having an argument with one of her friends, they didn't use the same method. I asked her why their communication was so different from what we were learning, and she answered, "Because we use Deaf Signs, these signs are for hearing people."

Also during this period, Steve challenged me to take another part-time course at Haywood Junior College. This was a pilot project with the "Head Start" program. Steve thought that since I had majored in education at WCSC, this might help me later on in my education. I was paired with a boy I'll call Jim, who had a hearing loss. So I became very interested in Deaf Education.

In the meantime, Letty and I started to drift apart. Although San Jose is not very far from Oakland, we didn't get to see one another as often as before. The last time Letty came to Oakland to visit me, I talked her into going to Geyserville to enjoy the spa. We spent a nice weekend there, naked from Saturday afternoon until Sunday evening when we decided to return to Oakland. Letty let me drive her VW back to town, and that's when we had a long talk that devolved into an argument. That was the end of our relationship. I took it philosophically because I knew I couldn't be the man she wanted, a man who would do "man's" work while she did "woman's" work. To my mind, there is only work to be done, period.

Mom's Visit to California:

Well, Mom arrived in California with our heirloom ring and a million questions. I picked her up at the airport and took her to Steve and Karen's place. They couldn't have been nicer to her. She stayed for two weeks, and I took her sightseeing all over Northern California. I borrowed my friend Marcia Thompson's car, a blue 1968 Chevy Corvette, and drove the three of us to visit Hearst's Castle in San Simeon. She really liked that trip. The castle impressed her, but something else did not impress her at all. After our visit to the castle, we stopped to get a bite to eat at a nice, out-of-the-way restaurant. However, I wasn't allowed in. Look carefully at this picture and you'll see the reason why. So Marcia and Mom bought some food to take out.

I thought it was funny, but Mom was appalled—at me. The sign said, "No Hippies Allowed."

Since I was working a lot, Karen, Steve, and Marcia kept Mom company and showed her some of the local sights. I took Mom to the warehouse to show her our progress and also to Shape Products to meet Mr. and Mrs. Gustafson. They impressed Mom, even though our staff was a motley-looking crew. Mom found them all very nice, and they all said nice things about me. I think that made Mom feel pretty good and not so worried anymore. That, and the fact that Letty and I were not getting married after all.

As I've said before, Klaus was a very skilled chef, and I asked him to make Mom a special dinner. Well, Klaus was dating a lovely, rich woman who had a house in San Francisco, and that's where we took Mom for the dinner. Klaus made Rouladen, Sauerbraten, and mashed potatoes with onion. Mom decided that she liked my roommates and all of Steve's friends.

Mom Gets High:

Wednesday nights at Steve's house were reserved for a big game of Hearts. Usually, there were four of us who played, but Mom insisted that she sit in and learn the game. Before each game, Steve and I would roll a bunch of joints and place them in shot glasses around the table before anyone arrived to play. In Hearts, if there are five players, the 2 of diamonds and 2 of clubs are removed, and each player will then have ten cards. If I remember, Richard Akutagawa (Aku) was one of the players, who else played in that game is anybody's guess. I remember Aku playing because, after smoking a joint, every other word out of his mouth was "fuck."

Mom was a lifetime smoker, and at that time her favorite brand was Salem cigarettes. So Mom would be smoking, and we'd be passing around joint after joint. Mom began delicately taking the joint and passing it along without trying it—at first. After the first hour of play, Mom began to take a draw of a joint, then another. After a few hits, Mom forgot where she was, that we were playing Hearts, and that if she had the 3 of clubs, she had to play the first card to get that round started.

Turns out Mom fell in love with Aku (was it the joints?), and when I asked her if she wanted to see Northern California and the Sequoia and large Redwood trees, she wanted Aku to come along. So Marcia, Aku, Mom, and I set off for Sequoia National Park. We not only went through the tunnel of a Redwood, but we continued on up into Oregon. I'm sure if Aku and I didn't have to work, Mom would have had us drive all the way into Canada. However, we had to get back to Oakland. Mom left a couple of days after that trip, and then my life turned into a crime drama, and I changed my path again.

Nearly Busted Big Time:

Further to all the above, the warehouse guys were looking to score some "easy" money to assist in our renovations. Clem had a friend called Crusty, who was a small-time dealer of grass and hash. Steve had a friend living in San Francisco, Nick, who was a big-time dealer of grass, hash, LSD, and cocaine. Crusty's cousin was also dealing, but in an international manner. The cousin brought 130 pounds of hash into the U.S. from Morocco and wanted to sell it quickly. I hooked Crusty's cousin up with Nick to unload 65 pounds of the stuff, and we'd get a cut of the profit. In the meantime, all of us in the warehouse were high nearly all the time on grass or other hallucinogenics.

Crusty's cousin, whom I'll call "Cuz" from now on, arrived at the warehouse with a bag of hash and a shaving kit, and another bag with a lot of clothes and LSD, Peyote, and Opium. I gave Cuz Nick's phone number and told him to call from a phone booth just down the street. I assume that's what he did because when he returned, he said they had a meeting set up for tomorrow night at Golden Gate Park. Great, all was set, and we would get a cut of Cuz's profit and taste opium and save the LSD for later. I stashed the LSD in a bucket from which we cut holes and used as a candle holder when we had parties.

That night I smoked opium for the first and only time. It hit me like a ton of sleeping pills. I could do nothing but sit in my favorite chair and stare at all the other people in our warehouse. The next day, we all went about our normal business and left Cuz, Crusty, and Nick to themselves. I had a delivery for Shape Products, and Clem was designated to accompany me because it was quite a lot of boxes that we had to bring onto the Army Post at Yerba Buena Island. We left Oakland around 3:00 and didn't get back until nearly 5:30.

So I asked Clem if he wanted to get supper at Laney rather than go directly home and have to cook. He said, "Naturally."

However, the most direct route to the college was past the warehouse. When we got near our home, there were about four Oakland police cars around the place.

We slowly went past, and then I quickly got to the phone booth. I called Nick and told him about the warehouse being busted. I also told him to get rid of what he had in his home because he might be next. He did get rid of a lot but forgot about his personal stash of about five pounds of weed.

Clem and I never got supper, rather we went to his mother's home in Berkeley and asked her what we should do. You see, she was what one considered in the late '40s and early '50s part of the "Beat Generation," but she was really just an activist. She tried to get marijuana legalized, abortion no longer a criminal offense, and homosexuality decriminalized.

Was she arrested? Yep, many times.

She advised us to stay with her, and she'd contact one of her lawyer friends. I called Steve from there and told him what happened, and he said that he already knew because Nick called him and was livid. Nick never spoke to me again after that.

Clem's mother got us in touch with an American Civil Liberties Union lawyer because she knew they wouldn't charge us an enormous amount of retainer fees to give us advice.

We were told to remain where we were and wait for information that they'd get from the police and let us know what the charges would be and where we could find Klaus, Crusty, Cuz, and our two newest roommates, Norris and Dave, who were in the warehouse when the cops broke down the door.

After what seemed like years, we were told that we needed to raise $500.00 for bail money. That money would be given to a bail bondsman who would put up the $500,000 to get our five busted "brothers" out.

We also found out that there was a warrant for our arrest as well because it was known that we lived in the same building.

Now I was in big trouble, but thought I could get out of it clean. Don't ask me why I thought that way, but Clem's mother was a very calming and reassuring person.

Clem and I took turns calling the various people we knew and asked them for a donation for the cause of getting our roommates out of jail. We managed to scrounge up nearly $400.00.

I had $150.00 in a savings account, and Clem had $80.00 cash, so after we drove around the Bay Area, we came up with the bail money, but it was General Gustafson, U.S. Army (retired), who delivered it. It turns out that his son was also a hash user, and Mr. Gustafson sympathized with our use.

However, we were dealt a shocking development, Klaus decided to act as a witness for the prosecution. He told them the whole scenario, leaving out Clem's and my names.

He gave himself up to squeal on Cuz and Crusty, but since he never knew Nick's name, he didn't say anything about him, even when he was asked. He said that he just knew Cuz would meet with someone from San Francisco to get rid of 65 pounds of hash.

The newspapers of that day made a big deal of the bust, but now, in 2021, I cannot find anything about that day. I *know* what happened, and I know what Clem and I did, but I can't find any corroborating articles in the newspapers of 1972 in the Bay Area. I'm very disappointed about that. But on the previous page is a picture of our front door after the police broke in.

After Klaus told the whole story about the deal they were involved in and all were released on bail, we returned to the warehouse and continued on with our lives.

Some people were very angry at Klaus for squealing, but I knew about his background and had no problem with his effort to stay out of jail. Klaus moved back into the warehouse as well, but Norris, Dave, and some of our "friends" refused to accept what he had done.

So Klaus decided to move out and move in with his beautiful girlfriend who had a house in San Francisco.

I Change Direction Again and Go On an Adventure with Mandrake:

At any rate, after that close call, I decided to straighten up and pursue a career in Deaf Education.

You see, after taking the sign language class in the Oakland Public School system and listening to my teacher say that to learn more, I should volunteer at the California School for the Deaf in Berkeley (CSD-B), I did.

Furthermore, the student I was paired with at Hayward College who had a hearing loss came with me to CSD-B to mix with the kids at the school.

He made a couple of new friends, and I decided that was going to be my career.

I figured that if I wanted to stop taking various hallucinogenic, I should get as far away from my user friends as possible. I had been an avid hiker and camper before and after my stint in the Marine Corps, so I decided to plan and take a hike in the High Sierra Mountains.

I read John Muir's book *The Yosemite* while in the Santa Rosa Jail and decided to go to the library and see if there were others. However, rather than reading other books written by Muir, I began to plan my hike.

I bought a good backpack with an aluminum frame, a cricket propane stove, two canisters of propane, freeze-dried food packs, a very good pair of hiking boots, and enough dog food to feed Mandrake twice a day for two weeks.

I thought two weeks in the wilderness would be long enough. I then found a long, thick stick that I decided to customize into a walking stick. I figured I was ready and got Aku to drive me to Yosemite National Park and began my hike toward Tuolumne Meadows.

When I finally got to the Meadows, I was pretty tired. The weight of the pack neared 100 pounds, and I got winded fast. I decided to quit smoking as well—for the time being.

The picture shows my first campsite.

On the tree to the left of my tent lies my backpack and the walking stick I made. Mandrake is sitting in front of the entrance, and I had already spread out my air…

CHAPTER 9:
BACK TO WEST CHESTER STATE COLLEGE (WCSC) - THIRD TIME IS A CHARM

So Bev brought me back to West Chester in the middle of June 1973. As I said previously, I had already applied to return to WCSC, was accepted and now all I had to do was register for the Fall Semester. Before doing that; however, I needed to get a job. I went to the unemployment office and looked at the jobs posting. I found one that would be perfect for me: a night watchman at an institution for mentally handicapped persons. The Devereux Foundation is a non-profit organization that has been serving mentally challenged youth and adults wince 1912. I worked at their campus that was located on a large piece of land between Downingtown and West Chester.

My working hours were from 11:00 PM until 7:00 AM. I was responsible for the care and safety of 40 male residents who ranged in age from 16 to 75. They were housed in two separate buildings; the Main Hall which slept 20 men who ranged in age from 16 to 32 and the honours building whose 20 men ranged in age between 35 and 75. I always brought Mandrake with me when I worked, and he was well received by all the residents I was responsible for. My job began with a spoken and written report of all the odd/bad behaviours of most of the men. In reality, they were very easy to deal with.

At 11:30 I made my first of 4 rounds of the buildings. In the Main Hall, I walked around all the bed rooms and checked to make sure the guys were sleeping. Most of the time, they all were. 99% of the time, those living there slept throughout the night. In the honours building, there were two men who rarely slept. One man was the 75-year-old, who had worked for the railroad for 30 years before he fell off one of the trains and knocked his head on the tracks. That caused him to lose memory and the ability to care for himself, which is why, with the railroad insurance policy, he was sent to live out his life at the Devereux Foundation. He couldn't sleep long, so he'd come out to the living room and smoke his pipe. His favourite tobacco was Captain Black Cherry, and I have to say, to this day, I like the smell of that tobacco. I never worried about him doing any harm to himself or the building. He'd be awake smoking from midnight until around 2 or 2:30, then he'd take himself to bed and sleep until 6:30.

The other man who had a hard time staying asleep was a man in his 40s who was probably on the autism spectrum and probably had Asperger's Syndrome. He was smart as a whip when talking about statistical things such as baseball batting averages, or the stock market, but he had a hard time just chatting. He was also a smoker but of cigarettes and had a habit of putting them out on the floor. I could usually get him back to bed after he smoked two. Then I'd pick up his butts and move on to the gym, where I'd workout for an hour or so then return to the Main Hall.

I'd do another round of checking, then go to the main office and work on my lesson plans. I was responsible for waking the residents for their day jobs at 6:00 in the morning. They all had their routines down pat. I woke each section by turning on the overhead lights in their respective rooms. After I awoke the Main Hall, I made it to the Honours building and made sure all of those residents were on the go; again, 99,9% of the time they all were well into their morning routines. When one wasn't getting ready for work, it was because they were sick and I notified the Health Unit about them.

I then returned to the Main Hall and checked up on them. One man who was in his mid-30s always had bad breath, I'd call it "sick" breath. So one morning I watched his bathroom routine (only the washing part) and noticed how well he brushed his teeth and used mouth wash. I couldn't understand why his breath smelled so bad, even after using the mouth wash. So I followed him into his bedroom and noticed a plastic container that was used to soak false teeth (Mom had a similar one). I asked him if he could take his teeth out of his mouth. He said, "Yes, want to see?" I said that I would, and he removed his set of upper and lower teeth.

The upper plate had mould on the part that fit over his gums, and the lower plate had food lodged between the plastic and his gums. No wonder he had bad breath. So from that day until I quit, the staff that worked with this man always checked his false teeth to ensure that at night, they were removed and placed in his container with Polident or Efferdent in it. And, every morning, I made sure that he brushed his teeth before putting them back into his mouth. His halitosis was cured.

My job at the Devereux Foundation paid me well allowing me to pay my tuition, share rent with Bev, drink, eat, smoke what I wanted and save money for the future. I was happy as a child with a free pass to DisneyWorld. I'm lucky in that I never needed a lot of sleep, so working overnight, taking a couple of cat naps between making my rounds and getting a nap before reporting to work was easy peasy. Since I needed transportation, I bought a Ford Econoline Van with the intent of turning it into a camper. Unfortunately, it wasn't in very good condition and only lasted me through the winter. I was lucky enough to sell it to an underclassman for $100.00 then in the spring,

Then serendipity hit me again when one of may colleagues told me aboutI a 1949 Plymouth 4 door sedan that was in tip top condition. There was, however, rust on the floor boards and the windshield wipers needed new rubber, but that was minor stuff to me.

The picture is exactly what the car looked like.

Same Colour, Tires And Markings.

The story about the Plymouth was that a farmer bought it new in '49. Used it to drive into the town for groceries and booze once a week. Unfortunately, he died a year later, and since his wife didn't drive, she put it in storage in their barn for the next 23 years. Whoever got it ready for storage did a great job. It was placed on a rack, the tires were removed, the battery wires removed, the oil drained, and the radiator filled with anti-freeze.

When I saw it for sale for $250.00 (yes I know, it seems as if most of my favourite cars cost $250.00), I had to buy it. I'm very glad I did. Although I had to pay another $100.00 to get it out of the barn, it was worth the extra cash. This wine coloured vehicle brought me to Nova Scotia to get a Master's Degree in Deaf Education and later brought me to live here in Newfoundland and Labrador.

I wasn't sure if I had to take regular courses or could spend this semester as a Student Teacher. So I contacted the professor who was to be my advisor. Mr. Cameron was the professor who taught Children's Literature, which I had taken in my second semester. Of course he didn't remember me, which was good because I only managed to get a D from that course. Anyway, he arranged for me to do my practice teaching during the Fall Semester.

I was assigned to the Old Forge Elementary School, where I was placed with the children with special needs. I loved it there. One student made a lasting impression on me. Gary Childress was a child who had cerebral palsy. He was confined to a back braced wheel chair, could only communicate with a special electric typewriter and was smart as a whip with a devilish sense of humour. His typewriter had a metal cover over the keys on which he could rest his right hand. His teacher or student support worker had to place the paper in the machine for him, and then he could communicate by painfully typing his needs, wants, and ambitions.

He loved watching baseball, and his favourite team, naturally, was the Philadelphia Phillies. On that team, his favourite player was their second baseman, Denny Doyle. He was always talking about him, so I suggested he write him a letter and ask for an autographed baseball. He was kind of hesitant to do it, thinking, I assume, that a big league player like Doyle wouldn't answer. However, Gary did write it.

We addressed the letter to Denny Doyle c/o Veterans Stadium, Philadelphia, Pennsylvania. Honestly, I had no idea the letter would get to him using that address, but to our surprise, about one month later, Gary got a return letter with an invitation to attend a Phillies home game as Denny's guest. Talk about excited! Gary saw the Phillies play the Chicago Cubs and he returned with two baseballs, one signed by all the Phillies and the other signed by the Cubs. Writing this now is bringing tears to my eyes, what a sap I am.

This school had a lot of different handicapped students as well as many specialist teachers and support staff. One of the support staff was a speech/language pathologist named Michelle. Michelle and I spoke often about working with kids that had a hearing loss. She introduced me to a couple of teenagers who had a fair amount of speech, but who preferred to communicate with each other in sign. So sometimes, I joined in their conversations. They both were pleased that there was a 'teacher' who knew how to sign and asked me to help them with a couple of their more English dependent classes, such as 'Civics' and 'History.' So not only did I make lesson plans for the classes I was teaching, but I also began tutoring these kids. Michelle was impressed, as I had hoped, and invited me to her house for supper on many occasions while I remained at the Old Forge Elementary School.

So I spent the first half of the semester teaching there, and the second half of the semester was spent at Smedley Junior High School in Chester, Pennsylvania. My supervising teacher, Mr. Deans, was apparently not very interested in actually supervising student teachers. My first day in his classroom, he introduced me, told me they were learning long division, and left the classroom. To say I was surprised is an understatement.

So I did what I thought would be appropriate—I asked them if they knew the times tables. Some raised their hands and said they were shown that last year, but nobody had actually memorized it. I decided that they had to learn the times table before they could think about learning long division.

As I began to write the times table on the chalkboard, one boy raised his hand and asked me about myself. "Where were you born?" "You're pretty old to be a student teacher, why?" "Who's your favorite baseball team?" "You like football? Who's your favorite football team?" I answered them and told them about myself, but I also asked each student about their favorite things and where school fit in with their favorites. That's how we spent the rest of the 50-minute class.

After the class, I finished writing the times table on the side chalkboard and prepared for the next day's class. The regular teacher came into the classroom just after the next class came in and asked me how it went with the previous class. I told him exactly what happened, and he said that that was a fine way to get to know the kids and that the times table was also a good idea. He then wrote in red chalk, "Do Not Clean This Board."

I guess I did a fair job. Old Forge Elementary gave me an "A" while Smedley Junior High School gave me a "B." I was a bit disappointed with the "B," but these grades still earned me High Honours and brought my GPA to 2.14, which was good enough to earn a Bachelor of Science in Education.

In the spring semester, I took three courses: Psychology of the Physically Handicapped, Abnormal Psychology, and Mental Health Practices. Since I had all night to study these courses, I managed to get a "B," "A," and "P," respectively, which brought my overall GPA up to 2.21. This was fine to graduate but not very high to submit to various universities to work on a Master of Education in Deaf Education. However, Bev talked me into applying to a variety of universities that offered that degree. So I sent applications to Western Oregon University, the University of Pittsburgh, and Indiana University of Pennsylvania. I guess because of my age, military experience, and work history, I was accepted at Oregon and Indiana, but their tuition fees were pretty much out of my reach.

Also, just before the Easter Break, one of my co-workers at the Devereux Foundation showed me pictures of his and his girlfriend's vacation in Nova Scotia. The province looked really beautiful, and I thought it would be an exciting adventure for Bev, Mandrake, and me to see the province during the Easter or Spring Break.

CHAPTER 10:
A MASTERS DEGREE FOR $1000.00 US

Bev and I enjoyed doing things differently. Since her car was newer and had plenty of space, we decided use it for our journey. She got an oil and filter change, all tires inspected, and was generally given the green light by a trusted mechanic that her father had been using for years. So off we went, with my intention of camping out in the KOA camp grounds that I read about. Planning the route we'd take, I discovered

that we could take a ferry from Portland, Maine to Yarmouth, Nova Scotia and then drive up the East Coast of the province, right through Peggy's Cove, which was one of the places my workmate raved about. Beautiful country! Bad timing! Camping out in April along the east coast of Nova Scotia is cold, wet and not for the faint-hearted or comfort-loving. Not only that, but the KOA camp grounds I was expecting to use had not yet opened for their season. Boy was I uninformed Peggy's Cove Lighthouse about Canada.

So we did the sensible thing, we slept in hotels and bed and breakfast places. We met wonderful people, such as Ivan and Nina Treen in Amherst, NS. Amherst was directly on the route we had mapped out and had an added bonus, the Interprovincial School for the Deaf (ISD) was located there. When we were in Halifax, I decided that it'd be an adventure to see if I could get a job in Canada as a Front Door Area Interprovincial teacher of the deaf. I was directed to the ISD in *School for the Deaf, Amherst, N.S. Amherst.*

Ivan and Nina ran a small motel of cabins in Amherst. Bev and I loved the place. It was near the school, downtown, and the stadium where a big spring concert was planned. So we stayed there and experienced the concert. I also stopped by ISD to fill out an application for a job. I figured that my sign language skill and Bachelor of Science in elementary education from West Chester State College would be enough to get me hired. WRONG!

Bev and I drove up the winding driveway together and parked directly in front of the entrance. I got out, put my fedora over my ponytail, buttoned the two middle buttons of my white Easton High School letter sweater, pulled up my leather-patched jeans, and clomped into the foyer of the school in my old Marine Corps issue boots. I must have been quite a sight to the receptionist as I asked her for an application for a teaching position. She smiled and asked me to take a seat and wait a second for the superintendent of the school to meet me. And then, serendipity struck again.

The superintendent of the school, Mr. Dan Jenkins, came out shortly, took a long look at this hippie sitting in the lobby of the school, blinked a few times, walked over to me, and shook my hand. After introducing himself, he asked me into his office. There we chatted a bit, and I explained to him my various experiences — Marine Corps hitch, the degree I'd be getting the next month — and demonstrated my signing ability. He told me that he only hired teachers who had a master's degree in Deaf Education, and after I obtained that, I could apply. However, since I was there, he'd introduce me to the director of the Learning Assistance Centre (LAC) program, Dr. Ann Kennedy, and I could apply to attend that program if I wanted.

Mr. Jenkins walked me through the school, showing me the various departments and down to the part of the ISD that housed the teacher training program. He introduced me to Dr. Kennedy and left us alone. I thought I saw a smirk on his face as he left; in retrospect, knowing what I know now about the two, he most likely did.

Dr. Kennedy was gracious and explained her program thoroughly. She also said that she was currently negotiating with the Université de Moncton in New Brunswick to get them to approve the program for a master's degree in Education. She said that she was 90% certain the program would be approved next June. She also told me the cost of the program was $1000.00 US, would begin in June of that year, and be completed in June of 1975.

I thought, *wow*. It took me ten years to get a BSEd, and I could get an MEd in only a year. Plus, I could earn money from the GI Bill as well. In other words, I could make money while getting a master's degree from a foreign country! What a great adventure this would be. So I quickly filled out an application for that program and promised to send my transcripts to her as soon as I could get them.

I was accepted into the program. There were only a couple of problems I had to overcome before I could leave Pennsylvania. First, I had to apply for and be given a student visa from the Canadian Embassy. No problem, I thought, but bureaucracy has a way of slowing down one's ambitions. I wrote to them and got a speedy reply saying that the application procedure would take about six weeks. That would have left me with very little time to drive an old car the 830 miles to Amherst, Nova Scotia. So I phoned them and asked for a face-to-face interview. They agreed, and I took the bus to New York City to their offices there.

The next problem was that I had to prove to them that I had enough money to live in the province without needing any social assistance. That meant that I had to show them a bank statement with at least $3000.00 US available for my use. Well, I had a savings account, but after Bev's and my vacation to Nova Scotia, the amount left was far less than the required amount. I told them that I didn't have a statement with me at that time, but I could send them a copy when I got back home. That was satisfactory. Luckily, Mom had some money in her savings from the settlement she got from Dad's life insurance and the sale of our home. She gladly lent me $3200.00 to put into a savings account to send to the Canadian Embassy.

The third problem was that I explained to them that I needed to take my dog, Mandrake, with me. They said that I had to get a certificate that stated he was healthy and had all his vaccinations by a certified veterinarian. That meant I had to spend more money before I could leave for the program. Well, if I had to get him checked out and vaccinated by a certified veterinarian, that's what I'd do — and did.

In the middle of May, I packed all my belongings into my 1949 Plymouth, loaded my dog into the front seat with my cassettes and tape recorder, and began this next adventure in my life. I was to be the only male among a class of eleven in the LAC. My erotic fantasies began immediately. I imagined nine beautiful, well-endowed Canadian women fighting over this sexy, ex-Marine hippie hunk. Okay, people, you can stop laughing now. My fantasies remained fantasies.

The program was to begin on June 6, 1974. I drove into Amherst on May 19 and went directly to the cabins owned by Ivan and Nina. They welcomed me warmly, asked me to tea, and we shared a lovely dinner and talk. I told them why I came back and asked if they knew of a part-time job I might get to earn enough money to pay my week's rent with them. Ivan said he wanted to paint the inside of a couple of cabins and that if I helped him, he'd drop the week's fee in half. I agreed, and we made plans to begin working the next day.

That evening I went to a pub on Victoria Street and met a couple of men. I told them what I was doing and that I needed a job that would pay cash and last only a couple of weeks. One guy told me about a painting job he'd give me, and if I completed it within three days, he'd pay me $200.00. I jumped at the chance, told him I'd meet him at the site the next morning at 7, and left the bar. I told Ivan about the deal and asked him if he minded if I worked on the cabins at night rather than during the day. He didn't, and all was arranged.

So for the next ten days, I scraped and painted a house on the outside and painted the inside of Ivan's cabins. I got paid the $200.00 the day before the program started and used it to open a bank account with the Royal Bank of Canada (RBC). I've been with that bank now for fifty years. I also transferred half of the money my mother gave me and was surprised that the $1500.00 actually went into my new Canadian account as $1485. Yes, in 1974, Canadian currency was worth more than United States money.

On June 3, I checked in with the director of the LAC program, Dr. Ann Kennedy. However, before I went into the school, I noticed a number of students on the front lawn playing football. I got my old 1950s-style football out of the trunk, and Mandrake and I ran to join in the fun. There I met a number of students, including Anthony Chaffey from Newfoundland. Newfoundland? The boys allowed me to join the game, and I was placed on Anthony's team. After fifteen minutes, the playtime was over, and they had to go back to classes. I went into the school and was met by Mr. Jenkins.

I said, "Hi, nice to see you again." Mr. Jenkins' right eye was twitching while he told me to accompany him to his office. I assumed he wanted to ask me how my trip was and generally welcome me into his ISD family. Wrong! His first sentence was, "You were observed participating in unacceptable behaviour with some students of the school."

I was stunned. I tried to think of something I did since arriving in Amherst that could have been thought of as unacceptable. Except that I was working illegally, all I did was play football and chat with some senior students since I got there. So I asked him what I had done that was "unacceptable behaviour."

This was not the correct thing to do with a staunchly conservative Welshman. It had the same effect as if I poked my finger in his eye, which actually began twitching uncontrollably. Mr. Jenkins coughed, walked slowly to his desk, picked up a small candy dish, and offered me a Canadian Mint. I declined politely, "No thank you. I'm not fond of Canadian Mints." Although I didn't think it possible, his eye began twitching even more.

In a barely controllable voice, Mr. Jenkins explained very carefully that there was to be an invisible line between the ISD students and LAC students. That line was the demarcation between professionals and students and was not to be crossed. He said that he watched me playing football with the students, and that was crossing the line.

So I made my second mistake with Mr. Jenkins. I said that I had a different philosophy of education—that I felt it was important to gain the trust and support of students so they would accept my pedagogy, and playing sports with them was only the first step in developing that trust.

Mr. Jenkins looked at me coldly and said very slowly, eye twitching like a turn signal and beginning to tear, "You are much too young and inexperienced to have a philosophy of education. Now, go carefully down to the LAC area of the school and speak with Dr. Kennedy."

I did as I was told. When I got to the LAC area, Dr. Kennedy greeted me with a smile and asked me to come into her office. She said that Mr. Jenkins had called her to complain about my interaction with the students. She told him that she'd talk to me about it, and this was what she was doing. She said that since I had just arrived and didn't know the expectations, this would be forgotten, but she understood that what I did was really not a problem. Mr. Jenkins was "old school" and wanted a wall between teachers and students so the students would "know their place in the school." Then she said that she agreed that establishing a rapport with any student is a good thing and was not crossing the line; however, unless you are the physical education teacher, it is best not to play football or hockey or any other game where there might be physical contact. Good advice she gave me at that time.

We then went into the conference, class, study, and library room where she introduced me to my fellow LAC students. My initial fantasy about being the only man in the program with nine beautiful women came true—the women were indeed beautiful. Three French-Canadians from New Brunswick, four English Canadians—two each from NB and NS, one of whom was Deaf—and two beauties from Newfoundland. Newfoundland?

We were given the syllabus of the program and a list of books we had to purchase. Then she distributed a mimeographed copy of an essay written by Thomas Mann and told us to read it carefully and write a criticism. It was to be in her inbox before class the next morning. So we now learned how we were going to get two years' worth of material done in one calendar year—begin immediately and work hard.

I also had to move into the dormitory for the LAC students, but they wouldn't let Mandrake stay there. ISD had a program for Deaf students who had other disabilities. This was a hands-on program situated on a farm. The students lived in the dormitory with the other students, but their education took place on the farm. They were taught how to care for cows, horses, sheep, chickens, and pigs and learned their language through that care. Anyway, Mandrake was allowed to stay there with those students and the other animals. Needless to say, he was a big hit with the kids and their teachers. The program was called "The 175 Program" because that was the address of the farm building.

This arrangement lasted for almost a whole month. After my classes were finished, I'd go over to the house with my assignments for that night, feed Mandrake, and take him for a run. Then I'd make something for me to eat and get to work on the books. The one restriction was that I had to be out of the building by midnight.

One time I had a project that had to be typewritten and handed in by the next day. We had to write a critique of the stages of cognitive development theory of Jean Piaget. I was using a 1927 Underwood typewriter that used to be my mother's when she was in high school. It was heavy, hard to use, and difficult to fix typing errors; consequently, I lost any sense of time and was in the building after midnight.

Superintendent Jenkins noticed that there was a light on in the building and knew I hadn't gone back to the LAC dorm. So he came over and loudly burst through the front door. Naturally, Mandrake ran to the door, barking and growling to protect me from the intruder. Jenkins quickly retreated but yelled at me to come to the door. With his twitching eye, he told me that I had to vacate the ISD premises the next day! I asked him if I was permitted to complete the courses at the LAC program, and he answered that he'd think about it and let me know the next day.

The next day I was called into Dr. Kennedy's office first thing in the morning. She said that I had to make a choice: get rid of the dog or find another place to live. Well, that was no choice at all. I told her that I'd find another place to live but asked if I was still part of this program. She said that she was the only person to decide who stays and who goes from her program. I didn't know it at that time, but Dr. Kennedy set up the LAC program from scratch and was very protective of it.

So that was the second time I got into hot water with the Superintendent of ISD. Right after class that day, I went over to Ivan and told him what happened. I then asked if I could stay in his cabins for the rest of the year and I'd pay him a monthly rent. He talked it over with his wife, Nina, and said yes, I could stay in the last cabin nearest the side road, because it was used as a storage unit, had no bed, and only a commode. On the bright side, it did have a fairly large oil space heater. So I arranged to pay them a small monthly rent and accepted responsibility for the oil bill. I also had to do the needed renovations to that cabin.

I told them that I had to be off campus after dinner that day and asked if I could move in right away. They agreed, and that's what I did. Since it was still July, I had no worries about being cold. They helped me move things around the cabin and found a good mattress, which I placed on the floor and used my sleeping bag for covers. They also found an old desk that I could use to type the papers I needed for school. I moved in that night.

So every day after classes, I came to the cabin, worked on the assignments until suppertime, ate, and then tackled turning the cabin into a place to live. The first thing I had to do was to put in a shower stall or bathtub. Since I had installed a bathtub in the warehouse and knew how to do that, they agreed to buy a tub that would fit into the available space as well as a small hot water heater. By the middle of the first week I was staying there, I had them both installed and working perfectly.

While tackling that problem, I discovered that the water pipe entering the cabin was above ground and would probably freeze during the winter, thus there'd be no water. Ivan told me that he had forgotten about that because it was second nature for them to turn off the water and drain all the pipes right after closing the cabins for the season. At first, I thought that I could avoid having the water pipe freeze if I kept the water running all the time. The problem with that was that their water bill would have been enormous, especially during the off-season.

Fortunately, one of the teachers at the 175 program with whom I was friendly told me about an electric heating line that I could use to wrap around the pipe.

That line would heat the water in the pipes just enough to keep it from freezing. I bought a long length at Canadian Tire and wrapped the pipe in it. Then I took fiberglass insulation and wrapped that around the line, and used duct tape to hold it all in place. Then I shoveled dirt around that. It worked like a charm.

The cabin was so small that there wasn't any room for a refrigerator, not even one that is used in hotel rooms. So what we did was to cut a hole in the cabin underneath the window and attach a wooden cabinet on the outside of the hole. Then we fastened a door for the inside of the cabin, and I had a natural cooler, which was fine during the winter months, but not so good in summer weather. The last thing we did to fix up the cabin for me to live in was to get a large, thick carpet to put on the floor. Not only did it make the cabin kind of cozy, but it acted as insulation. I was happy with the renovations we did on that cabin and enjoyed my stay there for the rest of the year.

August and September saw no new problems for me. I made friends with the physical education teachers by playing one wall handball with them and joining in their wrestling practices. I learned a lot from them.

In October, Dr. Kennedy decided that we should all go to one of the first meetings of the Association of Canadian Educators of the Hearing Impaired, ACEHI, held in the Maritime Provinces, specifically in Halifax. Dr. Kennedy commandeered the school van for the ten of us to travel to the meetings, and I was permitted to drive us to the hotel in Halifax with Dr. Kennedy acting as the navigator. The drive to Halifax was problem free, and the meetings were interesting. I have to say that I learned about the different approaches to Deaf Education in the different provinces that were represented there. The meetings were all day on Saturday. We spent the night in the hotel where the meetings were held and planned to set off back to Amherst right after breakfast Sunday morning.

Unfortunately, it began to snow overnight, a lot. It was also very windy, so we had to drive back to Amherst in a van that didn't have snow tires during a blizzard. Again, I drove the van. What usually would be a two-hour drive from Halifax to Amherst turned into a six-hour nightmare trying to navigate our way along the Trans-Canada Highway, CTH. I doubt that I went faster than 50 km/h the whole way. There was a lot of tension in the van, so I put on the radio, and Dr. Kennedy began a sing along with the girls. This eased the tension quite a bit.

Just outside Amherst, one of our guest teachers had a house, and Dr. Kennedy thought it would be a good idea to stop there and spend the night, but the teacher's house was on a plateau in which one had to drive up a steep hill, and that hill wasn't plowed. So that idea was scrapped, and we trudged along the CTH back to the ISD. When I drove into the school's driveway, there was a big cheer from everyone except me.

I was very tired and just wanted to get in my car and get back to Mandrake and the cabin. I parked my car just in the driveway of my cabin and got Mandrake from Ivan and Nina's cabin. I took him out for a walk, bought a quart of beer, went into my cabin, started the oil heater, and stripped off my wet clothes. I drank some beer as I changed into warm, dry clothes and crawled into my sleeping bag. Eight hours later, Mandrake woke me up to go outside.

I had a hard time opening the door and saw how much snow had fallen overnight. According to the weather report, it was around 18 inches or 35 cm. I shoveled out a path from my door to my car and from my car to the road. Then I went back into the cabin, got us some breakfast, and left for school. When I got there, I discovered that the school was closed, but the LAC program still had classes.

Because of that freak, early blizzard, the Treens closed their motel that day and left for their winter home. Fortunately for me, Ivan's mother, Florence, was staying in her house for the winter, and she and I became good friends. She loved dogs and accepted Mandrake and me into her house twice a week for a home cooked meal. To this day, in my opinion, her baked beans and homemade bread are the tastiest I've ever eaten.

After classes were over, and we got our assignments for the next day, I went home and began to shovel the snow up the walls outside the cabin. There was enough snow to cover half the walls, and much of it had already been blown up the sides as well. My little ice box that Ivan attached to the cabin was covered, and I decided to see how well it would keep food cold. We went to the grocery store and bought some milk, cereal, cheese, butter, strawberry jam, peanut butter, and whole wheat bread. Then I bought some Canadian Club whiskey and beer. Mandrake already had his stash of food, so I only bought him some milk bones and dry food.

It snowed again later that week, then it snowed almost once a week for the rest of the year. In total, Amherst had over 100 inches of snow that year, or 254 centimeters. I had all the insulation I needed to keep the heat inside that little cabin.

Oh yeah, did I tell you that the water didn't freeze, and the hot water heater worked like a charm? I am very proud of what I did that year to keep working on the master's degree.

November and December were uneventful, except that we all had a nice Christmas holiday, albeit with an assignment to read and write a report on "The Conquest of Deafness" by Ruth E. Bender. I flew home and spent Christmas with my family, while Mandrake boarded with Florence. I read the book and did the assignment. Then I got Bev to come up to Martin's Creek and take me to her apartment in West Chester. She did, even though she was going to her own home to spend time with her parents. That was fine with me because I had two other women I wanted to share time with as well, Michelle and Nicky, a thirty-year-old divorced woman whom I met in a bar through a mutual acquaintance.

New Year's Eve was an event that almost had Bev throw me out of her apartment and life for good. We went to a party that was hosted by some of her colleagues in the school where she worked as a science teacher.

Their apartment was also in West Chester, but in a more ritzy part of the town. I bought a bottle of tequila and two lemons. Bev brought a bottle of Bacardi Rum and coke. We had a great time, especially the men who spent much of the time in front of the television watching Penn State play Alabama in the Sugar Bowl. Penn State lost a close game, 13 to 6, and I drank the whole bottle of tequila. Then I started on Bev's rum. By the time we all went out on their balcony to sing Auld Lang Sign, I was drunk and don't remember anything. Bev told me that I decided to pee over the balcony. The other guests and our hosts were angry as hell at me and ordered us to leave. We did.

When we got back to Bev's apartment, she asked me something like, now where should we go. She was obviously being sarcastic, but my answer was, "Take me to Oakland, California." She was not in the mood for that answer and left me in the car all by myself.

I don't know how, but I made it up the stairs to Bev's apartment and threw up in her toilet. I awoke the next day naked, in the bathtub, in cold water, with vomit all around me. Bev was gone, and I was on my own to clean up myself and the apartment.

Since I had to be back in Amherst by January 5, and it was now January 2, I didn't have much time to make up with Bev so she'd drive me to the Philadelphia airport. Luckily, she accepted my apology and allowed me to buy her a nice meal.

On the 4th, I flew back to Halifax airport and got a ride back to Amherst. I immediately went to Florence's, gave her the gift I brought, and brought Mandrake home. I didn't feel well and had a hot toddy and went to bed.

When classes started again on the 5th, I showed up but felt and looked terrible. I was coughing and had a fever. Dr. Kennedy sent me home to get well and said that she'd send assignments for me to do while I recuperated.

She did, and I tried to do them, but was too weak. As a matter of fact, there were two days that I couldn't stand up to let Mandrake out to do his business, I had to crawl to the door. It was the same to feed him and make sure he had enough water. I had no medicine to take, so could only wait it out and drink lots of water.

I couldn't eat anything, which was probably why I was so weak. Fortunately, the bug I had finally left me after four days, and I began to do the assignments. Unfortunately, the assignments were all turned in late and were not done very well.

It's hard to know what was expected when you're not in the class to listen to the instructors and know what they wanted, it's easy to do a poor job.

One of the interesting aspects of the program was the number of practice teaching placements you did. The first three were actually within ISD. We each spent a week in a classroom in the junior, intermediate, and senior departments.

Then we spent two weeks in what were called then outclasses.

These were classrooms that were located in a local school that had at least eight Deaf, Hard of Hearing students living in the nearby area.

I was placed in the city of Truro. After our experience in that setting, we were to evaluate that system, basically review the pros and cons of that system of education for our students.

The classroom that was set aside for the D, HH students in Truro was located in the basement of the school.

These eight students ranged in age from six to fourteen, and some had an additional disability. So the teacher there had to make lesson plans for one first grader, three third graders, three fifth graders, and one in the tenth grade.

To teach in this manner on a five-hour day and also plan for the students to participate in gym activities, where the only real integration took place, was basically impossible.

After talking with the teacher and teacher's aide, I learned that they tried to integrate some students in the regular classroom for specific subjects, such as math.

It wasn't possible due to those teachers' inability to communicate with the students, and there were no interpreter services available.

During recess period, if there was bad weather—which happened often during my time in Nova Scotia that year—the teacher would have to create fun activities within their classroom. I tried to show the kids some gymnastics and various movements to work their bodies and burn off extra energy. In this picture, I'm demonstrating how to do a headstand. The boy to my right was actually able to do one right away. The girls all learned as well, eventually.

I came away from this experience with the understanding that this kind of environment was not conducive to providing the best setting for the students to reach their potential at all. The students were very enjoyable to work with and were capable of understanding what was taught, but by the very nature of the situation, were unable to actually reach their full potential. My written evaluation of "outclasses" reflected my understanding very forcefully. Dr. Kennedy didn't like the tone of my report but did agree with the assessment.

Although I had a couple of run-ins with Dr. Kennedy about grades and choosing a topic for my major paper — she didn't want us to take the time to write a thesis — most of the months after my illness went smoothly.

My major paper was about balance among the Deaf. All of the experts in the field at that time wrote that Deafness caused poor balance. But watching the wrestlers in ISD win match after match against hearing high school teams, and knowing how important balance is for wrestlers, I thought that either balance could be taught or that only Deaf people with a sensory-neural hearing loss would have their balance compromised. So I went about trying to prove it.

ISD had a trampoline team as well, and those students could do things I couldn't do. So I began testing the balance of as many students at ISD as I was permitted, and compared it with the balance of some of the teachers, including the gym teachers and myself. All the subjects would stand on a small balance beam first on two legs with eyes open, and I would time how long it took for them to fall off the beam. Then I had them stand on two legs with their eyes closed, then one leg with eyes open, then one leg with eyes closed. I was getting a fair sample to compare when we went on a "Spring Sojourn" to various schools for the Deaf in the United States. That was when I was thrown off the trip — but not out of the program.

Before the sojourn, we had to select a residential school in which to do our last practice teaching. Two girls, Ellen and Tish, began educating us about the virtues of Newfoundland. Ellen had (still does have) great legs, was very intelligent, the daughter of the principal of the school for the Deaf, and had the unique ability to trip up stairs while carrying a glass of beer and not spill a drop — even though her knees were bruised black and blue. Tish was drop-dead gorgeous, intelligent, and had a Deaf sister who was her inspiration for entering this field. They spoke of their home as if it were the only logical place on earth for anyone to live. Newfoundland?

Later on during the year, I met a number of Nova Scotians who had visited the fair province of Newfoundland and returned with wonderful stories of adventure and wonder at the friendly people who had so little but shared so much. I also discovered that the ratio of women to men in St. John's at that time was five to one. Mmm, I thought, this seemed like a great place to visit. Especially since there must have been a conspiracy among the women of the course to avoid being alone with me at any time for any reason—especially on a date. I couldn't believe they all had so much willpower to resist my American charm. Yep.

So when it came time in the program to choose a residential school in which to practice teach for a month, I chose the Newfoundland School for the Deaf. Not only to learn from their master teachers but to check out the greatest natural resource Newfoundland offers the world—their ladies. I was not disappointed.

We were going to take the ISD van for this sojourn and visit the Clarke Oral School in Boston, the American School for the Deaf in Hartford, Connecticut, the Marie Katzenbach School in Trenton, New Jersey, and Gallaudet College in Washington, DC. We were provided a per diem for food, but Dr. Kennedy arranged for the motel rooms and paid for them. I thought I would be driving, as I had when we went to Halifax and had had a lot of experience driving in the USA, but I was wrong—again. The vice principal of the ISD elementary school, Mr. Al Gillis, would be coming with us and do the driving. He and I would share a motel room for the journey. That seemed fine until the first night we spent together. Al had what we now know would be called sleep apnea and snored loudly—all night.

Needless to say, I tried to wake him up or to stop his snoring by getting him to sleep on his side. But sleeping on his side made no difference, he snored just as loudly and just as long. So that night, I took a pillow and blanket, went to the van and slept on the bench. When the sun came up, I returned to the motel room and took a shower while Al continued to snore. We got back on the road and continued down toward Boston where we were to visit the Clarke Oral School for the Deaf. Although the highways in Massachusetts are four and six lanes, Al had no problem getting us to the motel, which was just off the I95 heading into Northampton.

After another nearly sleepless night, I was getting irritated, but didn't say anything and watched the students interact in this beacon of oralism. What I and the girls from Newfoundland noticed was that when the kids were sure they couldn't be observed, they signed to each other.

Interesting!

The next school we were visiting was the American School for the Deaf in Hartford. At that school, which was opened by Thomas Gallaudet and Laurent Clerc in 1817, we didn't have to go to a motel. The superintendent of the school asked us to be his guests in his home. This semi-mansion had six guest rooms, just enough for three girls to share a room, one for Dr. Kennedy, and one each for Al and me. I was looking forward to a good night's sleep, but Dr. Kennedy decided that Al and I were to share a room. Not only were we to share the room, but this room only had one bed, so I was given a cot to sleep in.

So I still had the snoring, but to add insult to injury, I had to sleep on a small cot. Actually, the cot would have been comfortable if I weren't so damned irritated by a lack of sleep. So I again went down to the van. However, this time I was found out, and before our tour of the facilities and visit with the students at this school, Dr. Kennedy asked to speak with me in private.

She wondered why I was seen in the van overnight, and I told her about Al's snoring and my lack of sleep for the past three days. She called Al in and asked him if what I said was true. He told her that it was and that he and his wife had to sleep in separate rooms because of it. I told her I had a solution where I could have my own motel room. I suggested that rather than me using the per diem for food, I could use that money to pay for my own motel room and would buy my own food using my credit card. She said she'd think it over. I felt that the problem would be solved.

The American School for the Deaf used sign language to teach the students. Not only that, but they taught the students current events, and when they found out that I had been in the Marine Corps, they asked me many questions about my tour of duty. I told them that I didn't go to Vietnam, but many of the men who were in my basic training platoon did, and that about half of them either were killed or wounded. Then we began talking about why we got into that war, and I told them about President John Kennedy's interview with Walter Cronkite and that, had he not been assassinated, we probably would not have escalated our presence in that country's civil war.

After that conversation, the physical education teacher came over to me and asked if I had ever coached football. I told him that I played football and coached wrestling but had never coached football. He said that if I was willing to learn how to coach football, he'd be willing to hire me to work there after I got the MEd in Deaf Education. I agreed that I would be willing to learn anything to work there and left the school feeling very excited.

Our next school to visit would be the Marie Katzenbach School in Trenton, New Jersey. That was a fairly long drive, and Dr. Kennedy decided to spend that night in a motel in New Brunswick, NJ. To get to that motel, we had to take an exit and make a left hand turn, but the exit we had to take was two lane and Al got into the wrong lane. So rather than take a right and then turn around, he stopped, tried to back up and move into the left hand turning lane. We nearly got rear ended and side swiped, but luckily, we didn't. Of course, being the US, there was a lot of horn blowing, which rattled Al more.

When we finally got to this motel, this would be the fourth night I'd be spending with him and not getting any sleep, unless Dr. Kennedy accepted my proposal. I actually thought she had, especially when Al told her that he had this problem breathing and his wife would often sleep in their guest room, or he would. So when we stopped at the office, I began to go into it with her to pay for a room for myself. She stopped me and explained that she'd get the rooms and I could pay my bill in the morning. I thought that seemed reasonable and went back into the van.

When she returned, she handed out keys to the girls and Al and told me to pick up my key myself. That I thought was strange, but went in and asked for a key to a room for me. Well, the motel had two separate buildings on two levels with a swimming pool between them. When I got out of the office, the van had gone down to the building on the bottom level, but my room was in the building on the upper level. Being already so damned irritated from a lack of sleep, I was livid. My suitcase, cassette player and cassette carrier were placed on the parking lot and the girls were all in their rooms. I asked Al, who was still with the van what was going on and he just shrugged his shoulders. Then Dr. Kennedy came out of her room with a letter for me. I opened it and saw that there was $150.50 in cash (the remainder of the per diem), and a letter 'excusing' me from the remainder of the trip. I was to find my own way back to Amherst and my own way to Newfoundland, where I was going to do my practice teaching.

I was shocked and wanted to ask her what the hell she was thinking and why I was being treated this way. My proposal didn't seem to be unreasonable, which Al even confirmed, but she just sat stoically at the motel desk and told me to leave or she'd call the police and accuse me of harassment. I left her room, picked up my stuff and walked to the room she got for me. I then walked to a liquor store and bought a bottle of bourbon and some coke, got ice from the machine and settled into my room. Watching television, I drank a few drinks and got into bed. I went to sleep immediately.

When the girls left the motel, they saw this sign that said, "Farewell John Read." They thought I paid for it, but it was actually for a staff member of the motel. But it sure was eerie. They took a picture of it and after graduating, gave me this copy.

The next day, I went to pay for the room but found it had been taken care of; I assume by Dr. Kennedy. So I began to hitchhike to West Chester. I was fortunate to only need a couple of rides to get there and placed my stuff in Bev's apartment. She wasn't home from school as yet, so I phoned Nicky to see if she was home. She was, and I talked her into coming over to Bev's apartment for a visit. I wanted a shoulder to cry on and some TLC. I got both, then Nicky had to go and pick up her son from school.

When Bev got home, she also gave me some TLC, then we talked about my next step. Should I quit or make my way back to Nova Scotia and on to the Newfoundland School for the Deaf (NSD)? I decided not to quit.

Bev called Canadian Airlines in Philadelphia and got me a flight back to Halifax. Of course, it had to make a stop in Toronto first, but after five hours I was back in Nova Scotia and able to get a bus into Amherst. This trip took me the better part of a day, but when I got back to the cabins and Mandrake saw me, boy, was I glad to be back. I took Mandrake for a long walk with Ivan and told him what had happened on this sojourn. He was sympathetic and told me that he'd do anything he could to help me get to Newfoundland.

I decided it would be cheaper for me to drive to North Sydney and take the ferry to Port Aux Basques (PAB) rather than fly directly into St. John's. It was cheaper financially, but I did pay in the form of sea sickness. My first experience on that ferry was brutal. At first, while still tied to the dock, I thought all would be fine. I even went to the bar and bought my first Newfoundland beer, an India Pale Ale. Now the ferry ride to PAB was supposed to be six to eight hours, but this time we hit a strong headwind. This caused a number of things to happen: first, the trip took around fourteen hours; second, the seas were rough; third, to save money I didn't rent a cabin so had nowhere to rest my head; fourth, I found out that diesel fuel was not kind to a person who was sea sick.

After ridding my body of the beer I had just had and food I ate for the past couple of days, I gathered a large bundle of napkins, laid down on the soft bench that circled the bar, placed the napkins under my chin, and didn't move for the next thirteen hours. I didn't have the courage to even venture down to the bathroom to pee. When we finally docked, I slowly made my way to my car and got in. I drove off the ferry and began to look for the road to St. John's when I saw a couple hitchhiking.

Naturally, I stopped and picked up a young man and woman. I asked them where they were going, and they were also heading to St. John's, so I had company and people who were familiar with the roads and could direct me to my destination. They were really a Godsend. They kept me company, spoke of their religion, Bahai, but didn't try to do any "conversion" like the Jehovah's Witness in California did. When I stopped for gas, they paid half, and I didn't even ask them. They lived in Mount Pearl, a town just outside of St. John's, and I drove them to their apartment and was invited in. Since it was late, they asked if I wanted to sleep on their couch. It looked comfortable, so I took them up on their offer.

The next day they gave me directions as to how to get to the school. I only wish they had drawn a map for me. I found the streets of St. John's fairly complicated but managed to find the school, which at that time was located next to the St. John's Airport. Had I taken a plane, I'd have been close, I thought, and probably could have walked to the school. Of course, it wasn't that easy. Anyway, I digress. When I found the administration office, I checked in with Mrs. Parrott, the principal of the school.

She was very happy to meet me and directed the Head Supervisor of the Residence, Mr. Cooper, to come over and help me to my quarters. Yes, I'd be living in their dormitory, in my own room, with a real desk, nice bed, and access to the kitchen. However, I didn't actually have to worry about cooking my own food—nope, I had free food from their cafeteria. Heaven!

My supervising teacher was Mrs. Ruby Hunt, who taught English in the Intermediate Department. She had some signing skills, but in all honesty, my signing ability far exceeded hers, and the students liked it. My time as a student teacher at the NSD was wonderful! They were very accommodating, especially with helping me with my major paper.

The physical education teacher, Mr. Cyril Coffin, arranged for me to continue my balance experiments with the students at the NSD. The vice-principal, Mr. Reg, helped me with the statistical side of my experiments, and I wrote up my paper before returning to Amherst.

I also made some friends in Mary Trask, business education teacher, and her husband, Mike, who became my handball foe and partner. The industrial education teacher, Dunne, invited me to his cabin on the Salmonier River for the May 24th holiday, which was an eye opener as to the Newfoundland weather. When we left for the long weekend, the weather was warm and sunny. At the cabin, the weather became a bit cooler, but was still nice enough for barbecues and beer outside. That Sunday, Mike and I got into Jim's little boat and chugged up the Salmonier River just to see the terrain and wildlife. As I was getting into the boat, Mike advised me to bring my warm coat because you never know how things might change. So I did.

We were motoring for a couple of hours and talking about everything under the sun when the winds changed direction. They had been coming from the south and were quite warm, but they quickly changed to the east, then from the north. We put on our warm coats, and Mike suggested that we head back to the cabin. After we turned around, it began to snow—wet snow—and it came down very gently at first. We were going downstream now, and Mike decided to pick up steam because the winds began to blow harder. By the time we made it back to the cabin, we were engulfed in a blizzard. We brought the boat ashore and ran into the cabin.

The heat of the fireplace and oil burner was very welcome as we stripped off our wet clothes. We were lucky to get back in as good a shape as we were, because in the newspaper later that week, there were stories about trout fishermen who were on the same river whose boat capsized and one drowned.

Mrs. Parrott was also a very good host to me. She invited me to her home for a meal of seal carcass. Since I never ate seal before, I thought it would be a treat. I had had venison, moose, and caribou and liked that wild meat, so I thought seal would give me the same delicious meal. I was wrong. I tried to eat the portion Mr. Parrott gave me, but I just couldn't. To me, it tasted like a combination of greasy fish and rancid moose meat. I apologized to her and said I just couldn't eat it all. I never said that I didn't like it, just that I got full very quickly that day.

Thermal Printer

As for my major paper, I needed to have eleven copies, one for each evaluator and one for Dr. Kennedy. Again, the NSD helped me out by teaching me how to use their thermal coping machine and letting me use the necessary papers to make the copies. Let me tell you, it was a very slow process. First you had to take a film like paper and place it on your master copy, then take a thin paper and place that over those two papers, then another film and finally the paper the ink would be copied onto. After you had the papers all lined up, they were fed through a thermal machine. After 90 seconds, the machine put out the copy you wanted. There was one problem, each page had to be done by itself, so page one's ink went through 11 times and became almost invisible. So I had to make three copies of originals. Being a smart guy, I actually typed 4 copies and the last copy I made, became the one I presented as my original.

My paper was only twelve pages long, the smallest paper presented to the evaluators. I really had no idea how to write a research paper, and Dr. Kennedy was not one of my most ardent supporters at that time, so she gave me very little help with either my research or the way to put the paper together. I later found out that she had approached each of the members of the evaluation team and told them she would like to see me fail the oral exams. I never failed any of the written exams, so her last chance was the orals.

At the end of May, I bid my farewells to the friends I had made at the NSD and began my drive to PAB and the ferry to Nova Scotia. I had reservations for May 31st, and this time I made sure I had a cabin. It was fortunate that I left for PAB on May 30 for the crossing because Newfoundland weather had another surprise for me. I left St. John's in the morning to a fairly nice day, but when I got to Gander, it began to snow. By the time I drove through the Wreck House area, I was in a full-blown blizzard. My windshield wipers would get stuck, and I had to lean out my window to free them, and the wind was so strong my heavy car shook like a baby's rocking cradle.

The blizzard forced the ferry to postpone its crossing indefinitely, and I was stuck in my '49 Plymouth for the night. My plan to have a leisurely drive back to Amherst and a restful couple of days with Mandrake in my cabin preparing for the oral exams had changed big time. I went into the terminal with my notes and tried to study for them there. It was impossible. The noise and hustle and bustle made it so I could not concentrate at all. So I went back to my car, covered up as best as I could, and slept. The exams were scheduled for June 4 and 5. I had planned to return by June 2, but the weather in Newfoundland changed that schedule drastically. I didn't have two days to prepare for the orals — I had overnight — so I crammed all night.

The ten-person evaluation team was split up into two five-person panels, each responsible for asking us about the academic side of the program, then for us to support our major paper. The exam lasted two days. That June 4th and 5th were very hot in Amherst, and the sport coats that I had — the ones that Chilli from Oakland had given me — were made of wool, therefore steaming hot. To add to that discomfort, I was nervous as anything. Consequently, I began to sweat profusely. Furthermore, Dr. Kennedy had made the schedule for us to sit before each panel, and I was scheduled last for both days. Needless to say, I practically destroyed both of the sport coats.

I have to say that each person on the panel was very fair with me, and although my paper flew in the face of other well-known and established experts in our field, their questions were pointed and they listened to my rationale carefully and without prejudice. As for the academic questions, the cramming I did the night before helped immensely, and I had no problem providing accurate answers.

Despite Dr. Kennedy's wishes, I passed.

I decided to pass on the graduation ceremony and had my degree sent to my mother's address in Pennsylvania. I also passed on the graduation dinner and dance, preferring to eat with Florence, Ivan, and Nina. After our dinner, I bought some grass and drove to the home of one of the gym teachers. There, Steve and his wife, Kerry, and I partied with joints and booze.

The next day, I was asked to come to Dr. Kennedy's office before I left to drive back to Pennsylvania. She presented me with a copy of the recommendation she wrote for me to use when applying for a teaching position. It wasn't flattering, but good enough for me to use — and I did.

CHAPTER 11:
FINDING EMPLOYMENT

I applied for positions in schools for the deaf in Pennsylvania, Connecticut, New Jersey, and New York. I also, at the behest of one of my classmates from Newfoundland, applied there as well.

I was offered a position at the Western Pennsylvania School for the Deaf at $16,000 per year. The Easter Seal Society in Bethlehem, PA offered me the opportunity to set up a preschool program at their facility for $15,500 per year. I was also offered a teaching position at the NSD at $18,000 per year. Remember that in 1975, the exchange rate between the US dollar and Canadian dollar was on par, so I decided to accept the NSD offer. I thought that I'd remain there for a couple of years and reapply to other schools down in the good 'ole U.S. of A.

Arriving On The Island Of Newfoundland - The Most Easterly Point In North America

In order to pay for this journey, I visited the local welfare office on September 1 and received a check in the amount of $154.00. This was just enough to pay for the ferry from North Sydney, NS to Port-aux-Basques, Nfld. and gas. After cashing the check, I said goodbye to Mom and my sister and her family and set off on the 1,500-mile journey to begin a career as a teacher of the deaf in St. John's, Newfoundland. My 1949 Plymouth Sedan was packed chock-a-block full with all my worldly possessions, food for the trip, and my dog, Mandrake.

The trip was fairly uneventful. Driving straight through to Amherst, NS, I stopped off at a friend's house at 1:00 AM Tuesday morning, September 2, 1975. Steve and Kerry welcomed me with a large omelet and permitted me to siphon gas from their four-wheel-drive Chevy truck. You see, there were no 24-hour gas stations open in Amherst back then, and I had only a quarter tank of gas left. The ferry was scheduled to leave North Sydney at 7:00 AM, and I had to get there an hour ahead of boarding. I left at 3:00 and drove straight on for two and a half more hours until I got to Antigonish, NS. There, the old darling began to groan and ping. From experience with my 1948 Chevy pickup truck, I knew I threw a push rod. I was now driving with five cylinders but couldn't stop; it was senseless to entertain the idea of repair or postponing the ferry ride—I couldn't afford to do either. So I prayed to my father to help me make it to North Sydney and into St. John's. Dad helped, and I got into line to board the ferry at 6:45 AM. (Yep, the ferry was late departing; not an unusual experience.) Thanks again, Dad and serendipity.

I had to put Mandrake in a kennel for the trip over, and I spent a fair amount of time sitting with him. I did manage to sleep for about seven hours of the ferry ride and left Port-Aux-Basques for St. John's at 9:00 PM. Naturally, I stopped off at the first gas station I found and filled up. Driving across the island of Newfoundland was slow going with only five cylinders working. I thought I could make it in another twelve hours but was wrong, wrong, wrong.

Going up the numerous hills on the Newfoundland portion of the Trans-Canada Highway was very hard going, and on a few occasions, I had to downshift into first gear in order to reach the top of the hill. Stopping only to relieve myself and get more gas, I arrived at the Newfoundland School for the Deaf during lunch break on the afternoon of Wednesday, September 3, 1975. I arrived three days after the school opened because of an error made by the Newfoundland Department of Education.

They didn't advertise my position Canada-wide before I was hired, and I couldn't get the work visa until they did and no Canadian citizen applied for my teaching position. Luckily, nobody applied and I got my work visa.

Arriving At The Newfoundland School For The Deaf (Nsd)

The NSD campus, if you could call it that, was on the outskirts of St. John's, halfway between the city and the town of Torbay. It was set up in barracks built for the American and Canadian soldiers during World War II alongside the airport's major runway.

The vice-principal, Reg, greeted me warmly as he was leaving the building for a lunch date. Mandrake didn't growl at him, so I knew he was a good person. He brought us into the school to my classroom in the senior department and said that I would be teaching Social Studies to seniors. When asked what curriculum materials and books were being used, Mr. Harte said, "Social Studies is the study of society. Teach the kids about social issues."

So here I was in St. John's, Newfoundland, with a car that needed repair, all my possessions in and on top of it, and my dog riding shotgun. So the next thing I did was to ask if he knew a place where we could stay until I found an apartment. He went to a phone and called Mr. Cooper and asked him if the room I used while practice teaching was still available. It was, so I drove to the residence and brought in some clothes. I asked about Mandrake and was told if he didn't attack the kids, he could stay with me for a short time, so long as the authorities didn't find out. Now I could concentrate on teaching and finding a place for us to live.

I made a sandwich and fed Mandrake, then returned to my assigned classroom in the senior department. I had no idea what I was going to teach, who I was going to teach, or how I was going to teach it. So I decided that for the first few days, I'd just talk to the students, get to know them, and take a cue from them. That was a very good thing to do, as it turned out.

Also, it so happened that the province of Newfoundland was in the midst of a general election. Voting was to take place on September 16th and would be significant because this would be the last election as a leader of a provincial political party for Joey Smallwood. For those who don't know, Mr. Smallwood was the driving force that got Newfoundland admitted into the Canadian Federation as the tenth province in 1949. He was also the Premier responsible for the establishment of the NSD.

This election was also important because none of the senior students knew anything about the elections. I also discovered that in the decade that NSD had been open, there had never been a student council. So I thought I could create a student council and teach the students about parliamentary democratic elections simultaneously.

Of course, I needed to learn about Canadian politics and the Parliamentary Democratic system as well. Fortunately, the school had a library with two encyclopedias, *Britannica* and *New World*. So I spent a fair amount of time reading. I also read their newspapers to find an apartment. More about that later.

I had a meeting with Mrs. Parrott and Mr. Harte about perhaps setting up a Student Council and my idea about teaching Parliamentary Democracy at the same time. Both thought it would be wonderful for the students as well as the school community, and so my career began.

VOTING

With the help of the Industrial Arts teacher, Jim, Ms. Clarke, Mr. Harte, and Mrs. Parrott, this project was very successful. We first held an assembly and asked for nominations for Secretary, Treasurer, Vice-president and President. The nominees were: Secretary, Annie, Roy, and Louise; Treasurer, Bernard, Sheila, and Gladys; Vice President, Brenda and Janet, and for President, Bernice and Colleen. A polling station was set up with Raymond standing, and Joan sitting and voting, with Gladys seated back to the camera. Then we set up polling stations, while the nominees campaigned by making signs, sharing their promises, and finally giving their campaign speeches, which called for another assembly.

COMMENTATORS

I applied for positions in schools for the deaf in Pennsylvania, Connecticut, New Jersey, and New York. I also, at the behest of one of my classmates from Newfoundland, applied there as well.

I was offered a position at the Western Pennsylvania School for the Deaf at $16,000 per year; The Easter Seal Society in Bethlehem, Pa. offered me the opportunity to set up a pre-school program at their facility for $15,500/year. I was also offered a teaching position at the NSD at $18,000/year. Remember that in 1975, the exchange rate between the US dollar and Canadian dollar was on par, so I decided to accept the NSD offer. I thought that I'd remain there for a couple of years and re-apply to other schools down in the good 'ole U S of A.

Arriving on the Island of Newfoundland - The Most Easterly Point in North America

In order to pay for this journey, I visited the local welfare office on September 1, and received a check in the amount of $154.00. This was just enough to pay for the ferry from North Sydney, NS to Port-Aux-Basques, Nfld. and gas. After cashing the check, I said good-bye to Mom and my sister and her family and set off on the 1500-mile journey to begin a career as a teacher of the deaf in St. John's, Newfoundland. My 1949 Plymouth Sedan was packed chock-a-block full with all my worldly possessions, food for the trip and my dog, Mandrake.

The trip was fairly uneventful. Driving straight through to Amherst, NS, I stopped off at a friend's house at 1:00 AM Tuesday morning, September 2, 1975. Steve and Kerry welcomed me with a large omelet and permitted me to siphon gas from their four-wheel drive Chevy truck. You see, there were no 24-hour gas stations opened in Amherst back then, and I had only a quarter tank of gas left. The ferry was scheduled to leave North Sydney at 7:00 am and I had to get there an hour ahead of boarding. I left at 3:00 and drove straight on for 2 1/2 more hours until I got to Antigonish, NS. There the old darling began to groan and ping. From experience with my 1948 Chevy pickup truck, I knew I threw a push rod. I was now driving with 5 cylinders, but couldn't stop; it was senseless to entertain an idea of repair or postponing the ferry ride—I couldn't afford to do either. So I prayed to my father to help me make it to North Sydney and into St. John's. Dad helped, and I got into line to board the ferry at 6:45 am. (Yep, the ferry was late departing; not an unusual experience.) Thanks again, Dad and serendipity.

I had to put Mandrake in a kennel for the trip over, and I spent a fair amount of time sitting with him. I did manage to sleep for about 7 hours of the ferry ride and left Port-aux-Basques for St. John's at 9:00 PM. Naturally, I stopped off at the first gas station I found and filled up. Driving across the island of Newfoundland was slow going with only 5 cylinders working. I thought I could make it in another twelve hours, but was wrong, wrong wrong. Going up the numerous hills on the Newfoundland portion of the trans-Canada highway was very hard going and on a few occasions, I had to down shift into first gear in order to reach the top of the hill. Stopping only to relieve myself and get more gas, I arrived at the Newfoundland School for the Deaf during lunch break on the afternoon of Wednesday, September 3, 1975. I arrived 3 days after the school opened because of an error made by the Newfoundland Department of Education. They didn't advertise my position Canada wide before I was hired, and I couldn't get the work visa until they did and no Canadian citizen applied for my teaching position. Luckily, nobody applied and I got my work visa.

Arriving At The Newfoundland School For The Deaf (Nsd)

The NSD campus, if you could call it that, was on the outskirts of St. John's halfway between the city and the town ion Torbay. It was set up in barracks built for the American and Canadian soldiers during World War II alongside the airport's major runway.

The vice-principal, Reg, greeted me warmly as he was leaving the building for a lunch date. Mandrake didn't growl at him, so I knew he was a good person. He brought us into the school to my classroom in the senior department and said that I would be teaching Social Studies to seniors. When asked what curriculum materials and books were being used, Mr. Harte said, "Social Studies is the study of society. Teach the kids about social issues."

So here I was in St. John's, Newfoundland with a car that needed repair, all my possessions in and on top of it and my dog riding shotgun. So the next thing I did was to ask if he knew a place where we could stay until I found an apartment. He went to a phone and called Mr. Cooper and asked him if the room I used while practice teaching was still available. It was so I drove to the residence and brought in some clothes. I asked about Mandrake and was told if he didn't attack the kids, he could stay with me for a short time, so long as the authorities didn't find out. Now I could concentrate on teaching and finding a place for us to live.

I made a sandwich and fed Mandrake, then returned to my assigned classroom in the senior department. I had no idea what I was going to teach, who I was going to teach or how I was going to teach it. So I decided that for the first few days, I'd just talk to the students, get to know them and take a cue from them. That was a very good thing to do, as it turned out.

Also, it so happened that the province of Newfoundland was in the midst of a general election. Voting was to take place on September 16th and would be significant because this would be the last election as a leader of a provincial political party for Joey Smallwood. For those who don't know, Mr. Smallwood was the driving force that got Newfoundland admitted into the Canadian Federation as the tenth province in 1949. He was also the Premier responsible for the establishment of the NSD.

This election was also important because none of the senior students knew anything about the elections. I also discovered that in the decade that NSD was opened, there had never been a student council. So I thought I could create a student council and teach the students about parliamentary democratic elections simultaneously.

Of course I needed to learn about Canadian politics and the Parliamentary Democratic system as well. Fortunately, the school had a library with two encyclopedias, Britannica and New World. So I spent a fair amount of time reading. I also read their newspapers to find an apartment. More about that later.

I had a meeting with Mrs. Parrott and Mr. Harte about perhaps setting up a Student Council and my idea about teaching Parliamentary Democracy at the same time. Both thought it would be wonderful for the students as well as the school community, and so my career began.

Trying to make this school election as much like the Provincial election, we set up a newsroom to broadcast the results in real time to the rest of the school. It worked perfectly; and I was amazed!

Just after the general election in the Province, the NSD held its election and the student council was formed. President was Colleen, a high school senior; Vicepresident - Brenda, a high school junior; Treasurer - Sheila, a high school senior; Secretary was Louise, a high school senior.

Their first order of business was to choose school colours (Red & Blue) and an official mascot (the Newfoundland Dog). Next, the student council planned a halloween party for the children under the age of 13 and a dance for those 14 and above. At the dance, we charged admission and sold snacks. The student council finally had an amount of money to plan other activities. The amount of money raised - $54.60.

Next they wanted to have a bon-fire for November 5. When I asked them why they wanted to do this, they said it was a tradition in Newfoundland. I asked them why it was a tradition and no one knew. So this was our next project; researching why there was an annual bon-fire on November 5. They discovered that the reason was a man named Guy Fawkes, who was part of a plan to blow up English King James I and replace him with a Catholic King. He was caught on November 5, 1605, tortured, and was to be hung as a traitor on January 31, but died before his execution. The students were fascinated by the story and wanted to know more about Parliament, which is what we studied for the rest of the semester.

We needed a way to get the students, bon-fire material, and snacks down to the site, Middle Cove Beach, so during a recess period, I asked some of my colleagues if they had any ideas about how to do this. Mrs. Gosse, a wonderful teacher and mother of a Deaf daughter, who lived in Torbay, a farming and fishing community, said she would ask her neighbor if he'd drive them down from the NSD. She did, and her friend, whose name I cannot remember, not only drove a tractor with a large trailer behind it, but filled it with hay for an honest to goodness hay ride. The students loaded the trailer with old wood, tires, broken furniture and anything else they could burn. Mr. Harte and I loaded my 1949 Plymouth with boxes of food, blankets and matches. Needless to say, a grand time was had by all. And there was a bonus: the students who were acting out stopped for some time. Unfortunately, I cannot recall exactly how long the calmness lasted, but the rebelliousness did subside for a period of time.

It is interesting to note that in Deaf Culture, friends, teachers, and famous people are given "name signs." Mine is an "R" moving left to right under my nose in the form of a moustache. Mrs. Gosse's name sign was the letter "G" moved up and down twice on the top of the head. The reason for my name sign is obvious, I have had a moustache since I was 20 years old. The reason for Mrs. Gosse's name sign was because she had a habit of "losing" her glasses, which the students saw were on the top of her head. The students thought that very funny and gave her that particular name sign.

As Christmas approached, the student council asked if we could put a float in the St. John's Annual Christmas Parade. I'm not sure if it was Mrs. Parrott or Mr. Harte who called the Downtown St. John's Committee to get the necessary information for NSD to enter a float, but we did get it. Next, we had to come up with a theme, and one of our more creative students, Craig, said, "Snoopy." So we decided to do a float based on the cartoon strip, "Charlie Brown."

At that time, the Arts and Culture Centre (ACC) was advertising a Christmas show called "A Charlie Brown Christmas." I went down to the ACC to see what I could find out. The director of the show was Sylvia, who showed me the set and promised that she would help in any way she could. So I set up a meeting with her and the student council and a couple of other students. She explained the play to the students and allowed them to explore the set.

We needed a truck to pull the float and a trailer to build it on. And Mrs. Gosse came through again. This time her neighbour brought a trailer down to the RCAF complex and backed it into an empty building that we had permission to use to build the float. He returned on Parade Day and drove us downtown and through the parade.

The high school students and many of the intermediate boys and girls all chipped in to design and build the float, after school hours. The float consisted of Snoopy sitting on top of his dog house, a fence surrounding the trailer, Lucy's Psychiatrist Booth, Linus and his blanket, a sign on each side of the fence with various sayings borrowed from the comic strip, Schroeder playing his piano (which was merely a keyboard donated by one of our teachers), and Snoopy as the Red Barron, complete with wings and "flying" around the float and crowd. Craig again came through by making a snout in the same colours and size as the Snoopy snout as shown in the comic strip. Industrial Arts cut a piece of ply wood into a 4' X 5' piece and laminated it for painting. Craig, again, used his imagination to paint an unofficial school logo for NSD. He used the recently adopted school mascot, the Newfoundland Dog, as the centre piece with the year the school was opened sandwiching the dog and spelled out the name of the school. On the day of the parade, we fixed it to the front of the truck.

The students went home for Christmas vacation in 1975 a very happy group of kids. As proof of this, the students who were acting out and punching holes in the walls of the school settled down during these events.

Finding A Home: Only In Newfoundland

Mandrake and I were still living in the residence until I found a place to live. I saw an ad for a 2 bedroom apartment in a neighbourhood near the school for $90.00/month and decided to apply for it. The owner, Fred, was Newfoundland's first Olympic representative for Canada as a race walker. He was in his 70s when we met, and it was a pleasure to be in his company. He still walked so fast that I had to jog to keep up with him when we took our dogs for a walk in the woods near the apartment Ferd rented to me.

The apartment building was close enough to the school for the Deaf that I could walk if (when?) my car eventually died. There were two other things that made it perfect for me—Ferd welcomed dogs, and he was willing to wait for his first rent check. Imagine it. A landlord who said, "I know you are a teacher and will get paid eventually. I also know the kind of character you are, so I'm not worried about it." My dog, Mandrake, and I moved into the apartment on the second weekend I was in Newfoundland.

However, there was a major problem with getting a paycheque. The first was with the pay scale. When September 15th (payday!) arrived, the two other graduates of the masters in deaf education program from which we graduated in June of 1975 did not get paid on the appropriate teacher certification level. Ellen, Tish and I made an appointment with the director of teacher payroll and began a 2-week argument that was eventually settled to our satisfaction. You see, the policy at that time was to recognize a master's degree from a two-year program only. We were able to convince the administration at the department of education to realize that they were penalizing people for being smart enough to complete a 2 year course in one calendar year. So, Tish and Ellen got their back pay on September 30th, but there was no paycheque for me.

This time I made an appointment with the director of teacher payroll, Bruce, and discovered that my application was filled out improperly. At that time, Newfoundland was a denominational educational system. However, since the Newfoundland School for the Deaf was ecumenical and being from the United States, I filled in the part of the application where it asked for one's religion "No Preference." Big mistake!

Not only did I have to choose a religion, but I had to get a character reference from a clergy-person of that religion in order to be paid. I chose the Roman Catholic religion, since that was the one I was raised in, and was sure my mother's parish priest would provide me with a character reference. Wrong! It took most of a week to find that out, and that meant my October 15 pay check would not be forth coming.

I was confident I'd get paid by the end of the month, however, because one of my fellow teachers at the school for the deaf had a brother who was a Brother and sister who was a Sister. Mary was sure her brother would give me a reference and set up a Sunday dinner party so he and I could meet. However, Mary's brother who was a Christian Brother refused to write a character reference for me. So now it was obvious I'd not get paid on October 30th. To this day, I'm sure his refusal was because I beat him at the board game Risk after Sunday dinner.

So, Mary set up another dinner party, this time on a Friday night. Mary's sister who was a Nun, was very nice and didn't play board games. We did, however, play canasta. The Nun and I lost to Mike and Mary, but the nun thought I was a good enough card player, and therefore a decent person, to write me a letter of reference. On the Presentation Sisters stationery, she wrote, "To the best of my knowledge, John Reade is a good character," and signed it. That was sufficient to get me paid. Unfortunately, for teacher payroll to get everything else in the application, teacher certification, insurance and income tax processed, my first paycheque wouldn't come until November 30th.

During all this time, Ferd let me remain in the apartment while the rent bills pile up. I developed a walking relationship with him and our dogs, and kept him apprised of the paycheque situation. After it was obvious I'd not be paid October 15th, he asked me how I was feeding my dog. I told him that Mandrake was being fed table scraps from the school and teachers who had me to their place for supper.

Ferd said that was terrible for such a good dog as Mandrake, pulled a money clip from his pocket, stripped off a 50-dollar bill and ordered me to get appropriate food for Mandrake.

When I learned that I'd not be paid until November 30th, I sold my car — broken push rod and all. I got $700.00 for it and gave Ferd the $270.00 needed to pay for September, October and November. He'd just have to wait for my regular pay to get the dog food money returned.

That's how I began my twenty-six-year career at the Newfoundland School for the Deaf. I arrived with about $5.00 in my pocket, was given the task of creating a social studies program for high school seniors, and never got paid for the first three months. But was never without. The teaching, residence and office staff took turns inviting me to their homes to break bread with their respective families, and I was permitted to live in an apartment for free by a landlord who also gave me money for my dog. This experience could only happen in Newfoundland!

The Nsd History

The Newfoundland School for the Deaf played such an important part in my life's story that I'd like to take a few pages now to tell the history of the school. Please remember that this is MY understanding and experiences with the NSD.

From personal anecdotes from four different individuals of different eras, the education of Deaf students before the NSD was opened meant a child as young as 7 years of age would be sent by ferry, train and bus to a different province over a thousand miles from home to learn about the three "R"s, Deaf Culture and socialization. To say that this type of education was traumatic would be like saying the Titanic was a wrecked ship; however, the parents of Deaf children in Newfoundland and Labrador knew they had no choice if their children were to have a chance of a future. As written in Carbin's book, "Deaf Heritage in Canada," Flora, one of the first Deaf Newfoundland children to be educated, attended the Ontario School for the Deaf in Belleville. She went there from 1944 to 1949. She then attended the Belleville Collegiate Institute from 1949 to 1954.

Ms. Clark then went to Gallaudet College in Washington, D. C. from 1954 to 1958. From her experiences in these educational systems, she recognized the need for Newfoundland to have its own school for the deaf.

As secretary of the Caribou Silent Club (the precursor to the Newfoundland and Labrador Association of the Deaf) she commenced strongly and with firm determination to lobby the Newfoundland Government to open a school in her home province.

From 1949, when Newfoundland officially became the tenth province of Canada, until 1964, the provincial government of Joey Smallwood continued sending Deaf children to residential schools for the Deaf in either Quebec or Nova Scotia. Children as young as 5 years of age would attend these institutions for ten straight months returning home only after the school year ended. Not only was that traumatic in and of itself for parents and students, the Newfoundland government of the day used a kind of quota system, based, as far as I can tell, on the number of vacancies the schools for the deaf had in Montreal or Halifax. If Montreal had 15 spaces, 15 Newfoundlanders would go there. The remaining children might then be sent to Halifax; that is until Halifax's quota was filled. The provincial government was not very discerning as to whom went where or who was permitted to go to school. As soon as the quotas for Montreal and Halifax were filled, the Newfoundland government stopped sending students, period. And it didn't matter to them who went where. At least once a brother and sister were separated sent to different schools in the same school year.

At that time, the cost of sending these children off for their education was $1400 each. The government of the day considered this the least cost option to educate these Newfoundland citizens.

When Newfoundland and Labrador became a province of Canada, a semblance of prosperity was brought to the many people living off the sea, forestry and subsistence farming. Parents of Deaf children began wondering if it would be possible to have their children educated at home. Fifteen years after joining Confederation, the parents got their wish, the Newfoundland School for the Deaf (NSD) was established. Thanks to the efforts of Flora, and the fact that the schools for the deaf in Montreal and Nova Scotia were over crowded.

In June of 1964, Newfoundland had 100 deaf children who were supposed to attend either the School for the Deaf in Quebec, or the one in Nova Scotia. Only 50 could be accommodated between the two institutions. So the government of the day decided that it was time to open a school for the Deaf in Newfoundland.

The NSD was first located at the U. S. Air Force Base Fort Peperrell in the capital city of St. John's. It was opened on September 22, 1964, with six teachers, twelve houseparents and an enrolment of fifty-four students. The school was operated by the Department of Public Welfare under the Director of Institutions, Mr. Rockwood.

Mr. Karl Cornelius Van was appointed the school's first principal in September of 1965. Mr. Van oversaw the moving of NSD in September of 1965 from its quarters in Building 1054 at Fort Pepperrell, to the former RCAF station in Torbay. The school remained at the site near the airport at Torbay for twenty-two years, eventually occupying buildings #2, #18 and #43.

The Royal Canadian Airforce (RCAF) built the barracks near the Torbay Airport in 1941 to temporarily house RCAF personnel during World War II. These buildings were opened in 1941, closed in 1946, reopened in 1953 and closed permanently in 1964. They were then renovated to become the Newfoundland School for the Deaf, a residential school to educate those Deaf and Hard of Hearing students from around the province, TEMPORARILY. These buildings, having been built during World War II in 1941, used lead based paint and crumpled up newspaper as insulation. The windows were a single glass pane, wooden framed with holes cut into the bottom of the frame for ventilation, and during the winter, a wooden slat was attached to 'close' off the vent holes. These buildings were approximately 300 feet from the main runway of the St. John's airport. To state that they were inappropriate as a setting for a residential school for deaf children is painfully obvious. But, of course, the government of the day knew these buildings were only to be a temporary site for the school.

The first graduates of this version of the NSD were Ivan, Rosemary, Judy, Myles, Vincent, Donald, Carol, Eugene and Roland. Although I don't know what each graduate of NSD in 1968 was employed as, I do know that all became productive citizens of Newfoundland and Labrador. (For a list of all graduates of NSD see Appendix two)

Three of the first group of graduates of the NSD included Ms. Judy, who attended Gallaudet College from 1968 until she graduated in 1973. Returning to Canada, Judy landed a job as an instructor at the Atlantic Technological & Vocational Centre located at the Interprovincial School for the Deaf (ISD) in Amherst, Nova Scotia. She worked there for the next six years. During that time Mrs. Shea continued to take college courses and became a certified teacher.

She married another Newfoundlander, Mr. Shea, and they looked for opportunities to return to their home province. In 1979 she applied for a position at NSD, and the Principal of the school at that time, Mr. Harkins, jumped at the chance to hire the first Deaf teacher of the Deaf in Newfoundland and Labrador. Mrs. Shea became the Home Economics teacher, a position she held with distinction for 26 more years. She was and remains the only Deaf Teacher of the Deaf in Newfoundland and Labrador. During the planning stage of the NSD that was located on Topsail Road. Judy was instrumental in its design.

Mr. Myles Murphy also attended Gallaudet College, A Business Administration major, Myles was in his fourth year at Gallaudet in 1971 when he failed one course in accounting. This course was not offered again until the spring trimester. While waiting to complete the requisite course, he was forced to live off campus.

The Department of Social Services and Rehabilitation had been covering the expense of attending Gallaudet through their Vocational Rehabilitation for Disabled Persons (VRDP) program for Judy and Myles; however, when Myles informed the department that he had to live off campus until he could re-take that course, VRDP cut his funding. Myles returned home to Newfoundland and took the equivalent accounting course at Memorial University of Newfoundland (MUN). It is important to note here, that although Myles is profoundly Deaf, he took this course at MUN and passed it without the aid of a qualified interpreter, notetaker or tutor. He tried to transfer the credit to Gallaudet. Upon presenting the transcript to the graduate office, he found out that Gallaudet didn't recognize courses from MUN. VRDP would not sponsor attending Gallaudet for one course, so he had no option but to drop out. Myles is the Executive Director of NLAD. Mr. Vincent Power became a certified cook and was employed at the NSD from 1971 until the school was closed. He was able to retire with a full pension from the Newfoundland Government. When NSD was opened in 1964, as stated previously, there were six teachers, twelve house parents and an enrolment of fifty-four students. It was located in Fort Peperrell for the first year, and the first administrator was Mr. Rockwood. It is obvious that the government of the day tried to find an administrator who had at least some idea of working with Deaf children. Mr. Rockwood's son was Deaf. The next year the NSD was moved to the former RCAF station in Torbay. Built in 1941, it remained part of the RCAF until 1946. It was renovated between 1964 and 1965 to house the NSD.

The Newfoundland School For The Deaf At The Torbay Airport

The residence of the NSD is on the left, the school on the right, in between the two buildings was a playground. As you can see, the buildings were in the shape of an 'H'. In the residence, the middle of the 'H' housed storage upstairs for the senior boys and girls, downstairs for the junior boys and girls as well as the office of the Supervisor of the residence and the laundry room. In the school, the bottom 'H' housed bathrooms, the art teacher's classroom and storage, the upper portion of the 'H' held bathrooms and the teachers' lounge.

Mr. Van knew how important it was to have trained teachers of the Deaf and made an agreement with the Smallwood government to help train the teachers working at NSD. Arrangements were made to help teachers learn about the oral method of teaching the deaf and many teachers got some training during the summer months at the Clarke School for the Deaf under the supervision of Smith College in Northampton, Massachusetts.[1]

Mr. Van came out of retirement to help establish NSD in 1964, and agreed to a two-year contract. During this time, he hired teachers, ensured they would get training in Deaf Education, set up a residence, hired house parents, including at least six Deaf adults, three women and three men, set up an amplification system in each classroom, and generally created a school. The one thing he did not do was to codify a curriculum, nor did he adopt the curriculum used by the Newfoundland Department of Education in 1964. Instead, he had his trained teachers of the deaf develop their own program in their various areas of expertise using the information they had learned from their experience at the Clarke School for the Deaf.

As a matter of fact, the department of education's curriculum stated the following:

The following Workbooks and Manuals not stocked by the Department of Education are available from the publishers named. Teachers will decide for themselves whether or not they wish to make use of any or all of these instructional and learning aids. (author's emphasis)

So it was evident that at that time, the department of education did not seem to have a standardized curriculum. Obviously this gave schools and teachers freedom to develop their own curriculum and acquire their own teaching tools. The NSD was no exception. Their curriculum consisted of auditory training, speech training, English language acquisition, art, mathematics, science and social studies. In 1974, as far as I could find out, the youngest student at the NSD was 4 and a half years old. The oldest student was 18.

Although Mr. Van was a strict oralist in his methodological approach to teaching Deaf students, he did hire half of the residential staff from the Deaf community of St. John's. One of the first Deaf residential staff he hired was a man named Hammond Taylor.

Hammond, a native Newfoundlander, was one of the many students who had to travel to the mainland for education. He told me he had been in three different schools in two provinces from the time he was 8 or 9 years old. He became interested in weight lifting at the school in Montreal and became a very good body builder. I don't remember if he entered competitions or not, but have seen

---

[1] personal knowledge from conversations with teachers at NSD in 1975.

pictures of him in poses. His body reminded me of the cartoon character "Alley Oop," a caveman. His body was very square, with a huge chest and large arms. Anyway, Hammond told me he had conversations with Mr. Van and was partly responsible for encouraging him to hire more Deaf adults to "mentor" the students. Whether Mr. Van knew it or not, he established a conduit for the students attending the NSD to learn American Sign Language (ASL) and Deaf Culture. Of course, at that time, neither of those concepts were part of the natural lexicon in Deaf education.

Upon fulfilling his two-year commitment, Mr. Van retired at the end of the school year of 1966 and was replaced by Mr. Carmichael.

Mr. Carmichael immediately began lobbying for a new school to be built because of the make-up of the buildings at the abandoned RCAF base in Torbay. He must have been fairly successful because the government of the day appointed an architectural firm to work with Mr. Carmichael to develop plans for a new school and paid for them to visit other schools for the deaf in the United States and Canada. Although preliminary sketches were drawn, because of financial difficulties plaguing the Province, this initiative was discontinued.

Mr. Carmichael remained principal of the NSD for the next seven years. He continued to lobby for improvements and upgrades of the buildings being used for the NSD, but was largely unsuccessful. He did work with the teachers of the school to establish a functional curriculum so that when the NSD held its first graduation ceremony in 1968, two of the first graduates, Judy and Myles, were accepted at the only liberal arts college in the world for Deaf students, Gallaudet College in Washington, D. C. Unfortunately, they would be the only graduates from the NSD to be accepted there until fifteen years later.

In 1966, Mr. Cooper was hired as a residential supervisor by Mr. Rockwood. Mr. Rockwood introduced him to the students coming back to the residence after being in school all day. One boy, Leonard, was a hard of hearing boy in the group and acted as an interpreter for Eric. During Eric's first day of working that evening, he wrote his name on the chalkboard in the common room and asked Leonard what time they had to go to bed. He was told 10:30.

Suppertime came and went, then homework time was completed and the boys settled in to play games and watch television. At 10:30 the boys went to bed quickly, and Eric wrote a description of his shift in the Report Book and said to himself, "Geez, this is easy."

The next day, Mr. Rockwood called Eric just before his shift and informed him that bedtime was actually 9:30, not 10:30. Eric said, "Boy, they got me good, so I decided to get them back." He got the boys in the common room again, wrote on the blackboard about the previous night bedtime, they all laughed, of course. "Then, I dropped the bomb, tonight bedtime is 8:30 p.m. I thought WWIII had broken out; however, the kerfuffle quickly settled. At 8:30 they went to bed, and I never had an ounce of trouble after that," Eric told me in an email.

Mr. Carmichael made Eric the Chief Supervisor of the residence in 1969. Eric said that the first thing he did was to move the office of the chief supervisor from the administration offices into the residence. Eric remained in that position until 1978. When the position of vice-principal-residence was created, Eric was demoted to supervisor. He said, "That was quite a blow. I had to have a job, so I had to do night shift, then eventually shift work with the senior boys until I retired." As a viceprincipal, that individual had to have a degree in education as well as Deaf Education; unfortunately, Eric had neither.

Under Mr. Carmichael's, and Dr. Norah Brown's guidance, the Newfoundland and Labrador Parents Association for Hearing Handicapped Children was formed. I believe the first president was a businessman named Bud Ozark, whose daughter was attending the NSD, and Mr. Laurence Cashin was either the vice-president or treasurer. Mr. Cashin had a son attending the NSD. Mr. Ozark and Mr. Cashin, with the guidance of Mr. Carmichael, formed an interdisciplinary committee consisting of the school principal, an audiologist, an otologist, and a psychologist to deal with the total management of hearing impaired children in the Province and lobby for a new school building.

The lobbying efforts were successful in one respect: responsibility for the operation of the NSD was transferred from the Department of Social Services and Rehabilitation to the Department of Education and Youth in April of 1971. This transfer was done in recognition of the fact that the school for the deaf was first and foremost an educational facility.

Mr. Carmichael earned a master's degree in Deaf Education from Smith College in Boston, Massachusetts. As stated in a previous chapter, Smith College partnered with the Clarke School for the Deaf in its Master's program. The Clarke School is renowned for its oral methodology of teaching Deaf students; therefore, like Mr. Van, Mr. Carmichael used the oral method of teaching in the classrooms of the NSD. He also followed Mr. Van ideology of hiring Deaf adults to work in the NSD.

The school hired many Deaf adults to work as food service workers, utility workers and, especially, residential staff so that students would learn about Deaf Culture and signed language. The Deaf adult staff accepted the responsibility of teaching the students about Deaf Culture and sign language, and at least one teacher contacted them to learn how to sign as well.

A Brief History of Deaf Education

This short history lesson, hopefully, will be helpful in understanding the importance of the paradigm shift in teaching the students of the NSD during Mr. Carmichael's tenure as Principal.

From the middle of the 1700s to the present day, there has been an argument as to the best method of teaching Deaf and Hard of Hearing children. Probably, the most famous individual purporting the use of sign language to teach the Deaf in North America is Thomas Hopkins Gallaudet. Thomas Hopkins Gallaudet, along with Laurent Clerc, opened the first school for the Deaf in North America that used sign language, the Connecticut Asylum for the Education and Instruction of Deaf and Dumb Persons, in 1817. Later, the name was changed to the American School for the Deaf (ASD).

Laurent Clerc was a student at the Institution Nationale des Sourds-Muets á Paris and later became one of the school's assistant teachers. This institution used sign language as its methodology of teaching the Deaf in France and was so successful that numerous schools for the Deaf that opened around Europe between 1776 and 1811 adopted this methodology. Thomas Gallaudet travelled to Paris in 1816 to learn this methodology. In June of that year, he returned to America to open his own school for the deaf. Laurent Clerc accompanied him.

To open this school, Gallaudet and Clerc travelled to various cities in Connecticut to garner support for a school for the Deaf. In October of 1816, they convinced the legislature to give them $5000.00 for the school. With private donations totaling $17,000, Gallaudet and Clerc opened their school on April 15, 1817.

Two years later, Clerc went to Washington, D. C. and met with the Speaker of the House, Henry Clay. Clerc pleaded for support from Congress to help fund ASD, and so impressed Mr. Clay that an act was passed that appropriated land for ASD and eventually $300.000. "Thus, education for the deaf was established in the United States, from the beginning, as a public responsibility." This success led to other states taking interest in educating their deaf students and opening state schools for the deaf, and all used the methodology of ASD.

As Gallaudet is the most famous teacher of the deaf using sign language methodology in the US, the most famous individual purporting the oral/aural method of teaching in North America was Alexander Graham Bell, the inventor of the telephone. This monumental invention actually came about because of his experiments with developing a sound amplification system that would enhance a deaf person's ability to hear speech.

Bell's grandfather and father were teachers of diction and elocution. His father, Alexander Melville, developed Visible Speech. This was a system of symbols that were designed as a pictorial abbreviation of the positions of the organs of speech while speaking. In 1871, Alexander Graham was hired by the Boston School for Deaf-Mutes to train the teachers there in Visible Speech. He later was hired by the Clarke School for the Deaf and later by the American School in Hartford, Connecticut. The following year, he opened his own training school for teachers of the deaf in Boston.

In 1876, Bell was credited with the invention of the telephone and patented it in March of that year. After patenting his invention, Bell married Mable Hubbard, a deaf woman who helped start oralism in the United States.

Contrary to popular belief, the controversy between teaching the deaf either orally or by sign language did not begin with a feud between Thomas Gallaudet and Alexander Graham Bell. Both methods had been used in various schools throughout the world since the 1700s. Both methods had success. In 1868, Edward Miner Gallaudet, Thomas Gallaudet's son, organized a conference of representatives from the schools for the deaf in the U. S. in Washington, D. C. At that time, there were twentyfive schools for the Deaf in the US, and 15 of them sent representatives to the conference. They unanimously adopted this resolution:

In the opinion of this Conference, it is the duty of all institutions for the deaf and dumb to provide adequate means of imparting instruction in articulating and lipreading to such of their pupils as may be able to profit in exercises of this nature.

In 1880, in Milan, Italy, there was another conference, billed as the Second International Conference of the Deaf. Although this was actually the first international conference, I believe it was billed as the second because of the conference previously mentioned. The Milan Conference was organized by the Pereire Society, which is an organization devoted to the promotion of oralism. This conference passed eight resolutions. The most controversial resolution was the first one:

The Convention, considering the incontestable superiority of articulation over signs in restoring the deaf-mute to society and giving him a fuller knowledge of language, declares that the oral method should be preferred to that of signs in education and the instruction of deaf-mutes.

The invention of the telephone got Bell world-wide acknowledgement and wealth.

One of the prizes he was awarded for the telephone was the $200,000 Allessandro Volta Prize. With this money, Bell created the Volta Bureau in 1887 "for the increase and diffusion of knowledge relating to the deaf." This organization has been publishing the Volta Review since 1899. This magazine is a professional, peer-review journal that publishes manuscripts devoted to promoting the development of listening and spoken language by graduates of schools for the deaf that use the oral method of teaching.

Due to the Milan Conference and the Volta Review, education of Deaf students in North America from the 1890s to the 1960s was done almost exclusively by the oral method.

Then a most significant hire by Gallaudet University happened in 1955, when Dr. William Stokoe joined the university as a professor and chairman of the English department. His observation of the students' conversations peaked an interest in their language. He developed a linguistics research laboratory where he studied their language intensely. In 1960, he published SignLanguage Structure, where he coined the term "American Sign Language," or ASL. This was followed in 1965 with A Dictionary of American Sign Language.

In 1972, Dr. Stokoe started an academic journal, which he edited until 1996. Dr. Stokoe's research and studies of ASL encouraged other linguists to analyze ASL to prove without a shadow of a doubt that ASL is a fully formed and legitimate language.

Arguably, the most influential publication about the linguistics of ASL was published in 1979. The Signs of Language was written by Edward Klima and Ursula Bellugi, two accomplished linguists who worked together at the University of California-San Diego around 1977. Dr. Bellugi is a cognitive neuroscientist and a psycholinguist, while Dr. Klima is a linguist as well as a psycholinguist. Together, they wrote, in my opinion, the definitive early work that demonstrated, linguistically, how ASL is a living, evolving language. Their studies have prompted many others to follow and support that fact.

Roy, a Deaf educator, who was the area supervisor of a deaf education program in Santa Ana, California from 1968 to 1973, coined the term "Total Communication." This philosophy of education maintains that each deaf student has the right to be educated in whatever form of communication that is most suitable for that individual — American Sign Language, oral English, and often, a combination of both. Schools for the Deaf in the United States began adapting their curriculum to adopt to Total Communication during the 1970s.

As stated before, Mr. Carmichael was an oralist and hired teachers who became trained in the oral method at Smith College in Massachusetts. However, sign language was used occasionally by some teachers and at least one administrator at NSD. In one edition of The Monitor, the official newsletter of the Catholic Archdiocese, there is an article about a Mass that took place on February 29, 1972. The Vice-principal of the NSD at that time was Mrs. Parrott, and she signed the Mass for around 40 Deaf students at the Marian Chapel in the Basilica. I believe it was she who began promoting the use of sign language in the classroom.

This is consistent with the North American movement of using Total Communication in many American Schools for the Deaf during that time period.

When I first got to the school, I heard rumours that there had been a "power struggle" between the principal and vice-principal of the NSD. It seems as if the vice-principal wanted teachers to be able to communicate the curriculum to the students using sign language.

Those teachers who had trained exclusively at Smith College wanted to continue using the oral/aural method of teaching.

Other teachers, saw where using sign language would be welcomed by the students. Two newly hired teachers who attended the graduate program offered by the Interprovincial School for the Deaf (ISD) in Amherst, Nova Scotia, were among those who believed in using sign language to teach their students. During their time at the NSD, they each became a vice-principal of Academics and one went on to become principal of the school, twice.

Reg was hired at the NSD in 1973. He had a brother who was Deaf, and Reg developed a sign system to use with his brother, Willy. He learned to use a more formal sign language while at ISD and became vice-principal the year before I joined the teaching staff. Miss Clarke was also hired at the NSD in 1973. If she had had previous understanding or skill at sign language, I do not know. But I do know that in 1973, Ms. Clarke developed a very keen knowledge and skill at communicating in sign. Her skills were often used for interpreting in many sensitive situations, including doctors' appointments and courtroom interpreting. She followed Mr. Harte as the vice-principal and later became principal twice. Actually, she retired as principal and later returned to oversee the closure of the school.

Ms. Clarke, Mr. Harte, and Mrs. Ellie Parrott, the vice-principal, formed the core group of advocates for the use of sign language in the classrooms of the NSD. From conversations with former or retired teachers of the NSD at that time, the discussions as to which methodology was best became pretty darned heated. I'm sure this animosity between the teaching staff wasn't lost on the students.

At the end of the 1973/74 school year, Mr. Carmichael decided to continue his administrative career at another school. Mrs. Parrott was selected as his replacement, and Mr. Harte was hired as vice-principal.

Mrs. Ellie officially took over the position of principal of the NSD in 1974.

In an email conversation with her daughter, a colleague, former classmate at the LAC, and retired teacher at NSD herself, Penney said:

…Mom was actually the first teacher hired at NSD by the minister of education at the time, Fred???

Actually it was either G. Alain or Henry (both held the portfolio in 1964)] with the understanding that she would travel to Clarke School for the Deaf in summers and complete her Ed of the Deaf. After several teachers were hired a Mr. Rockwood was hired as the principal/administrator he was followed by the Van and the Dave. She did (go) to Smith college, as a matter of fact we all did, we travelled to Clarke with her.

At the time she was already questioning the Oral approach to education of the Deaf. She had met some of the adult Deaf who would work in the dorm and others who had travelled to Montreal and Halifax for their education…

The students who attended the school that first year in Pleasantville had already attended school where there was sign. She learned from them in attempts to present the curriculum. She would bring the older students home and teach them in the evening and learn from them. She also did some one-on-one work with some of the adults to learn sign.

She knew she was not a great signer but was determined to include sign in her communication and make it possible for her students and friends to do whatever they wanted to do. She spent countless hours volunteering in all kinds of situations always explaining that she would not take pay as she was not qualified. As she interpreted regularly in churches we as kids attended services everywhere! And I think she spent more time doing homework at our home with her students than she spent with us!

Under Mrs. Parrott's leadership, the NSD was able to increase the services offered to the students when a pre-vocational building was opened, and three programs were added to the curriculum: Industrial Arts, Business Education, and Home Economics. To provide the best programs possible, the three teachers, Mr. Dunne, Mrs. Mary, and Mrs. Stella (respectively) visited five different schools for the Deaf in Canada to observe these programs already being taught to borrow the best ideas from each place and incorporate them into their individual fields. Again, these programs became first class and provided senior and intermediate students with an opportunity to broaden their social skills as well as decide if any of these vocations were worth their effort to pursue upon graduation.

Integration of the students of NSD was also a goal of this administration. Integration, not inclusion — there is a big difference between the two educational concepts, which will be discussed in more detail later. Integration is used to fit an individual student's needs and abilities. It was done at least once a year before I arrived at the NSD. Principal Parrott writes in the first NSD newsletter printed in 1975:

Kimberley Wells is attending school this year in her hometown, Corner Brook. Luedee is in a regular Grade III class at St. Andrew's School, St. John's.

Both of these students were profoundly deaf and had attended the NSD for at least the earliest portion of their academic career. They were integrated into the regular school system because of their ability to do the required schoolwork with little supervision of an itinerant teacher. As a matter of fact, I only learned of one itinerant teacher working at this time, Mrs. Sheila; however, despite this lack of adequate support, they succeeded.

Furthermore, students were encouraged to be integrated into society in at least one other way. Again, quoting from Principal Parrott's newsletter contribution:

During the summer vacation two of our students, Louise, and Derrick were invited to partake in the 4-H Provincial week (August 4–13). This meant travelling by bus from St. John's to Stephenville and visiting points along the way. Ms. Whiteway (the school secretary) accompanied them as escort. The week's activities concluded with a banquet at Colonial Inn. We were more than a little proud that both Louise and Derrick had been nominated for the "best All-round student" award. Louise and Derrick received a spontaneous standing ovation when they went forward to accept their awards.

In 1975, Mrs. Parrott hired three new teachers who were all fairly skilled in the use of sign language. Ms. Beehan, Ms. Parrott, and I were all hired upon completion of a Masters Degree program in Deaf

Education. Ms. Beehan had a sister who was deaf and learned to sign from her. Ms. Parrott was Mrs. Parrott's daughter and probably learned to sign by sharing time with her mother and the Deaf adults and students that her mother brought into their home.

After Mrs. Parrott became principal of the NSD, there were still many teachers hired by Mr. Van and Mr. Carmichael who firmly believed in using the oral method of teaching students. When I started teaching at the NSD, most of the oralist teachers were in the pre-school: Mrs. Sheila; elementary school: Mrs. Marion, Mrs. Nita. Since there was never a formal philosophical decision made as to methodology, a conflict arose between the teachers, administrator, and residential staff. As I said while discussing Mr. Carmichael's principalship, this conflict must have been felt and acknowledged by the students, because they began to "act out."

By "Acting Out" I mean that they began to rebel, some physically and others by being obnoxious. A few rebelled obnoxiously physical by punching holes in the hallway walls, throwing rocks at windows of abandoned buildings, skipping classes, and challenging any teacher who had the temerity to try and correct their behaviour. During my first three years at the NSD, the students became more and more incorrigible. The guidance counsellor and principal both believed that these teenagers would "come around" with love, understanding, and respect. In the meantime, some of the students were getting more and more out of control.

Here are a few of the things some of the older, stronger bullies were doing around the school:

- An intermediate school boy threw rocks at a teacher's car because she had given his class a test that afternoon.
- A student got on a bus that was going to take the students who lived in St. John's home, stole the emergency ax, and threatened to beat up a teacher's car with it.
- A boy walked down the high school corridor and punched a hole between two classrooms, then walked to the foyer and punched another hole in the wall next to the front door and began tearing the sheet rock apart.
- A boy poured a can of coke all over a teacher's desk and test papers while she was correcting the papers and sitting at her desk. He did it in such a way as to have scared the teacher half to death. She was afraid to move and began to cry. The student laughed and walked out.
- An intermediate student pulled out a knife and threatened a teacher with it.

When these incidents were brought up to the administration, the principal asked if the teacher had said or done something to provoke the student. Mrs. Parrott always believed that there were two sides to every story and wanted to get the student's perspective about each incident. This also caused the teachers to doubt that the principal cared about their well-being.

The teacher who became frightened when a can of coke was poured on her work quit. The teacher who disarmed the student who had a knife and brought the student and knife to the principal's office became upset that the principal told the student to apologize and sent him along his way. Then the principal reprimanded the teacher for putting his hands on the student. Forming the student council and planning events with them helped, but something more had to be done to try to get the students to cooperate with the teachers and learn the curriculum.

After the Christmas vacation, Memorial University of Newfoundland was hosting an Atlantic Canada wrestling tournament. At that time, I was a certified wrestling referee and worked during that tournament. Participating in this tournament was a team from the Interprovincial School for the Deaf (ISD), which was located in Amherst, Nova Scotia. We hosted a couple of get-togethers with the athletes from ISD and brought students from NSD to MUN to watch the action. They were very excited when two of the ISD students won medals. I don't remember which ones, but I think one was gold and another silver, which means two Deaf students either went undefeated or lost only one match. Very impressive performance from a small school of Deaf students. Naturally, the boys wanted to begin wrestling as well.

So I spoke with the physical education teacher, Mr. Cyril Coffin, who thought it was a good idea.

That perhaps the energy they used up in practice and competition would alleviate their acting out, which began again after the Christmas vacation.

Quite honestly, it was not successful.

The leaders of the group acting out didn't want to participate in practice to learn techniques and do strengthening exercises.

Instead, they used the time to bully those students who were participating. Later, I found out that the bullies would gang up on those students individually and threaten them to either quit or get beat up. Naturally, the wrestling club faded quickly.

To raise money for the student council, a number of activities were planned. They included: an arts and crafts sale (items made by students in art class), a raffle of two handmade cushions donated by President Colleen Power's grandmother, the design of an official school crest (and an attempt to copyright it), a benefit concert performed by Joan Morrissey (a well-known and popular local country-western singer), and a spring equinox dance.

What actually happened? An in-house arts and crafts sale, an in-house raffle of the cushions, and a spring equinox dance.

As these activities were taking place, the boys, and some girls, continued to act out. As the year went by, there were more and more holes being punched in the corridor walls. As stated earlier, the Newfoundland and Labrador Parents Association for Hearing Handicapped Children was formed in 1970.

This Association eventually morphed into a Parent Teacher Association, and in 1975 a teacher was elected president for the first time. Mr. Dunne, the industrial arts teacher, took over as president and thought that a way to curtail the damage being done to the NSD buildings was to get a new school built.

To that end, he brought in the St. John's Fire Commissioner to evaluate the safety of the buildings being used for the NSD.

The Commissioner found that the buildings were unsafe to the extreme. The lead-based paint was not only detrimental to the health of the students; it was also very flammable.

The fire extinguishers for the buildings were actually water pipes that transverse across the ceiling of each classroom and outside the dorm rooms.

This would have been acceptable had they been in working condition; however, the nozzles were rusted, and there were blockages throughout the pipes. In other words, they wouldn't prevent a fire from spreading quickly if one began.

The final straw was that the insulation used by the RCAF in 1941 was newspaper that, after twenty years, was dry as tinder and would act exactly as that if a spark made its way into the walls.

With all the holes that were being made by angry, frustrated students, the chance of igniting the insulation increased tenfold. The government's answer was to quickly plaster over the holes and later paint it to match the decor of the school. Furthermore, having the NSD PTA bring in the Fire Commissioner to evaluate fire safety at the NSD made a number of people in the Department of Education very angry.

This was conveyed to the principal of the NSD, who expressed her dismay to the president of the association. In retrospect, this was a warning to Mr. Dunne to watch his "Ps" and "Qs" or face consequences.

Mr. Coffin, myself, and the guidance counsellor established the disciplinary committee to see if we could develop a strategy of disciplinary action that would convince the students to stop this behavior. As I recall, the first meeting of the committee was in mid-May. The ideas discussed included detention, fines, withholding of privileges, and extra homework.

Mrs. Parrott and the guidance counsellor believed that there was no such thing as a bad child and believed that more love and understanding of the boys and girls would alleviate the situation.

Unfortunately, it was so late in the school year that graduation ceremonies, end-of-the-year concert, and final exams had to be prepared; the result was that nothing was actually put into practice.

So Mr. Coffin, Mr. Dunne, Mr. Harte, Mrs. Trask, Mrs. Woodford, and the executive of the student council decided to try and establish some amount of pride in the NSD itself. How this was going to happen, we had no idea as yet, but we thought developing pride in themselves and the school would be a very good first step.

The first thing I thought we should do was to give the student council more responsibilities and perhaps have a student representative or two on the disciplinary committee.

The president of the Student Council was a senior girl named Colleen Power. We asked her if she would like to sit on the committee. She declined, but suggested that the Vice-President join since Brenda Muller would remain at the school for the next year. So it was settled, and Brenda, who the next year became the president, joined our Disciplinary Committee. I have to say that she was an asset to our efforts to curtail the boys from acting out; most of them liked her and paid attention to her cajoling.

A few weeks before the end of the school year, Mr. Dunne bought a new home just around the corner from his current abode. The weekend prior to the graduation dinner, Mr. Dunne asked Reg and me to help him move into their new place. He also asked a few of the senior boys. He bought beer for the adults and Spruce Beer, a nonalcoholic beer, for the students. Unfortunately, one boy found out his girlfriend was pregnant and was very concerned and frightened. Being so very upset, he began to pour real beer into an empty Spruce Beer bottle. He did this again and again and got very drunk. When we discovered what he had done, we immediately took him back to the dorm to sober up. At that time, we had no idea about his girlfriend.

The houseparent in charge of the boys' dormitory at that time was concerned about the boy and called the school nurse. The nurse assessed the student and said to just let him sleep and have him clean up his mess the next day. She made her normal report about seeing the student and thought that was the end of it.

The principal read the report and called the department of education. The director of special schools decided to reprimand Mr. Dunne, harshly. He was given an alternative: leave the NSD by transferring to another school or be charged with contributing to the delinquency of a minor. In retrospect, however, we believe this harsh response was because of him calling the Fire Marshall to assess the school building's fire safety, thus embarrassing the government. At any rate, Mr. Dunne found another teaching job in a downtown St. John's junior high school and completed his career with ease.

I wrote a letter in support of Mr. Dunne and brought up the report by the Fire Marshall in my letter. I was called on the carpet for this letter and was told by the principal that she was very disappointed in me for doing this. I said that I was disappointed in the way Mr. Dunne was treated, which was why I wrote the letter in his support.

The remaining time during the spring of 1976 was to plan and execute a wonderful graduation prom. We got the Lions Club of Mount Pearl to donate their facilities, had friends and family member musicians donate their time and skill to play for the graduates during the dance, and got our food service workers to create a dinner to remember for the graduates. Actually, the student council developed the menu so that each grad had at least one of their favourite foods on the table. It was a night to remember. We decided to ask the mayor of St. John's, the first woman mayor in the history of the province, Mrs. Dorothy Wayatt, to give a speech to the grads. She accepted enthusiastically.

When September of 1976 arrived, I was married and had moved into the house in which Carol, my wife, and I still live. More about married life later on. I was transferred to the intermediate department and was assigned the classroom across the hall from Ms. Dunne, Jim's sister.

After meeting with the disciplinary committee and having the goal of trying to get the students to feel pride in the NSD, Ms. Dunne and I thought we would try teaching our students as a team. By working together with our two classes, we would be able to support each other, teach those subjects in which we were most accomplished and use positive reinforcement rather than threats if the student didn't comply with our assignments.

Ms. Dunne taught English and math, I taught social studies and science.

Taken prior to tour

Our students were receptive to this situation, for the most part. Two students were bullies and very disruptive in class; however, with the help of the new 'Superintendent' of NSD, formerly the principal, Mrs. Parrott, the guidance counsellor, Mrs. Marie, and the new vice-principal, Ms. Clarke, we coped with their behavior for most of three months. However, these two students were very much out of control. They would bully other students whether a teacher was around or not. We'll call them Bob and Jack.

For the first half of the school year, Miss Dunne and I had a pretty successful situation.

Bob and Jack, not withstanding, our team teaching approach was rewarding to the students as well as to us as educators.

We developed a behavior modification system in which the students were required to amass 20 points in two weeks.

They were awarded a point for completing their homework assignments, wearing their hearing aids (a school requirement), being friendly to each other (no bulling) and using good manners around other teachers. Those who earned the 20 points were taken on a field trip every second Friday.

One of the more memorable field trips was to the Holyrood Electrical Generating Station, which was actually called "The Thermal Plant."

We were greeted by the Superintendent of the Plant, Mr. Rex Gillard, and the Public Relations Representative, Mr. Noel Halfyard. The visit could not have been better. I believe it was Mr. Halfyard who wrote about our visit in their monthly newsletter.

1976 also saw the hiring of another teacher with a master's degree in Deaf Education, Miss Jane House. Jane was assigned to the intermediate department as well, albeit with a younger group of students. One of the first things Jane did was to bring her copy of the World Book Encyclopedia into her classroom. I must say that these books got a lot of use, by the students and many teachers as well.

I asked Jane if she would like to help with the student council. She said she would, but we should make the organization more inclusive and suggested we get representatives from the intermediate department as well. We did. The elections that year included two additional representatives, one from the intermediate department and one from the older students in the junior department.

After the election, we began planning for another Halloween Party and dance. This time intermediate students were included in the dance, and we also asked students from the Pinegrove School to join us. Pinegrove School was a special school for children who had been labeled "developmentally delayed." One of the teachers there, Mike Trask, was married to one of our teachers. He was a gym teacher and member of their student council mentors. It was a very nice dance and a fairly successful fund raiser.

Next up was Guy Fawkes night, unfortunately our hay ride couldn't go ahead this year due to our Torbay friend being out of the province for most of the month of October. We did manage to get the students back to Middle Cove Beach, along with the fixings for a huge bonfire and snacks.

Our last project of 1976 was to plan for the annual St. John's Christmas Parade. Working on the school float was an opportunity for all the students to become involved in a creative, cooperative manner.

The theme for this float was "A Charlie Brown Christmas." The Evening Telegram, the local newspaper, wrote the following about our float, SNOOPY SHARP:

One of the sharpest looking floats was modelled after the Peanuts cartoon, complete with Snoopy and his house and Lucy's Psychiatric Booth.

After the float was the Christmas concert and finally a much-appreciated holiday.

When we returned to the business of teaching our students, Miss Dunne and I were enthusiastic with the outline of the plans we discussed during the holidays. We were going to use many 'hands-on' techniques to get science concepts understood; Miss Dunne was going to use the students' holiday stories as a beginning to create English lessons, and math was going to be focused on earning and distributing money. 1977 began well, the lessons were catching on with the students, and we two teachers were enjoying the camaraderie and success of our efforts. Unfortunately, Bob and Jack began to bully and disrupt our classes again—not only the classes in which they were assigned, but other intermediate classrooms as well.

Another time, when I was teaching a science lesson about kinetic friction, I explained how friction was used in the past to create fire. I said that two objects rubbed together get hot and can burn. To demonstrate, I asked the class to take one hand and grab hold of the opposite wrist and quickly rub it back and forth. I demonstrated how to do it on myself and told them to try it on themselves. Jack tried it on himself and then decided to do it to a classmate. This used to be called a "Chinese Burn" and is done using two hands, squeezing the other person's arm very hard and rubbing quickly. Chinese Burns really hurt! The other student began to cry; which Jack thought was really funny. So I took Jack's arm and showed him what that felt like and told him to never do it again to another student. Jack ran out of the classroom and to the Superintendent's office and told her that I hurt him.

The Superintendent called me into her office and ordered me to apologize to Jack and write a letter of apology to his parents. I did as I was told; my letter was written and sent on February 11, 1977. I suggested that Jack be required to write a letter of apology to the student he initially hurt. Jack did and, as far as I was concerned, the problem was rectified.

Although we had many problems with Bob and Jack, they were handled as best we could, usually by getting the help of either the vice-principal or superintendent. Unfortunately, they were not the only boys who were acting out.

In April of that year, John was angry about a test that his English teacher gave that afternoon. He went into the classroom, where the teacher was correcting the test papers she had given to her senior students, and poured a can of soda all over her desk and ruined the papers. I was leaving the building at that same time when I heard the teacher crying and beginning to clean up her desk. I went in to comfort her and saw what had happened. She told me who had done this. I thought he should clean up the mess and went out to bring him in to apologize and clean up the classroom he destroyed. He refused, and I tried to coerce him to return to the school. The vice-principal saw what was happening and told me to just let him alone. I began to explain what had happened, and Miss Clarke told me she knew all about it and was taking care of the situation. Later in the month, John was suspended. I was also reprimanded for trying to coerce him to clean up his mess and apologize to the teacher.

The disciplinary committee met to discuss the situation with Bob, Jack, and two other students who were in the senior department. We met with the school administration with a number of ideas as to how to handle these unruly boys. In the student council, Miss House and I asked the executive what they would like to see happen with these students. Their ideas were fairly drastic because they were, understandably, afraid and fed up with these boys. One of the ideas they came up with was to kick them out of the school for good. Obviously, this could not be done, but I took that idea to the committee for a discussion. Interestingly enough, Mr. Coffin, Mr. Harte, and I thought that idea might have some value.

The committee set up a meeting with the superintendent and vice-principal as well as Mr. Dicks, supervisor of institutional schools, to see what we could do. The idea of expulsion of the boys was not an option; however, Mr. Dicks thought that the boys might benefit from being in a completely separate environment during school hours and be taught differently. So the four boys were placed in a special class with one teacher, Ms. Beehan. What she did with them is information I do not have, and after speaking with her, she doesn't remember very much either. She does, however, recall that she had a provincial car with which she could take the boys on outings around the city.

This accommodation solved the immediate problem for the rest of the school year, and we concentrated on teaching and planning numerous fun activities and fund-raising for the student council. Much of the time was spent planning for the upcoming graduating ceremonies and prom dinner and dance.

Jane and I brainstormed who we could get to give the graduates an inspirational speech. We decided to ask Mrs. Dorothy Wayatt again, and she accepted with grace. We were very happy when she accepted our offer. We managed to get the Lions' Club venue in Mount Pearl to donate their building and catering service. We got the food donated by the food service department of the NSD and got the younger student council members to make tissue flowers and centrepieces for the dinner, and again the graduates got to choose a menu of their favourite foods. With a sigh of relief, the 1976/77 school year was over.

Helen and I found out that we would have the same students for the 1977/78 school year and decided that we had to continue using the behaviour modification system that we developed the previous school year. With the help of the guidance counsellor, we got the full cooperation of the administration, superintendent, vice-principal, guidance counsellor, and Mr. Dicks from the Department of Education.

We set up the contract system during the first week of school. The incentive to fulfill the contract was field trips away from the school. We did change our perspective with the field trips this time; we decided to arrange the field trips for every two weeks as before, but this time have them correspond with and enhance our planned science and language lessons. To fulfill the contract, the students had to earn a specific amount of credits in the two-week period prior to the field trip. If I remember correctly, they had to earn 40 credits this time around. To earn credits, each student had to wear his or her hearing aid and attempt each lesson by doing homework and participating in class. They could earn extra credits, which may be carried over into the next two-week period, by demonstrating good manners, politeness, and helping others. If a student did not earn the required credits, that student was to remain in the dormitory and complete schoolwork that was previously covered in class.

The administration and Department of Education arranged the transportation needed and provided the administrative support that was required to get permission to go on so many field trips, as well as allowing us to use official government stationery to write to the various establishments we wanted to take the students to visit.

Little did I know that this program would get me in big trouble as well. When we began this program, Bob and Jack decided that they weren't going to participate. However, when I announced where we'd be going on our first field trip, Jack decided to participate after all. He began two days after his classmates and tried very hard to make up the delay. He managed to fulfill his contract, but because of his behaviour the previous week, the administration decided that he could not go on this field trip.

Since Jack was in my homeroom, I was given the task of explaining to him that he would have to remain in school this time. Because the decision to exclude Jack from the field trip was made by the administration, I asked the vice-principal to be with me when I spoke to Jack. I was expecting that she would help explain why Jack was going to be left behind, but she did not say anything to him at all. As I was explaining the situation to him, and ensuring him that if he continued with his good behaviour in the future, he'd be on our next field trip for sure, I also tried to explain that had he been more polite to other students and other teachers, he could have earned bonus points that might have persuaded the superintendent to allow him to go with his class despite his previous behaviour.

As I was conferring with Jack, Bob came into my classroom. He got behind me and was telling Jack how to respond to the explanation. Bob also broke into the conversation and stated that neither he nor Jack would do any schoolwork while his classmates were on the field trip. Miss Clarke did not attempt to correct him nor did she intervene to tell Bob to leave the classroom. So I turned around and told him to leave my classroom. He smiled at me and shook his head "no." So I began walking toward him and backed him to the door. He threatened to hit me and said that he'd like to kill me. I told him to go ahead and try. Instead, he left, and I closed and locked the door.

I returned to Jack and continued to let him know how proud I was of him for trying so hard and ensured that if he continued his change of behaviour, for sure he'd be with us on the next field trip. Jack left with that understanding, and Miss Clarke and I discussed what had happened with Bob. She told me that I handled Bob very well, and we left for the night.

The next day, Helen and I took the students on their field trip. It was very enlightening, and the students learned a lot. Upon returning to the school, I was told by the vice-principal that Superintendent Parrott and Mr. Dicks wanted to see me. I asked what's up, and she said that she wasn't sure. I went to the superintendent's office and was greeted coolly by Mrs. Parrott and Mr. Dicks. I was handed a letter that said, in essence, because of my actions with Jack and Bob, my services with the Department of Education would be terminated after the end of the school year.

To say I was shocked is not a strong enough reaction to this letter. I was unable to think straight, say anything, or hardly breathe. I had only been fired from a job once before, and being fired for this situation was, in my estimation, very wrong. I went home, had a drink, and discussed the letter with my wife. She read the letter again and again. I then decided I would fight this with everything I had and began to write a rebuttal letter.

I wrote a six-page letter to the Director of Special Services, Mr. Andrews. In that letter I listed everything our students and ourselves had to deal with concerning Jack and Bob. In that letter, I suggested that a meeting be held with Mr. Andrews, the superintendent, a representative of the Newfoundland Teacher's Association (NTA), and me to further rectify this entire situation. A meeting was held, and I stated that I felt Mrs. Parrott placed Ms. Dunne and me in the situation with Bob and Jack because of our affiliation with Mr. Jim Dunne at the end of the previous school year, which was described earlier. (Ms. Dunne is Jim Dunne's sister.)

Mrs. Parrott vehemently denied my accusation and stated that all her actions were in the best interests of the students, and that after her conversation with the vice-principal about how I had "threatened" Bob, she HAD to take extreme action. Mr. Andrews and the NTA representative conferred, and I was placed on a one-year extended probationary period. That meant I was able to continue teaching at the NSD but had to follow every and all directions made on me and my time by the superintendent sitting and vice-principal. I was relieved to not have to worry about being dismissed and went back to focusing on the system Helen and I set up and student council activities.

Unfortunately, the boys' behaviour got worse day after day. Bob and Jack took turns "teasing" me every day. I had a metre stick waved in front of my face and under my chin until it struck my neck. I got up from my desk quickly and walked to the phone outside my door to call the vice-principal for help. The boys ran away. I was told to "fuck off" many times, Jack made a fist and put it under my chin forcing my head back, and Bob pulled out a pocket knife and threatened to kill me with it. I took it away from him and brought it to the superintendent. Fortunately, another teacher was a witness to that threat and supported me in my action. Finally, that was enough for the superintendent to suspend the boys for two weeks.

As the first part of the 1977/78 school year ended, the focus was again on the float for the Christmas Parade and the concert. The Lieutenant Governor, The Honorable Gordon Winter, and his wife attended the concert and, in his remarks, spoke about the behavior of the students, their politeness, and friendliness.

1977 ended with the Department of Education searching for a principal of the NSD, since Mrs. Parrott was now the superintendent. Mr. Harkins was one of the applicants for the position and accepted it in February of 1978.

However, Mrs. Parrott decided to retire at that time. In the interim, Mr. Dicks took over the Superintendent's position, and Ms. Clarke filled the role of principal, albeit temporarily.

Big Changes To NSD:

Mr. Harkins accepting the position of principal was the beginning of the most radical and continuous changes to the education of Deaf and hard of hearing students in Newfoundland. In April of 1978, Mr. Harkins arrived in Newfoundland and rented a suite at the Karwood Cabins. The next day, as he was beginning to get settled in, he got a phone call from Dicks, who told Mr. Harkins that he needed to come to the NSD for a meeting with him.

Mr. Harkins took the position of principal with the understanding that Mrs. Parrott would be the superintendent and was surprised that she retired just before he got here. So when he got to the NSD, he met Dicks sitting behind Mrs. Parrott's desk. He told Mr. Harkins to sit in the chair facing the desk and ordered tea from the kitchen. He then told Charlie that since Mrs. Parrott resigned and since he was leaving to attend a conference, Ms. Clark, the vice-principal, would run the school until Mr. Dicks returned.

Charlie told Mr. Dicks that he had been principal of two other schools for the Deaf in the United States and he'd take over immediately. If there were some aspects of the school that were unique to Newfoundland, or some local knowledge that he needed to know, then Ms. Clarke could fill him in; otherwise, Mr. Harkins would be principal. To say that Mr. Dicks did not make a positive impression on Charlie would be like saying Secretariat was a race of a horse. And to say that Charlie rubbed Mr. Dicks the wrong way was like saying fingernails on a chalkboard made a bad noise.

When Mr. Harkins left the NSD that afternoon, he contacted the director of special education, Mr. Andrews, and asked him who Dicks was. He then said that Mr. Dicks was not to return to the NSD without first asking permission from the principal, or Mr. Andrews could begin searching for another person to take the job. Mr. Andrews agreed to Charlie's demand, and I don't remember seeing Dicks at NSD again.

Mr. Andrews also told Charlie that the Deputy Minister of Education would like to meet him. Mr. Roebothan had a niece who attended the school, so it seemed a logical assumption that there would be strong support for the NSD. However, when Mr. Harkins met Mr. Roebothan, the first thing the Deputy Minister said was, "Don't ever ask me for a new school for the Deaf." Not "welcome to Newfoundland," or any kind of small talk, which was very strange indeed. Of course, by the time 1987 came, there had been a number of other Deputy Ministers of Education, and Charlie was able to successfully get a new school built. (Private conversation with Charlie)

The New Principal Introduces Himself And His Sign Name: When Charlie returned to the school, he held an assembly in the multi-purpose room to introduce himself to the students and staff. There he explained that he had been principal of the Mystic Oral School for the Deaf, the Senior Department of the Western Pennsylvania School for the Deaf, and that his name sign was an "H" handshape motioned to the bridge of his nose, which is similar to the sign for 'strict.' He also explained that he was also fair and if the rules were followed there would be no problems.

He then met with the staff individually to get an idea of their concerns, student expectations, and goals for the school. He found that the overall, most serious concern that was expressed by all was student behavior. Charlie's next series of meetings was with the disciplinary committee.

During one of the meetings, I mentioned that before teenage students will listen to an adult, they have to have a fear of that adult. Mrs. Warren argued vehemently that students should never have a fear of adults; adults should show love and respect for them, and they would then return that demonstrated attitude. My argument was to ask her how the students were returning the love and respect the teachers had been showing them. Mr. Harkins then stepped in and showed support for my argument, albeit with a different concept to fear. He said they should develop an aversion for being disciplined rather than fear the teacher.

Since Mr. Harkins' principalship began near the end of April, he decided that implementation of a concerted disciplinary plan would begin in earnest in September of 1978; however, that did not mean he would accept the continued disregard by the students toward the school building, schoolwork, teachers, or just bad behavior.

Mr. Harkins Is Tested And He Asks For Help: His first big test came from a senior student who was in a classroom in which students blocked the entrance. Charlie got them to disperse and saw a student exposing himself to the teacher. He removed the student from the classroom, took him to his office, and read the riot act to him. That student developed into a very respected member of the NSD and, as an adult, a leader within the Deaf community.

Another time his reputation for strictness was tested was when a senior named Billy decided that he wasn't going to bother with homework, or even stay in the classroom. Mr. Harkins saw him wandering around the school and asked him where he was supposed to be. Billy decided that he didn't have to answer him, so Mr. Harkins invited him into his office. When he sat down at his desk, Billy went in and was asked again where he was supposed to be. Billy shrugged his shoulders and refused to answer. Mr. Harkins gave him an ultimatum: go back to class or be sent home. Billy decided to leave the office.

Mr. Harkins slowly walked after Billy, who just as slowly backed away from him. When Billy went into the hallway between the junior and senior departments, Mr. Harkins phoned me. He said that Billy was in the hallway and he wanted Billy back into his office. He asked me if I would stand at the other end of the hallway and keep him from running out of the building. I told him that I had been put under extended probation, but he said, "Don't worry. I got your back." So I gave my class some seat work to do, told Helen what was happening, and asked her to check in on my students as I might be gone for an extended period. I then went and stood in the hallway. Billy was in the middle of the corridor, near the teacher's lounge, when he saw me. He looked at Mr. Harkins, back at me, and decided to try to run through me. It didn't work. I tackled him and held him down on the floor until Mr. Harkins arrived.

Mr. Harkins calmly walked up to Billy and gestured for him to come back to the principal's office. Billy shook his head "no," so Mr. Harkins gently placed him in a wrist lock. He could hold Billy with one hand and with his other hand flexed his index finger in a 'come with me' motion. Billy shook his head again, and Mr. Harkins applied pressure to Billy's wrist. He screamed loudly, which brought teachers and some students out into the hallway to see what was happening. Mr. Harkins crooked his finger again, and this time Billy quietly and slowly got up and went back to the Principal's office. That evening, Billy was suspended from school and sent home for the remainder of the week.

With that action, a number of changes began to happen. When Billy's parents called the Department of Education to complain that Billy was suspended, the Department supported the principal's action, thus giving Mr. Harkins the unwritten power to continue with his ideas for running a successful school for the Deaf. The students began to understand why Mr. Harkins' name sign was the same as the sign for 'strict,' and their behavior began to change.

Priorities:

From his interviews with the teaching and residential staff, Charlie developed a list of priorities to use in improving the NSD. These priorities included: establishing discipline, hiring more staff (teaching and residential), improving the food service, improving morale, and transportation.

His number one priority was to upgrade the food service. He developed an interesting perspective while serving in the Army Reserve—good food equates to good morale. One thing that was definitely needed at the NSD was better morale, by the staff and especially the students. One of the first meals he experienced at the NSD was previously a dietary mainstay—spaghetti on toast. Yes, the cooks would open a number of large cans of Heinz spaghetti, heat it on the steam line, and ladle it over two pieces of white bread toast. No wonder the students were rebellious.

A close second priority was to hire teachers that had a Master's Degree in Deaf Education. To that end, he travelled to Amherst, Nova Scotia, where the Masters in Deaf Education program was still in existence. His recruitment was very successful, and by the start of the 1979/80 school year he hired three Newfoundlanders, P. P., D. S. (assigned to the senior department), and A. E. (intermediate department), and two teachers from out of province, J. S. and S. L. (kindergarten).

Budget Changes: After studying the budget for the NSD, Charlie determined that there was sufficient financial support from the government, but the money was misspent on too many superfluous staff; for example, there was a night watchman on duty at the same time as residential staff, three cooks in food service when one or two at the most would suffice (especially when the cooking seemed to be opening large cans of spaghetti), and at least three extra utility workers who were responsible for cleaning the school. By eliminating these extra staff members, he freed up money he could use in other areas, such as hiring a dietician and an audio-visual technologist.

Because of our disciplinary meetings and the approach to discipline that Mr. Harkins was planning to take, the guidance counsellor decided to resign from the NSD. So the next thing Charlie had to do was find a guidance counsellor who had a background in Deaf Education. Since a Teacher of the Deaf would probably not be able to immediately satisfy the provincial qualifications to be a guidance counsellor, Charlie began interviewing candidates for the position at the NSD. One candidate stood out for two reasons: first, he was willing to attend the National Technical Institute for the Deaf in Rochester, New York, to get the necessary training in the psychological assessment of Deaf children, to learn which tests to use and how to interpret the results with Deaf children; secondly, because of his background in working with Canadian Army Cadets.

So Jack J was hired in July of 1978. When he was introduced to the staff, he told us that he knew little about the Deaf and just started to learn sign language. In an email, Jack sent me the following:

I asked that I be allowed to go into classes to observe and almost every teacher was comfortable with that. Charlie wanted me to get some specific skills and the most important one was assessment of children who are Deaf and hard of hearing. In February of 1979, I spent 2 weeks with Michelle Boyer at Rochester School for the Deaf focusing on psychological assessment and we also dealt with academic assessment.

During my first and second year at NSD, I spent time arranging for children to travel home as we had established a school schedule that allowed us to send the children home on a weekly basis for children Grand Falls and east, and all children went home every 6 weeks, in October, November, December, February, April, and May.

As I started working at NSD, one of the first things we were dealing with was discipline at NSD. The older kids were frequently rude and unruly. It was decided by Charlie in discussion with myself, Clarke and Cyril Coffin that we would put a system in place where students would get a 1-hour detention for anything they did in school. Children would not be sent home for breaking the rules, they would just be given detention. At the start, the detention room would be full and 2 teachers would sit with the students and Charlie, Clarke and myself would be on hand to deal with anyone that refused to do things. The system took a long time to catch on, but eventually the numbers decreased dramatically and student behaviour improved dramatically.

The Kids Get Home More Often — Parents Happy:

When Charlie got to the NSD, students living in Mount Pearl, a community about 15 kilometers from the school, were required to stay in the residence. Understanding that parents would prefer to interact with their children daily, he arranged for students living in Mount Pearl to be driven to a drop-off point in that community—I think it was at the Mount Pearl Hotel on Park Street.

There, parents would meet them and bring them home.

The parents were a bit conflicted; they were happy to have their children home every night, but were unhappy about having to pick them up at that drop-off point in the middle of the afternoon.

When they complained to their Member of the House of Assembly (MHA), Neil Windsor, he summoned Charlie to his office to express his discontent about having his constituents complain about picking up their children at that location at that time of the day.

Mr. Windsor was a member of Premier Brian Peckford's cabinet, perhaps the Minister of Finance or of the Treasury Department. So Charlie explained that he'd love to drop all of them off directly to their homes, but, "I need some busses and drivers. That will resolve both of our problems."

Mr. Windsor's response was, "You got me, didn't you?"

So the school got a couple of 15-passenger school busses and two drivers. He also pondered a way to get students from remote community's home quickly during the Christmas holidays. Brain storming with the president of the Parents Association, Mr. Laurie Cashin, the idea of using a helicopter to fly them came up. Mr. Cashin's brother, Peter, was a Member of Parliament. He set up a meeting with the MP from the Southern Shore District and a prominent member of Prime Minister Pierre Trudeau's cabinet, Mr. Don Jamieson.

From that meeting, Mr. Jamieson convinced the Canadian Armed Services to permit their Search and Rescue helicopter to fly students living in Grey River, Burgeo and Ramea home. In Grey River, there was no place with enough room for the pilot to safely land, so he placed the rear wheels onto the wharf, lowered the rear loading dock and the students got off and ran into their parents' arms.

The picture was taken of the first helicopter ride to Grey River. Santa, played by Hammond Taylor, dropped them off and gave their parents little gifts.

Developing Professional Services:

There were so many changes happening during the first two years that Mr. Harkins became principal, that it is a challenge to remember them all. During the summer of 1978, Clarke, Bill Snow, a Deaf houseparent, Beehan and I formed the Registry of Interpreters of the Deaf - Newfoundland Chapter (RID-NC). In this way, we would be able to begin charging various government departments and other organizations for providing interpreting services. During the first year, our invoices were mostly ignored; however, by the next year, some departments began to pay our bills in full. With that money, we could begin to improve our skill level by organizing and bringing in other interpreters to provide workshops for us and other interested people.

Charlie also discovered that the Newfoundland Teachers Association (NTA) supported special interest councils. In order to avail of that resource, he suggested to me that I explore the idea of establishing a council of teachers of the Deaf. So during our Christmas holiday of 1978, I set up a meeting with a member of the executive of the NTA and learned of the process we needed to follow to become a special interest council of the organization. First we needed to have an approved constitution, approved first by the expected membership then by the NTA itself.

I began writing a constitution from a template I was given by the NTA librarian and set to work tweaking it to fit the specialty of teachers of the Deaf. After a couple of drafts, in February of 1979, I presented it at a staff meeting, and they approved it. I then took it to the NTA executive. A week later, the Newfoundland and Labrador Council of Educators of the Deaf (NLCED) was formed. Election of officers was held during one of our Friday meetings, and the NLCED was formed with 5 executive members: President - Ms. Tish , Vice-president - John *Reade, Secretary - Ms. B. O'R, Treasurer - Ms. J. H. and Communications Director - Ms. A. E.*

Another important priority was to raise the expectations of the Deaf community, staff, parents and government as to what Deaf students can accomplish. The NLCED through professional development grants provided by the NLTA, provided the funding necessary to bring in guest speakers from various backgrounds and various careers to give workshops to the staff and parents. One of the first workshops we funded was to bring in Kirtchner and his wife. Mr. Kirtchner was an administrator at a school for the deaf in the US, the president of the national RID, and, most importantly, a firm believer in the use of "total communication" in teaching Deaf students. Mr. Kirtchner gave his workshop to us in May of 1979

After his workshop, Charlie formed the sign choir. By focusing on interpreting the lyrics of popular songs of the day, we were forced to think about the underlying meaning of them. Thus we began to sign concepts rather than English. It was our first introduction to American Sign Language (ASL). We discussed the lyrics to Barry Manilow's song, "I Can't Smile Without You" and listened to it so often that to this day, I can remember every word and learned to hate the song. Other songs we worked on included John Denver's "Sunshine On My Shoulders," and Carol Kings "I Feel the Earth Move Under My Feet."

Drama Club Opens New Skills And Ideas For The Students:

During this time frame, Ms. Tish wanted to improve her interpreting skills and asked for a leave of absence to take a semester at NTID. This was granted and she enrolled that summer. While there, she became enthralled by the NTID acting troupe. She decided to become involved with Theatre of the Deaf and brought her enthusiasm back to the NSD. In order to establish a Drama Club at the school, Mr. Harkins decided to bring members of the NTID drama department to Newfoundland to close out the 1979/80 school year with an Acting Workshop.

The NTID acting troupe that came to the NSD was composed of two Deaf actors.

L-R: Patricia, Paul, Patrick, Paul and in the back, Jerome and Paul, both members of the National Theatre of the Deaf (NTD) in the US, and Patricia, Jerome and Bruce. Mr. Harkins asked Mr. Greybill, a veteran of the stage both as an actor for the NTD and a drama teacher, if he would like to meet a few government officials. Mr. Graybill agreed and Charlie took him to the Confederation Building to meet Mr. Roebothan, Mr. Andrews and a few others. He was hoping to introduce Mr. Graybill to the Minister of

Education, Ms. Lynn, but that was not to be. So he left her a ticket to the performance, 'Hand Dance,' that was to be held at the Holy Heart of Mary High School Theatre on the weekend.

The parents were invited to attend this workshop, as were all the students. To say it was well received would be equivalent to saying that the Stanley Cup is the most important series of hockey games in the world. The students proved to be natural actors, the parents were impressed with the various activities that the company brought, and the few government officials that stopped by were pleased that we pulled it off without any additional help from their coffers.

The review by the Evening Telegram's theatre critic, Paddy, said,

"Handance, directed by Jerome, is something for everybody, young and old, a series of lively presentations by writers with such varying talents as James, Anton, and Lewis."

In his second-to-last paragraph he stated,

"It was absorbing and moving to appreciate this new world that can be opened up for our deaf community in Newfoundland, a taste of hopefully much more to come."

And that's exactly what happened, until the NSD was forced to close.

That year was also the last time the NSD graduation ceremonies were held at the Provincial Recreation Centre. From then on, the end of the year brought a workshop for parents and staff, and a graduation ceremony held at various locations, often at the Memorial University's Queen's College.

The success of the workshop by the NTID Acting Company brought so much excitement to the Deaf community as well as the performing arts community here in St. John's that Mr. Harkins decided to invite another NTID Acting Company to visit, hold a workshop, and perform their children's show. Sunshine Too was a professional troupe of Deaf and hearing performers. They were here from December 7 to 13, 1980, and gave a performance at the Memorial University's Little Theatre Sunday afternoon for parents and students of the NSD, but it was open to the public. The theatre was filled to the brim.

Sunshine Too performed songs, ASL poetry, poetry, sign-mime, storytelling, and scenes from different plays. After that performance, they moved to the Holy Heart of Mary Theatre and gave a similar show for various elementary and high schools in the St. John's area. These were done on Tuesday and Wednesday, December 9 and 10. On the eleventh and twelfth, they held classes for the students of the NSD. The members of Sunshine Too were Ed, Joyce, Pete, Mitch, Debbie, and Ogden.

These two theatre endeavors inspired Ms. Tish to establish the NSD Drama Club.

DRAMA

Ms. Tish developed a venue for the students to showcase their impressive talents. It was called "A Night At The Nickel." This was in reference to the first movie theatre in Newfoundland, the Nickel Theatre. This theatre opened in 1907 and showed silent films for $0.05, thus the name "Nickel." So Ms. Beehan, wrote a script for the students in which there would be a series of skits much in the vein of the silent movies.

There were the Keystone Cops, Snideley and a damsel in distress, ASL poetry, a mime about a mixing bowl, stick-ups, flying saucers, and just about anything she could think of for the students to act. We all thought they were so good, we tried to convince her to enter it in the Provincial Drama Festival. I don't think it was an actual entry, but was a demonstration piece and was given high praise by the adjudicator.

Here are some scenes that were used in the 1981 yearbook.

The Only Army Cadet Corps Made Up Of Deaf Students And Leaders:

While Ms. Tish was bringing in Deaf theatre performers from the States, Jack actually fulfilled the promise he made to Mr. Harkins during his initial interview and started up the 2965 Army Cadet Corps at the NSD. He contacted the Army Cadet Office in St. John's and explained what he wanted to do. The Company Commander at the time wasn't very supportive of the idea but told Jack that in order for him to consider a Deaf Cadet Corps, there were three things he had to set up: first, he had to get a sponsor; second, the Deaf Cadets would not be allowed to attend the annual Cadet Camp in Ontario; and third, there had to be an Army-based sign language to be used.

Mr. Harkins had a friend who was part of the Stokers Group of Rotary, a service club made up of the richest people in St. John's. His friend told Charlie that the group wanted to fund something for the school on a one-time basis. Sensing a promising contribution to the NSD, Charlie told him to contact Jack. When he did, Jack spoke of needing a good sponsor to establish an Army Cadet Corps.

Charlie's friend took this information back to the Stokers Group of Rotary, and they discussed the whole concept. Some of the members of this group included John Murphy, owner of a discount store on Water Street and later mayor of the city; Mr. Reid, the son of the developer of the Newfoundland Railroad System; and Jay Parker, owner of the Parker/Monroe Shoe Company. They discussed the idea and agreed to fund this unique program to the tune of $1,500 for the first year.

During the course of the thirty years that the Newfoundland School for the Deaf Army Cadet Corps 2965 existed, the Stokers Group of Rotary provided continuous funding and were responsible for ensuring this enduring, completely unique experiment remained a source of education, enjoyment, and accomplishment. When I say unique, I use the word as it's meant to be used—"having no like or equal, unparalleled." It was and remains the only cadet corps in the world made up entirely of Deaf and hard of hearing individuals.

To develop the corps, Jack set up a Thursday meeting for all those students interested in joining and began the task of teaching the unique signs that would be used to convey various military orders such as "attention," "stand at ease," "left turn," "forward march," and more. New signs never needed to be developed, as the signs already used by staff and students at the NSD were given an additional meaning when used in this military setting.

Knowing commanding a Cadet Corps would be a huge undertaking, Jack sought help from some of the other staff members and got it. First on board was Mr. Cyril Coffin, Vice-Principal of Residence, Jack's brother, Bill, Vice-Principal of Academics, sister, Jackie Clarke, Rose Daley, a houseparent, Jacques Monfette, teacher of the Deaf, and last, but surely not least, Des McCarthy, a fellow Bell Islander and former Cadet Corps member himself.

Jack planned two annual weekend camping outings as well as two overnight sleepovers.

These were very successful, so successful that Jack approached the St. John's Army Cadet Corps headquarters and requested that they be allowed to send NSD Army Cadets to the Summer Cadet Camp. In 1983, he got permission to take NSD Cadets to the Army Summer Camp in Penetanguishene, Ontario. Those in attendance were Michael, Kevin, Alfred, Dale, and Wade. At the end of their deployment, Kevin returned to the school with the shadow rank of Sergeant, and Wade returned as a Lieutenant.

Remembrance Day Ceremonies:

After ten years as the Commanding Officer of the 2965 Army Cadet Corps, Jack stepped down, and Des took over. Des remained in that position until the school was closed in 2010. One of the most significant events during Des' tenure was to establish a tender, informative event surrounding the November 11th Remembrance Day Commemoration.

He contacted one of the Canadian Legions in St. John's and asked if any of their WWII Veterans would be interested in sharing any of their experiences during the war with the students at the NSD. At first, only a couple said they were interested. He organized a Cadet inspection for those vets, who showed up in their uniforms, and proceeded from there. I can remember the first one vividly, as I did a lot of interpreting for the students after we moved into the theatre for a question period, and the students had a lot of questions.

Perhaps it was because of all their questions that the men opened up about some of their experiences. One man told the story of the ship he was serving on being torpedoed by a U-Boat. While telling that story, he became emotional and had to stop for a bit before finishing up. The students, God bless them, noticed his reaction and did not follow up with any other questions.

After the question period, Des organized a little party for the adults in the meeting room at the NSD and thanked the men with a snack bar and something to drink that would be fitting for old soldiers.

Obviously, the first group of veterans who participated were impressed enough to return to their respective Legions and talked about how great their experience was, because in the years that followed, this commemoration became very popular and more veterans returned the next year and every year after that. A difficult thing that Des and his corps had to deal with was the fact that over the years, the participants began to pass away.

A Major Change:

A major change to the structure of the NSD was made by a minute in the House of Assembly. The school day began at 8:30 and ended at 4:00 rather than following the schedule of all the other schools in the province. By doing this, he was able to close the school at noon on Friday. When that happened, as was described previously, all the students east of Grand Falls-Windsor were transported home every weekend. This also improved the behavior of the students by getting to see their parents more often. Furthermore, the parents began to show more support for the school.

Mr. Harkins also decided to make some very important changes to the internal structure of the school. He requested the addition of another administrative position to the NSD, that of Vice-Principal of Residence. I believe this was one of the main reasons graduates of the NSD had so much success academically and socially from 1979 until the day the school was closed in 2010.

The administration of the NSD looked like the pictures.

Friday Afternoon Meetings:

Charlie also began to have Friday afternoon meetings with mandatory attendance. After the initial grumbling, the teachers began to understand his ideas and concepts much better and got on board with his program. Of course this wasn't easy. Sometimes the discussions were very heated, but Mr. Harkins eventually convinced us that he had a plan where within five years many of the graduates would be going to Universities, Colleges and other post-secondary institutions.

That promise came to fruition with the graduating class of 1983 when Kevin, Alfred and Paul were accepted into various post-secondary institutions in Canada and the United States. Mr. Kevin was accepted into the Drama in Education program at the University of Windsor. Mr. Alfred and Mr. Paul were both accepted at Madonna College in Livonia, Michigan. Both entered the teacher training program, Alfred with the goal of becoming an industrial arts teacher, Paul an educator of mathematics.

A Very Successful Pilot Project:

Another reason for students' academic success was the development of a research program developed by the Faculty of Medicine Telemedicine-telehealth at Memorial University of Newfoundland (MUN). "In 1977 the project's objective was to find a way of teaching parents how to develop their deaf children's language and communication skills as early in life as possible." [2] This project was supervised by Dr. Clare NevilleSmith and handled by Ms. Beverley O'Reilly.

Videotape machines were purchased and distributed to parents in seven areas around the province. Video tapes were produced by teachers at the Atlantic Provinces Resource Centre for the Hearing Handicapped in Amherst, Nova Scotia. Each month an instructional tape was distributed to the participating families as well as a visit by Ms. O'Reilly who demonstrated how to put to use the instructions given on the video tape She then followed up with weekly phone calls to make sure the families remained comfortable with the instructional techniques.

In September of 1978, the NSD took over the program with Ms. O'Reilly, a Master Degree teacher of the Deaf, being hired by the NSD to continue the program, named the Home Centered (sic) Videotape Program.

Later, the name was shortened to the Home Parent Program; however, the process remained the same until there was a change in ideology at the Department of Education after the provincial election of 1989 (more about that later, much more).

Many of the participants of this program went on to get post-secondary degrees upon graduation from the NSD.

_____

[2] Sheila Gushue, Information Officer, (Medicine), March 1979, The Gazette (p 5-6)

Bev had to advise the parents as to the best educational placement for their children when they became kindergarten age. Jack Jardine helped her with that advice. Part of the Home Parent Program was to have the parents come into the NSD and see what type of education we offered. It also gave Jack Jardine the opportunity to test the children and determine their English language skills to see if they could compete with hearing peers. One of the tests was the Peabody Picture Vocabulary Test, which he used to see if the students understood one or two-word sentences and could comprehend simple and/or comprehensive sentences.

When Mr. Coffin was chosen to become Vice-Principal of Residence, there was a need for a physical education teacher. Mr. Harkins asked Ann to take over the physical education program. She agreed to do it for a short time, but she was mostly interested in being an itinerant teacher.

So at the end of the school year, Mr. Harkins asked me if I'd be interested in this position. I said yes, and Ann became an itinerant teacher.

Physical Education - The Reade Way

During that summer, I participated in weekend workshops that were presented by the Canadian Association of Physical and Health Education Resources (CAPHR) and offered at MUN during the summer of 1978. I learned a lot from those workshops, most importantly, to ask the students what they enjoyed doing. I also learned that there were a couple of ways to approach teaching physical education: focus on two kinds of sports—lifetime sports and team sports. Lifetime sports were activities such as handball, squash, swimming, skating, badminton, tennis, and weightlifting. Team sports included volleyball, basketball, soccer, baseball, and kickball.

When I contacted the director of the Provincial Recreation Centre about setting up the P.E. program for the NSD, I told him my plans, which were very different from what Mr. Coffin had been doing. I was told that to use the swimming pool to teach the Red Cross badge program in swimming, I first had to be a certified lifeguard.

MW with her medals

So I contacted the Red Cross, and they directed me to the Royal Lifesaving Society's Bronze Medallion course. The course was beginning in a few weeks and would take place on three successive Saturdays at the Mews Centre Swimming pool. It turned out that one of our students, MW., wanted to get a summertime job as a life guard, so we both signed up for the course. I interpreted for her while participating in the program myself. We both passed, although, truth be told, MW was a much stronger swimmer than I.

MW won a silver and three bronze medals at the Canadian National Swim Trials for the Deaf and was named to the Canadian team that competed in the World Games for the Deaf in Cologne, West Germany in July of 1981. However, her place on the Canadian team was jeopardized by her Newfoundland provincial coach. I don't remember the whole story about this situation, but I do remember that Mr. Harkins, Mr. Laurie Cashin and the provincial minister for sports had to do some arm-twisting to ensure Marjorie did participate in Germany.

Ms Clarke had to take some personal time to accompany MW on her trip to Cologne because she missed the official flight with the rest of the Canadian team. As I recall, MW participated in the breaststroke and came in 4th in the world, but did not bring home a World Games for the Deaf medal.

The swimming program was very popular, even in the winter when the water in the pool felt pretty cold when one jumped in. Before and after swimming, the children

had to take a shower. Before so they didn't bring any mud or other strange things that would compromise the cleanliness of the water. Afterwards, so the chlorine could be washed off their bodies. They weren't always thrilled with the showers, but they did take them, and dried off both with towels and the blow dryer that each locker room had.

For the kindergarten and children in the Home Parent Program, I set up a vinyl splash pool. Filled it with water from the regular pool, but let it warm up for the little ones. After they got wet, we then transferred to the shallow end. There was always a volunteer parent or another teacher with me for those youngsters. Once the kids became acclimated to the water temperature, I would have them jump into the pool, into my arms. Then I'd swing them around, dunking them up and down into the water, making sure their head did not go under, and let them stand by the deck while we persuaded another child to jump into my arms.

The first time a kindergarten boy jumped into the pool, he inadvertently defecated. It rose to the top of the water and floated around. We really had to scramble that day. We cleared the pool of all the students, cleaned up the boy, and informed the supervisor of the Rec Centre's pool. The rest of the swimming classes were cancelled, and the pool was closed until the filters had the opportunity to cleanse the water. After 24 hours, the pool was tested for any bacteria, and the pH balance was restored to normal. That was embarrassing!

Getting Teachers Involved In After-School P.E. Activities:

I thought many of the younger students would want to participate in off-campus athletic activities with local children their age. I found out that there was a basketball program for students aged 5 to 12 that was taking place in many different locations across the city. It was called Youth Basketball Canada (YBC) at that time; since then, it has changed its name to Junior NBA Canada. I contacted the director of the local YBC program—who, coincidentally, was also located at the Provincial Recreation Centre—and talked about getting interested students involved. To my surprise and enjoyment, this program was integrated by gender as well, boys and girls on the same team.

My idea was to have interested NSD students placed on different teams in an attempt to have both genders of Deaf students integrated with hearing peers. In order to do that, I needed the support of five other staff members to act as interpreters, chaperones, and assistant coaches. I spoke about the concept with Mr. Harkins, who thought it was a good idea and suggested I ask Mr. Coffin if he had any ideas on how to make it happen.

So Mr. Coffin and I met and discussed the idea. He also thought it had merit, but when I asked if he could ask his residence staff for volunteers, he said they were too busy doing other after-school programs to participate in the YBC program, but he'd be happy to help organize transportation to the various locales. So at one of the Friday afternoon meetings, I described the YBC program and asked if anyone might be willing to give up four hours a week so our junior and intermediate students who were interested could participate in the program. To my surprise, I had more than enough teacher volunteers to ensure the program was successful. Some teams even had two teacher volunteer/interpreters/coaches.

All the games between teams happened on Saturday mornings, but the YBC practice schedule for the six teams was broken up into different blocks for different teams at different gymnasiums around the city. So I divided our interested students among the various teams, placed the volunteers with students who were in their homerooms as much as possible, wrote up the schedules for the teams, and passed them out. The program was very well received, but, to paraphrase John Lennon, sometimes life gets in the way of your plans. And that happened with this program as well. Sometimes the volunteers could not make a practice session because their home life, naturally, took precedence. When that happened, I filled in, and on a few occasions, Mr. Coffin helped out. The overwhelming feeling among all the staff was that the students' extracurricular activities would not be cancelled if at all possible, and that included the YBC program.

The intermediate students all participated in the swimming program, of course, but in the gym, we did a number of fun things. Sometimes I'd set up an obstacle course where the boys had to climb a rope, jump over the vaulting horse, weave between pylons, and slide under ropes. Other times, we played kickball, or as it became known later, soccer baseball. Later, we'd play frisbee, basketball, handball, racquetball, volleyball, and so on.

Gymnastics – Me? However, there were a number of intermediate girls who wanted to do gymnastics. At first, I didn't understand what they wanted to do; the sign they used was one I understood to mean "ballet." However, after a number of questions, one of the girls did a cartwheel in front of me and said, "That." Again, I had no idea how to coach or teach gymnastics, and yet again, the offices at the Provincial Recreation Centre came through. The CYGNUS Gymnastics Club of Newfoundland shared their office with another sport upstairs, and I trotted up to that office once I knew someone was there.

Dr. Gordon greeted me warmly and listened closely while I told him what I needed from CYGNUS. Again, there was complete support from a sports association. He gave me a copy of the CYGNUS schedule when they used the Rec Centre for practice and told me to bring the students whenever I wanted.

The next time I had these girls in a class, I told them what I did and asked who wanted to join the club and learn gymnastics. They all enthusiastically wanted to participate. There was one student who lived in St. John's and would need to miss her bus home on those practice nights (I believe there were two per week). The food service staff and the residence staff made accommodations for Paula to stay after school, do her homework with the girls in the residence, and accompany all the girls over to the Rec Centre just before practice time.

At the first practice, I introduced the girls to the various coaches. One coach, in particular, took a great interest in working with our NSD girls. JS took to communicating with them like a fish to water. She became the unofficial personal coach for them and taught them how to work on the uneven parallel bars, balance beam, and some beginning tumbling. I was amazed at how naturally flexible all the girls were. Trying to do a split was no problem. I was also encouraged to see that they were able to balance on the balance beam fairly easily, even being able to do the split on the beam. Thus further supporting my Major Paper Theory—HA!

A Death:

One evening after the practice session, while Janet and I were putting away the gymnastics equipment, a man came running out of the swimming pool and yelling for help. He needed someone who knew CPR. Well, both Janet and I had first aid training from the St. John's Ambulance, so we volunteered to help out. In the 1980s, it was the standard to do artificial respiration while another person did chest compressions. We got into the pool area and saw a man lying on the deck at the deep end, face up and obviously in distress. Janet immediately began chest compressions, and I began artificial respiration. We continued this for what seemed like forever, but probably only 15 or 20 minutes. After a few compressions, he threw up in my mouth. That was terrible; worse, the man died.

Cygnus Gymnastics And The Provincial Gymnastics Association:

The Provincial Gymnastics president, Dr. Gordon, invited Canada's national gymnastics coach, Ms. Pope, to come to Newfoundland. He wanted her to give advanced coaching techniques to Newfoundland's coaches and some of our promising athletes. Ms. Pope brought Sherry Hawco, the national champion on beam and floor exercise, to accompany her and demonstrate her training techniques as well as routines. In July of 1982, Dr. Bennett's lobbying came to fruition, and three of NSD's gymnasts were invited to attend. I was there to interpret and act as a kind of chaperone, but because our gymnasts were female, I was only needed to interpret.

This was an intense training session that required the participants to remain together, eat together, and train together for the five days of the workshop. On the first night, one of our gymnasts decided that she just couldn't stay in the camp overnight. She lived in the city and needed to go home overnight. After trying to convince her otherwise, it was decided to let her go home and return early in the morning for breakfast with the other participants.

Participating NSD students.

When I asked the high school students what they wanted to do during physical education, I got many different answers. One boy wanted to do track and field. Since I did not have the knowledge or skill to coach track and field, I got a meeting with the president of the provincial track and field association, Mr. Chris Pickard. He agreed to meet with Paul and see if he had any potential. Mr. Pickard was impressed with Paul's natural ability and agreed to be his coach. For the first couple of sessions, I went with Paul and acted as an interpreter, but from then on, Paul went to practice sessions on his own.

Paul and Elvis both enjoyed handball, and that was a sport I could coach. I spent many hours playing the sport in high school, when I lived in California and after I got to Canada, in Amherst and St. John's.

After school, we began participating in the Newfoundland Handball Association's practice sessions at the Provincial Recreation Centre and participating in their tournaments. In 1980, the YMCA opened a new building that had two full-sized handball courts. For the next two years, the three of us participated in all the tournaments.

Handball champs

Above is The Evening Telegram's picture, hosted by the Handball Association at the YMCA. Paul, Newfoundland Handball Champions. Paul won the boys under-19 provincial open championships in the top row, 3rd from the left. Elvis is next to and Elvis was runner-up in 1982. I won the Men's "B" championship that year, and the three of us represented Newfoundland in the Atlantic Open Championships in St. John, New Brunswick, in May of that year.

Paul made it to the semifinals in the under-19 tournaments, but had to resign due to bleeding blisters in his feet. At the time he stopped playing, the game was tied. Elvis played well and managed to come in third in the consolation round.

For the junior department, as stated previously, I used the pool at the Rec Centre, but often their gym time was in the multi-purpose room on the first floor of the main school building. It was also where the P. E. teacher's office was located. Mr. Coffin had gathered some interesting gym equipment to be used in that small space.

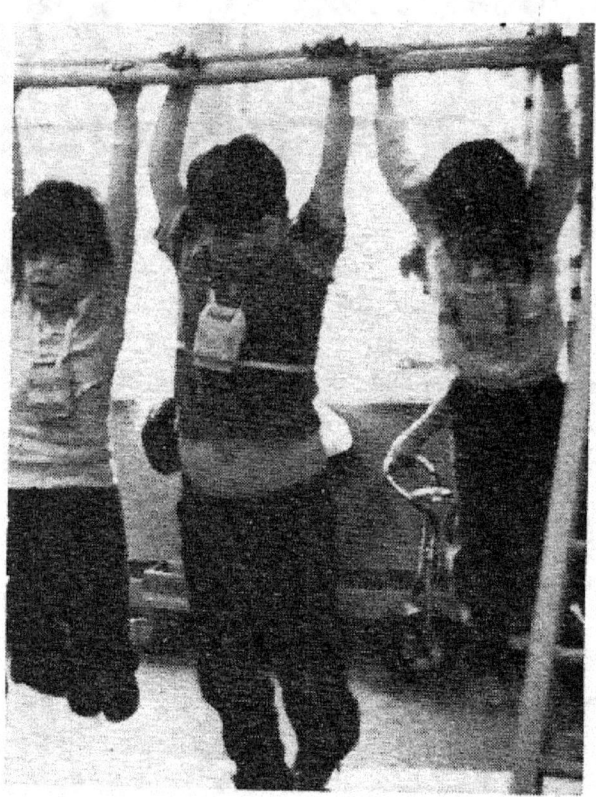

My gym classes with the junior students were divided into blocks. To warm up, I would have them move around that space the way we would imagine different animals would 'walk.' For example, I ask them how a duck walks.

Then show them my version of a duck walk and have them copy me. We'd do elephants, camels, cats/dogs, birds, rabbits/bunnies, and even snakes. Then we'd follow up with an obstacle course, or races either on foot, hands and feet, crab walk, or on a small scooter (a board with four roller skate wheels attached to it). After each class, I'd walk the students back to their classroom and explain to their teacher what we did. That way, the teacher could use the gym time activities as a language lesson.

The kindergarten was housed in a separate building, a block away from the regular school building. For that department, again, there was swimming at the pool, but their gym classes were held in a vacant room on the second floor, above their classroom, as well as the industrial arts, business education, and home economics classrooms. Their activities were similar to the junior department's, with one exception—they were of shorter duration and changed quickly.

One activity they enjoyed was playing on the wooden monkey bars that we had in that area. I would place a mat under the apparatus and let them do whatever they preferred.

Physical Rehabilitation:

The next thing I had to learn as the NSD physical education teacher was to become trained in physical rehabilitation. Over the years, we have had students who had multiple disabilities. These students needed to have daily rehabilitation exercises, and taking them to the Janeway Hospital's Rehab facility was not an option. So I took workshops with the director of that program in order to learn the proper techniques to use with these special students.

One junior student with whom I worked for a number of years had cerebral palsy. I must say, he was a pleasure to work with — always smiling, trying hard to do what he was supposed to do, but often in pain, especially with crawling. Another junior student was burned severely and had to learn to walk, run, and generally move after that horrendous accident. These special kids often made my day and sometimes caused me to reflect on how life can throw hand grenades at your head. Working with these students helped me develop an ability that came in handy after I retired from the NSD.

More Master Degree Teachers Arrive:

In 1980, Mr. Harkins recruited quite a few more people from the M.Ed. The Deaf Education program is still taking place in Amherst, Nova Scotia. That year, B O'D, B Mac, Janey, EJ, Joan R, Muffin, Jacques, DMac, and Ms. Shea joined the teaching staff. After three years, the entire teaching staff had either a Master's Degree or specific training in Deaf Education, with one exception. The exception was Ms. Shea, but she was and remains the only Deaf teacher of the Deaf who worked at the NSD and had experience as a Home Economics teacher in Amherst.

Jacques, as one might tell from the name, was a native French-speaking young man. The Director of Special Education, Mr. Andrews, was a francophile and questioned Charlie as to Jacques' English-speaking ability and whether he would be a good fit for Newfoundland. Charlie calmly explained that since he interviewed Mr. Monfette over the phone, and since Charlie didn't speak French, Jacques' English was obviously suitable.

He also hired the husband of one of those recruits, Mr. CJ, as a dorm counsellor. Chris was an athlete in university and graduated with a degree in Physical Education. So it was only natural for me to cultivate a relationship with him. Chris played football, basketball, and volleyball in university and was a nationally certified coach and referee in basketball and volleyball.

Some of the senior boys wanted to form a volleyball team, so I approached Chris to see if he'd be willing to coach our team. He agreed, and we set up a practice schedule. The boys had seen volleyball on television and had an idea of the game; however, they needed to learn some basic skills and rules. Chris was a very knowledgeable coach but didn't yet have a good grasp of signing, so my job, mostly, was to interpret for him at first. It didn't take long before the boys could understand what Chris wanted them to do and how to do it.

Back In The Classroom:

I remained as the physical education teacher until 1984. Chris graduated from the Master's program at Amherst, and Charlie hired him to be the physical education teacher. I was happy to be heading back to the classroom, but a bit distraught that I would no longer be working with all the students in the school. That was the best part of being the P.E. teacher.

In the 1981 Speech from the Throne, Premier Brian Peckford, a former teacher, announced a five-year plan of action by his government to improve business opportunities, promote the exploration of offshore oil, and upgrade educational services in the province, including building a new NSD. Mr. Harkins made sure educational opportunities for Deaf children were included in that plan by meeting with the Deputy Minister of Education repeatedly and eventually getting to speak directly with the Minister of Education, Ms. Lynn Verge. The Department of Education agreed to hire a specialist in Deaf Education to conduct a thorough review of the NSD facility and programs and to report back to them within a year of being hired.

I'm proud to say that I was partly responsible for Charlie recommending Dr. Kennedy to perform this important task. As I said previously, Dr. Kennedy was formerly the Director of the Master's Degree in Deaf Education for the Université de Moncton, and we had a poor student-teacher relationship. However, at that time, she was a consultant in the education of hearing-handicapped children in the Calgary School Board in Alberta, and despite our problems in 1974, I thought she'd do a fair review and help us get the school we needed.

In January of 1981, Dr. Kennedy began her review of services provided to the Deaf students of Newfoundland and Labrador by going to Wabush, Goose Bay, Corner Brook, and Gander to interview parents of students attending the NSD from those communities. She said she wanted to get their perspective on the progress they felt their children were making, both educationally and socially.

She also accepted briefs from the NLCED, RID–Nfld Chapter, and the Parents Association. In an interview conducted by the *Evening Telegram*, Dr. Kennedy said that the NSD teachers were using excellent methods and the students were progressing well academically, despite working in "less than ideal surroundings."

Although her written report was to be submitted in March of that year, she sent a draft of her report to the NSD, NLCED, and the Parents Association for our review. We did this thoroughly and sent her our suggestions for revision. Happily, she included nearly all of our input in the final report, which was used as the basis to fulfill the promise of a new NSD made in the Speech from the Throne in 1982.

We Train Real Professional Interpreters:

Dr. Kennedy wrote a compelling critique of the interpreting services being provided to the Deaf community at that time. The RID–Nfld Chapter did all of the interpreting for the Deaf community voluntarily, although we did send bills to specific organizations such as political parties and governmental offices. Whenever a payment was made, it went into an account that was used to reimburse the volunteer interpreters for parking fines and, occasionally, a hotel room.

These interpreting assignments included being called on to interpret for the Royal Newfoundland Constabulary (RNC) and/or the Royal Canadian Mounted Police (RCMP) at all hours of the day and night. Many a time, I was called out of bed during the early hours of the day to facilitate communication between the police and a drunk driver who was Deaf or to help a doctor explain the injuries an accident victim who was Deaf had sustained.

We also needed to interpret for individuals who needed medical treatment. We tried to pair the gender of the individual who had the doctor's appointment with that of the interpreter, but sometimes it just wasn't possible. That occasionally led to the individual refusing to keep the appointment because of the sensitivity of the problem.

However, the most unique interpreting we did was in cooperation with CBC News and Avalon Cablevision. In 1979, CBC News would air its *News Digest* on Saturday evenings. *News Digest* was a review of the previous week's top news stories around the province. It took over a year to work out all the details of the program, but when the technicians at Avalon Cablevision understood what we wanted, and CBC permitted us to have a script of their program ahead of time, we began to take turns interpreting...the weekly *News Digest* once a month.

It was a difficult interpreting session at first because each part of the script was timed down to the half-second, and the anchor, Glenn Tilley, had to get his dialogue finished in that specific time frame. We would sit with him at first and listen to his delivery so we might be able to get the meaning of that script to fit with his pacing. After the first few times, and the way the program was set up, we just began to "go with the flow," so to speak. Avalon Cablevision set us up with a split screen where we were on the right half of the viewer's screen and CBC on the left half. It was very successful, and the Deaf community loved it; however, all good things must come to an end, and after three years, CBC decided to cancel *News Digest*.

Partially due to Dr. Kennedy's critique, in which she acknowledged that the service being provided was adequate but took energy away from the teachers who comprised the RID at that time, the situation began to shift. Around the same time, the Kennedy report was published, the NCCD received a grant from the federal government to hire an individual who was qualified to teach ASL interpreting. That person was Mr. Still.

Eight people signed up for the course, which was held at the NSD in Building Two, above the kindergarten classroom, the Home Parent Program office, and the workshop area (industrial arts, home economics, and business education). The seven women and one man went into a complete immersion of ASL—eight hours a day, five days a week, for one full year. After a few weeks, most were skilled enough to begin participating in social events with the Deaf community of St. John's. This served a number of purposes: the students became familiar with the way each Deaf individual signed, the Deaf community became familiar with the future interpreters who would be serving them, and the community in general learned how to use professional interpreters rather than the teachers who had been acting as interpreters.

By having this interpreter training course at the NSD, the individuals participating could also watch the students communicate with each other during lunch, recess, or just walking around the buildings on their breaks. Quite honestly, this was another of Charlie's goals in changing around the culture of the NSD — broadening our reach into the Deaf community.

At the end of the course, four full-time, trained, professional interpreters were hired by the NCCD, and an office was established above the building that housed the Gaze Seed Company. Mr. Still remained as the executive director and interpreter supervisor, Myles Murphy was hired as a researcher at first and later became office manager, and M. Sh. was the secretary, who handled time sheets and scheduled interpreter placements. The four interpreters hired were M. Parsons, Mrs. Peddigrew, Ms. McCarthy and Mrs. Reade, my wife.

One of the best outcomes from creating interpreter services was that teachers no longer had to interpret during school activities such as workshops, assemblies, meetings and awards ceremonies during school closings.

What Makes A Good School For The Deaf:

In a conversation I had with Charlie over a few beers one Friday afternoon, he told me that he believed a good school for the Deaf was like a three-legged bar stool. The school was the seat, and each leg represented the government (necessary for the funding), the parents (necessary for lobbying the government and providing support to the school), and the Deaf community (necessary for supporting the students and initiating them into Deaf culture).

So by 1981, as stated previously, Charlie convinced the government to pay for a consultant to evaluate the educational programs and facilities of the school, as well as change the hours of the school day and the time of year the school opened and closed; got the parents' association to organize parents from all parts of the province to raise $50,000 to purchase a large bus capable of driving students home every six weeks (we called it the Blue Bomber); began educating various politicians and the general public about the unlimited capabilities of Deaf adults by bringing in the NTID and the *Sunshine Too* acting troupe of Deaf performers, as well as Deaf guest speakers for parent workshops and graduation ceremonies; established the NCCD and got that organization to establish an interpreter training program; established the NLCED and got that organization to develop workshops in which teachers, government officials, and parents could participate; hired a skilled dietitian who created a nutritional, delicious, educational dining experience for staff and students; incorporated a pilot project from MUN into the school's preschool program; completely changed the administration; established a means to get the students home to their parents every six weeks; set up annual SAT testing for all the students; and finally ensured that graduates of the NSD would be accepted at various post-secondary institutions. Not a bad first three years of accomplishments during a twenty-three-year tenure as principal. And he lived by the principle he established — by getting government support, establishing a good rapport with parents and the Deaf community.

Never Stop Lobbying:

Due to the promise of a new school, 1982 began with very high morale throughout the school — students, teachers, dorm staff, and parents. However, in politics, promises made during an election are kept about as often as the temperature in the Arctic gets above 30° Celsius.

So Mr. Harkins began to establish a plan to use should the Peckford government decide to renege on its promise of a new NSD. The idea was to set up a letter-writing campaign to the various Members of the House of Assembly (MHA) in each student's electoral district, asking what that individual would do to make sure a new NSD would be built. This campaign included members of the Deaf community and their friends and neighbors, the NSD Parents' Association, interpreters of the NCCD and their friends and relatives, and the NLCED executive, who were also responsible for ensuring that the Newfoundland Teachers' Association was on board with the building of a new NSD.

The reasons for building a new school in a different location were obvious. After all, the buildings the NSD used were only meant to be temporary placements. Since the students and staff moved into those buildings in 1965, that "temporary" placement had stretched to seventeen years. Not only were the buildings unsafe, but being so close to the airport runway most often used was also a cause for concern. Commercial airplanes landing and taking off just 300 feet from the school and residence posed a real danger — one crash could kill everyone inside. But there was another serious hazard: the noise level was often unbearable.

Neither the Liberal government of Joey Smallwood, which opened the NSD, nor the Progressive Conservative government of Frank Moore was concerned by the loudness of jet planes taking off and landing so close to a school for the Deaf; after all, these kids couldn't hear anyway. None of these government officials had a good understanding of sound, I suppose. Because if they did comprehend decibel levels and the damage done to the auditory nerve by extremely high dBs, then they willingly established a situation where children could be permanently damaged and didn't care. Therefore, I chose to believe in their ignorance.

When jet planes take off, they have to rev up their engines. This is a very loud process that caused the windows of the school to vibrate, the air to become pungent with jet exhaust, and the noise level in and around the school to become unbearable. Hearing aids amplify all sounds by as much as 90 dB, but are usually set between 50 and 70 dB. Jet plane engines produce levels of sound between 120 and 140 dB. So students wearing hearing aids at their normal settings could possibly have between 190 and 210 dB of sound going through their auditory nerves into their brains when planes took off or landed. It's no wonder the children often complained of headaches and refused to wear their hearing aids.

This information was pounded into the politicians' heads, figuratively speaking, in an attempt to reinforce their desire to move the NSD to a more suitable location and building.

While that lobbying effort for a new NSD was going on, we continued to develop our courses, preparing senior students to take the public exams, intermediate students to take their SAT tests, and the junior students to stay happy in a supportive, encouraging, yet competitive learning environment. NLCED planned workshops for the teachers during the various breaks every six weeks, extracurricular activities continued to be planned and executed, and staff morale varied according to the temperature of the government.

Although it was unknown by most of us at the time, in 1981, the architectural firm of Sheppard and Associates submitted a proposal to the Peckford government to design a school specifically for Deaf and hard-of-hearing students. They were awarded the contract early in 1982.

Preparation For The New Newfoundland School For The Deaf:

Charlie assembled a committee that consisted of the president of NLCED, the vice-principal of residence, a representative of the Canadian Paraplegic Association (CPA), a representative of the Deaf community, the school's educational audiologist, Beaton Sheppard, and himself. This committee was responsible for helping Mr. Sheppard design the school to meet completely the various needs of teaching Deaf and hard-of-hearing children.

It was proposed that members of the committee and a couple of representatives of the provincial government tour the newest and best schools for the Deaf in North America to get ideas for the construction of the new NSD. From a conversation I had with Beaton Sheppard, the schools they visited were: The Robarts School for the Deaf in London, Ontario; five different schools around New England; the Pennsylvania School for the Deaf in Philadelphia; Western Maryland College; and Gallaudet University. Also, so Beaton could develop a better understanding of what was needed to fit the needs of these special students and teachers, he spent a number of weeks at the NSD, observing classes and sharing time with students and staff in the residence.

By the time Beaton Sheppard was ready to design the new NSD, he had information about wheelchair accessibility from the president of the CPA and a long-time teacher at the NSD; the necessity of sight lines and appropriate lighting without glare from Mrs. Shea (the only Deaf teacher of the Deaf that NSD ever had); the importance of acoustics from the school's educational audiologist; the need for after-school activities from the VP of residence; and the need, rather than the desire, for a theatre designed to meet the needs of a Deaf audience.

From all this information, he decided that it would be appropriate for the areas of the school that created noise (industrial arts, gymnasium, theatre, and generator room) to be separated from the classroom area by a long corridor. Each classroom would have its door at an angle so that noise from other classrooms would be limited. There would be carpeting throughout the school to eliminate reverberation. Each department would have its own set of bathrooms, and there would be areas of natural lighting—what he liked to call "nooks"—one between the intermediate and senior departments and another in the residence between the intermediate and junior dormitories.

The guidance counsellor's office was next to the library and opposite the intermediate classroom pod so that he would be readily available to help control pubescent traumas and dramas, as well as have easy access to conduct any necessary research.

During the week of May 14, 1985, the Department of Public Works and Services called for tenders for the construction of the new NSD. Our school would be 90,000 square feet, cost $10,000,000 to complete, and could accommodate 110 students from across the province, 80 of whom could live in the residence.

In the Department of Education Newsletter, Volume 6, No. 4, of May 1985, they wrote:

Sound

Although located in a central, busy area of the city, there are many architectural features designed to eliminate environmental noise. Such noise creates vibrations that are sensed by the Deaf, which interfere with hearing aids and the audiological equipment in the school.

The buildings, to be placed below street level, are surrounded on two sides by 15-foot-high earth "berms" (an architectural term for a high mound of earth). These features effectively deflect sound over the top of the buildings.

Other provisions for reduction of sound interference include the architectural separation of activity areas in the building, offset doorways in all classrooms, full-height floor-to-roof-deck walls, fully carpeted floors, and specialized surface shapes and textures.

Lighting

For a Deaf person, sight is the most important channel for communication.

Lighting, therefore, becomes one of the most important considerations, as concentrated visual attention is demanded in learning situations. Relatively minor lighting problems can, therefore, cause significant interference in student attentiveness.

Research has shown that illumination levels of 150 foot-candles are the most effective for speech reading. Although this is much higher than normally lit classrooms, provision for this level of illumination has been made in the school's fluorescent lighting system.

This system also includes dimming and spot-lighting capabilities for situations where lip-reading is not required and for situations where simultaneous translation of audiovisual projection is required.

Further lighting control has been gained through the critical placement of windows in north-facing walls, which effectively provide a constant level of diffused light without strong shadows and glare.

Although there were cuts made to the original concept of the new NSD—such as making the theatre seating smaller than originally designed, the gymnasium floor space smaller by one basketball court, and changing the floor covering from hardwood to a linoleum surface with a spongy undercoating—the basic educational and residential design remained intact.

When the tender was called for the building of this version of the NSD, there were more bright smiles among the students and staff of the school than there are lights on Water Street during the Christmas holiday season.

We couldn't wait to move in, and the two years it took to complete seemed to take two decades. When the school closed over the May 24 holiday break in 1987, no one wanted to go home.

We had spent the last couple of months gathering those items we wanted to bring into the new school and discarding those that would be of little benefit in this modern building, built specifically and especially for Deaf and hard of hearing students. Boxes were stacked in each classroom, ready to be picked up by the moving company and distributed into the new NSD.

Then we moved in and were greeted with these sights:

Skylit halls, a resource centre, science and computer labs as well as home economics, the guidance counsellor's office where the round window is, and the intermediate department.
A Bright Beautiful Dining Hall

After moving in and getting the students settled into their new environment, the teachers began allowing the artistic side of the students to shine.

The students painted murals about the stories they were reading or wrote themselves or the science or history they studied.

In the residence, murals were drawn on the walls of the elementary playroom on their bottom floor.

As you can see above, our physical education teacher has a lot of sporting activities going on in the NSD. Softball, badminton, weight lifting, Taekwondo, and, most popular, wheelchair basketball were just some of the sports the students participated in.

Our wheelchair basketball team competed in a number of tournaments and actually won a couple, although I cannot tell you which ones they won.

Taekwondo was started at the school by one of our female teachers who worked in the intermediate department. The school in which she participated needed a different space to train in, and she asked me if they could use our gym three times a week after school hours. I set up a schedule for the various groups who wanted to use the NSD gymnasium to practice and train in, and went from there. Ms.

Peters was involved in a number of activities, and I was asked to interpret for the three intermediate students who became involved in the martial art. So I began interpreting quite often so the students could train. When Ms. Peters left Newfoundland to teach at another school, I became the full-time interpreter, and I thought that perhaps I should join the NSD Taekwondo school as well. So at age 49, I became one of the oldest white belts in Newfoundland.

First Date With My Wife:

If you remember, I said that in 1976, I got married to Carol. Some of the teachers and I would frequent a bar called "The Four Ace" in a mall. Actually, I began going there back in May of 1975, but Carol didn't remember me at all. She said it was because I had long hair pulled back into a ponytail, a goatee, and a mustache, and she just did not like "hippies." In September of 1976, I was getting paid on a regular basis, had my dream job, was playing handball three times a week, going for long walks with Ferd and our dogs, bought some new clothes, and got a haircut.

One Tuesday evening in early March, around 5:00 PM, Reg and I were having a few beers and discussing the students who were acting up at the school. Carol was serving us. I told her that I thought she was very attractive and that I'd like to get to know her. She basically said something like, "Go fly a kite!" When she brought us our third or fourth beer, she overheard me tell Reg that this was my last one because I had to get Mandrake out for a walk. She said, "How long has your dog been locked up in your apartment?" I said, "Since 8:30 this morning." She replied, "If you let me take this beer you just bought and toss it down the sink, I'll consider going out with you." I said, "Okay, I'll see you later, bye, Reg."

So I went home and got Mandrake. We went for a long walk, then about an hour and a half later, I returned to the bar with Mandrake. I asked Carol for some water for my dog and told her that there was a Barbra Streisand movie playing at the Arts and Culture Centre the next night. Would she go with me? She said she would, and that was the beginning of our relationship.

I brought some popcorn with me when I picked her up, and popped two large brown paper bags full. One for Carol's family and the other for us to take to the ACC. After all, one cannot go to a movie without eating popcorn, right? Well, Carol thought that was a foolish thing to do because the ushers wouldn't let us into the theatre with a bag of popcorn. She was wrong. The movie was *Funny Girl*, and some of my favourite Streisand songs were in that movie: *People, Don't Rain on My Parade*, and *My Man*. The people sitting around us smelled the popcorn and turned around to look at us. So, naturally, I passed the bag around our area and shared most of it. When we got it back, there was maybe a quarter of the bag left.

After the movie, we met Reg and his newest girlfriend at a club near my apartment. We had one drink and left for my place so I could let Mandrake out again. What really impressed me about Carol was that Mandrake took an instant liking to her. He would start wagging his tail when he saw her and never barked at her. However, the same couldn't be said for Reg's new girlfriend. He was very wary of her.

I always wanted to be able to say to my guests, "What would you like to drink?" and have any kind of alcohol and mix that they would want. So I bought a flask of everything: vodka, Scotch, rye, rum, gin, Tia Maria, and a bottle each of Piat d'Or white wine, red wine, sweet vermouth, and a dozen beers. When I asked Carol what she would like to drink, she said, "Yes." So, being a wise guy, I poured a bottle cap of each kind of alcohol I had into a large glass with a lot of ice. Naturally, she refused to drink it, so I had to try it. I wound up throwing it down the drain. If I recall correctly, she wound up having a Scotch and water.

I had a small cassette player, put on *Chicago Transit Authority's* first album, and we danced to it. Reg and his girlfriend left early, then Carol had to go to the Four Ace to close up, so the three of us piled into my new car, a blue VW, and drove to the club. After she closed up, she took the cash in a deposit bag and dropped it into the Canadian Imperial Bank of Commerce slot. I then drove her home — but not directly. I thought I'd show off how fast Mandrake was, so I let him out of the car and had him follow us. I went up a hill and decided to drive down a small alley behind the new City Hall building. Big mistake. The alley turned into a path that went sideways down a hill, and the car began to lean down toward the top of the building. Carol demanded that I stop and let her out. I did. Then I tried to back up out of danger. That didn't work either, so I also got out.

By now, it was nearing 2:00 AM, and I needed to get someone to tow my car out of danger. We weren't far from Carol's house, so we walked there to use her phone. All I can say is that Carol's mother was not pleased that I brought her daughter home at such a late hour and let me know it without mincing any words. I recall her saying, "You brazen son of a bitch, get the hell out of here!" She did relent enough for me to use her phone book, and fortunately, there was a 24-hour towing service just down the street from City Hall. As I was leaving, Carol asked me to call her and let her know we got home safe and sound. So Carol and I ended our first date on that cheery note, and I walked back to my car to await the tow truck.

That little adventure cost me a fair amount of cash, but the car was saved, and Mandrake and I went home. After getting ready for bed, I called Carol to let her know we were safe and sound. Then we began to talk about the discussion we had between dances — whether or not it was all right to burp and/or fart in your own home and not excuse yourself. Yes, a stupid argument, but fun, and we continued that talk for another half hour until Carol's mother told her to hang up and "…let that poor man get some sleep before he went to work." We did, and I slept straight through until 8:00. Three whole hours. Then I got up, let Mandrake out, took a fast shower, gave him some food and water, whistled for him to come back home, got some toast, and made it to the school just before class time.

We dated exclusively from that time on until June of that year. After another long night, I rolled over in bed and asked Carol to marry me. She said, "Are you serious?" I said, "Of course." Then she said, "Yes." We were going to have a small, quiet wedding with only our mothers, Carol's daughter Holly, the maid of honour, and the best man present. So after the NSD closed for the summer break, I went home to bring my mother up for the wedding.

My sister and brother-in-law began to make hurried plans to come up to Newfoundland for my wedding. Although I would have loved to have had them there with me, since it was only going to be a small, intimate affair, I talked them out of changing their original vacation plans. I told them it would be better if they took their time and came up for a nice, long, relaxing vacation the next year.

My Dad And I Were More Alike Than I Thought:

When we were discussing our wedding plans, I thought it would be cool to be married at Flatrock, where there was an outdoor Grotto with an altar and the Stations of the Cross winding around a rocky hill. It's beautiful. Carol liked the idea as well, so we made arrangements to speak with the parish priest about it.

The priest declined to allow us to have our wedding there and refused to preside over it. I assumed that he probably didn't want to make it a precedent; however, what he said was, "We don't present the sacraments outdoors, so your wedding is out of the question." Well, his lie burned my butt, and I said something like, "That's horse shit. I was in the service and took communion outdoors. Isn't that a sacrament? The Marine Corps priest had no qualms about doing that." The priest didn't care for my response to his lie and said something like we shouldn't even be allowed to be married in the Catholic

Church. Bottom line, we had to get married in the Marion Chapel in the Basilica. So, we had our first date in March of 1976 and got married on August 27, 1976. That was 49 years ago at the time of this written account.

Famous Actors In Newfoundland:

Around April of that year, the big news around the province was that the Dino De Laurentiis Company was going to film a major motion picture in... Newfoundland.

The film was **Orca** and starred Richard Harris, Keenan Winn, Will Sampson, Bo Derek, and Charlotte Rampling.

The company rented out a floor in the Newfoundland Hotel for most of the cast and crew. Carol's brother, Robert, was playing in a band called

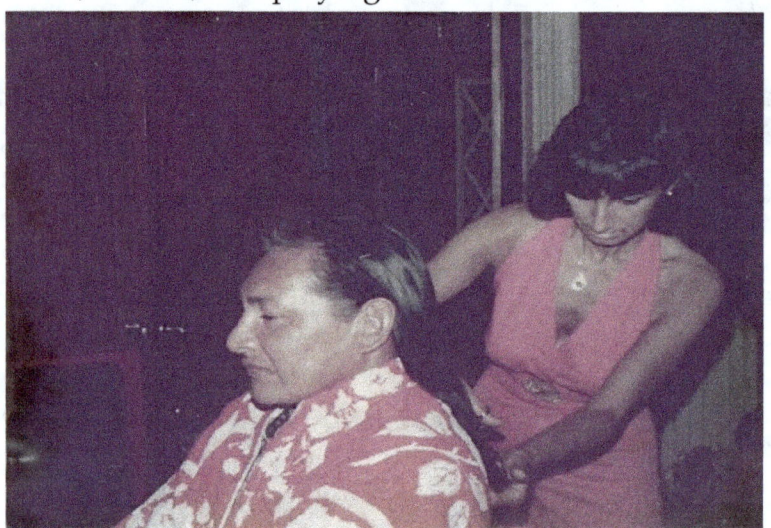 

The Echoes that had a long-term gig at the hotel's bar, The Killock.

Well, Kennan Winn began coming to the bar just to listen to them and struck up a conversation with the boys, Bob McDonald, Wally Cobb and naturally Robert, who was the drummer, front man and did impersonations.

The band had to play until 1:00 and at 12, Robert called his mother and asked her to make a Lebanese meal for the boys and a surprise guest.

Around 1:30 in walked Robert, Wally, Bob and Keenan. Carol got a phone call, she called me and we went to the party as well, after she picked up our go-to sitter.

Kennan asked Robert if he wanted to come to the next day's shoot and meet some other members of the cast.

Naturally, he accepted the invitation and a friendship between the two began.

For the rest of the time the film was being done, Kennan Winn and Robert partied at home, and Robert's mother, Mary, made many dinners of Lebanese cuisine.

Some of the film crew had accommodations at the Battery Hotel.

One evening, Carol, her friend and her aunt went to the Battery Hotel for drinks.

While there, Carol saw Will Sampson talking with a couple of men at an adjacent table.

We both had seen the movie *One Flew Over the Cuckoo's Nest* recently and were impressed with Mr. Sampson's height and acting.

So Carol decided to try and meet him.

She got a stick of Juicy Fruit gum out of her purse, walked over to the table and said, "Gum?"

At the same time, she offered him the stick of Juicy Fruit. If you've seen the film, you know the significance of that question.

He laughed quite hardily, but one of the men sitting with him became very annoyed and told her she was rude for interrupting their conversation.

Carol replied, "Well, if I didn't interrupt you, I wouldn't have been able to meet you, would I?" Will Sampson laughed again and asked her to join them.

She did.

They also became friends, close enough so that Will let her cut his and his son's hair.

Carol also showed Will and his son how to eat Newfoundland lobster with taboulé and baked potato.

The Wedding Plans Change:

So, as Mom and I began our journey to Newfoundland, Carol and her family were having a good time with various members of the cast of *Orca*, while Carol's friends and other family members decided that we were NOT going to have a small, quiet wedding. No, sir, they planned an entirely different occasion.

One longtime family friend, Pat Sheen, told Carol, "By God, if you're not having a wedding party, I'm having one without you." Pat was a chef with Marine Atlantic and had a very nice home in Mount Pearl. His downstairs was decorated like a disco club, and that was where they decided to hold the reception. Pat also catered our reception at a cost of $100.00, and he gave Carol $3.00 change. That included a full turkey dinner, prime rib, and a large wedding cake. The beer distributors for the club contributed two cases of their product and we bought spirits and wine. So all in all we spent nearly $400.00.

Pat's wife, Muriel, set up the living room so that the dinner could be a buffet style and she sprayed CONGRATULATIONS, JOHN AND CAROL, on the mirror. Although I was a bit miffed that our original plans had been changed because my sister's family wouldn't be there to witness my marriage, I got over it. Especially when my mother became a fan of Carol's uncle Mickey, who was one of the band members and was a very good vocalist. She especially liked his rendition of *Ave Maria*. Every time he began to sing, Mom got tears in her eyes. That's Uncle Mickey below, wiping a tear from his eye.

Oh yes, the band that played at our wedding; they were THE cream of the crop when speaking about Newfoundland musicians. Carol's family were all musicians; her uncles had a band called the Michales' band from the 1940s through to the '60s. They were so popular that they played everywhere around the Island. Her uncle Freddy travelled around Newfoundland and Labrador with Frank Sinatra's band during World War II when Frank visited the US Servicemen who were stationed in Newfoundland. Her brother-in-law, George "Buddy" Pennington, was a drummer in the United States Air Force Band with Leo Sanderval, a trumpet player and Ralph Walker, a jazz pianist. I already told you about her brother, Robert's band, who impressed Keenan Wynn, another brother, Vince, played saxophone, and finally, the last member of our marriage band was her oldest brother, Frank, who began playing drums as a teenager with Michael's band and toured with them as well.

They were all well known amongst the working musicians of Newfoundland, and there were so many musicians at the reception, the music literally did not stop. When one member took a break, he was immediately replaced by another very talented musician. In the picture, the guitar player is Bill Burke, behind him on the drums is Frank, playing sax is Vince, on the keyboard is Ralph Walker, and blowing the trumpet is Leo Sanderval.

Carol's matron of honour was her oldest sister, Mona. Many years before our marriage, Carol spent some time at Mona's home in Tucson, Arizona. While visiting, Carol discovered that Mona's husband was not the kind of man the family thought he was, and Carol was distraught about her discovery. She mentioned her concerns to Mona and, as I understand it, that initiated a conflict between the two sisters. Carol thought that if she asked Mona to be the matron of honour, they'd end their feud. Although she was nervous about asking her, Carol finally phoned Mona and talked about her presence as part of the wedding. It worked. They buried the hatchet.

My best man was my last roommate and the vice-principal of the NSD who greeted me at the school the day I arrived, Reg. Mom really liked Reg and was pleased that I had made such a good friend so quickly in Newfoundland. Reg was a very good hockey player, actor, teacher, administrator and friend. We shared a house near the university and Health Science Centre for a few months after I met Carol.

The picture is our wedding ceremony.

The priest is Father Green, Mona in Yellow, Carol, me, Holly and Reg. The picture was taken after the ceremony with our mothers looking very pleased (hmm, maybe not), Holly looking very bored (hmm, very obvious), Carol looking scared about taking this big step and me looking very pleased with myself for marrying a beautiful woman, with my mother by my side and getting one up on my mother-in-law (hahahah).

Actually, Carol's mother was a big help to us.

After school, Holly would walk down the hill to 199 Gower Street, Sittie's home, where she'd wait for me to pick her up after I was done teaching at the NSD. The picture was taken at our house on Portugal Cove Road. We had just got done moving in and were celebrating. Mom scrubbed all our cupboards and sat down on our couch. Reg and I decided to sandwich her while we each had a drink and I was telling them a story about our honeymoon.

Honeymoon?

One might ask, "Where did you go on your honeymoon?" Our answer would be, "Clarenville." Yes, that's where we decided to spend our first few nights as a married couple, the Holiday Inn in Clarenville, because it was close enough to drive in Carol's 1965 Buick Skylark convertible, it had a swimming pool and a decent restaurant.

Unfortunately, after we took a swim in the pool, Carol got sick and spent the rest of the first day of our honeymoon in bed.

I brought her food and drinks, but she preferred to sleep. So that night I watched hockey in the hotel's lounge and had a number of drinks.

The next day, we drove to Gander where there were stores open on Sunday and bought some medicine for Carol.

Even though she was very sick, she posed for a picture at the Gander Airport Monument, looking beautiful as a model, don't you agree? `

The day after the picture was taken, we returned to St. John's and began moving into our first and only home.

Carol at Gander Airport

58 Portugal Cove Road:

Funny thing about our house, we bought it before we were married, and I agreed to the purchase sight unseen.

Well, that's not exactly right, we bought it from a woman who was a regular at the Four Ace Lounge and who had us to her home for a couple of parties. I did agree to the purchase over a phone call from Carol, who said, "I found a house for us.

It's in the East end of the city, has a good fire place, floors strong enough to hold your water bed and a big backyard for Mandrake to roam around in. We've been in it before, it's Liz's old house." I asked, "How much?" She said, "$46,500." I said, "Buy it!" We're still living in it all these years later, and it's still strong enough to hold a water bed, the fire place still works well, the back yard is too damned big for me to mow anymore and the only animal we acquired ourselves is a Tuxedo cat we call Max although he was originally named Gilbert. However, we've been adopted by our neighbour's elderly grey cat named Bo.

Using What I Learned Working My Way Through College:

When we were younger, I did most of the repair and renovations myself. We had a very small deck in the back of our house, which was not useful at all; so I spent our first winter together cutting down trees at my friend Mike's property. He and I designed a deck and planned out what lumber I'd need, and where to get the trees milled. That spring, I loaded a trailer with ten foot logs and took them to a mill in Torbay. So for about $300.00, I had the necessary wood for my back deck. Then that summer, I built a deck that was 46 feet long, 10 feet wide and 10 feet off the ground. I used creosote as a preserve, and the deck lasted for over 35 years; albeit with a couple of add ons and repairs. The next year, I built the decks we still have in front of the house. They're over 45 years old and only had a few 2X4 boards replaced. Oh yeah, the railing on one deck was removed and not replaced.

Five years after moving in, I had to re-shingle our roof. I hired one of my students to help, rented scaffolding and did the roof. The shingles had a 25 year guarantee, but they lasted 34 years because I used so much roofing tar.

Some of my other handiwork was to put in a pedestal sink, install a lighted medicine cabinet above said sink, and generally do whatever repairs had to be made around the place.

Having all those "Joe Jobs" that I had working may way through college certainly paid off. Now, I can just barely crawl under the kitchen sink to tighten a nut. Age!

Although your mind says you can do something, your body tells you to "pack off."

Lesley Is Born:

In 1977, Carol became pregnant. She was a bit skittish about telling me because she thought I wanted to wait until my additional probation was completed thus job secure, but I was very excited to hear that news. I wanted at least a son and a daughter and would have welcomed more; however, Carol had a different mindset. So after our daughter, Lesley Marie, was born on March 16, 1978, Carol had a tubal ligation. I can understand why she didn't want to give birth to more children, it was obviously very painful for her. I am still amazed at how strong her grip became as she squeezed my ring hand and during the final push, bit my stomach. I still have a mark there.

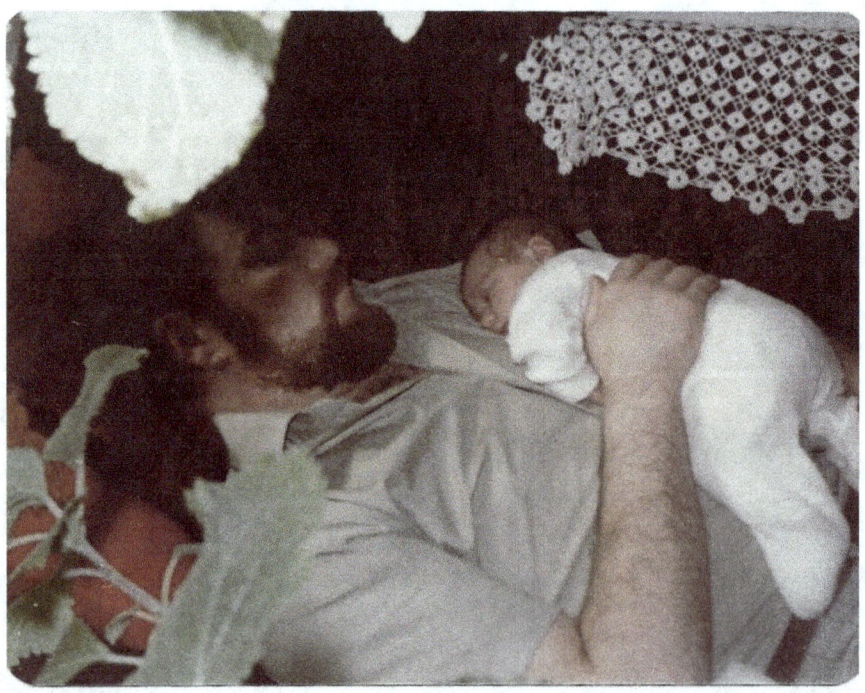

To say I was proud to be a father is like saying it's good to be alive. Carol refused to breastfeed, so I gave Lesley her first meal. I also went into the nursery at the Grace Hospital and changed my daughter's diaper, washed and dressed her. Since Carol had to recuperate from the tubal ligation, we came home from the hospital ten days later. We knew we would need a permanent baby sitter because Carol could not take any time off from the club. She was responsible for doing the ordering of goods and all the administrative work. As a matter of fact, the day after giving birth, her brother, Vince. phoned me and told me to bring the club's books to her to update and write the cheques to pay the staff. Her brother-in-law, Buddy Pennington, who usually did the books, was on an extended holiday down in the states and her brother didn't know how nor was he interested in learning how. So that was left for Carol to do.

There was my wife, just after giving birth, propped up in her hospital bed, the utility tray across her middle, an accountant's book open and the cheque book resting underneath that book checking all the figures on her calculator and entering them in the appropriate place in that large book. There was nothing I could do to help, so I just took Lesley and did whatever I could with her. After three days of paternity leave, actually just given time off by Charlie, I went back to the NSD, but I left as soon as I could when my duties were over, again with Charlie's permission.

We decided to ask my mother if she'd be willing to come back to Newfoundland for a year or so to help us out. She jumped at the chance. Not only to help us out, but she developed a strong friendship with Carol's sister, Rita. So during the day, Mom would take care of Lesley, and at night, she'd go to Rita's club on Water Street and "help" out. Of course she'd also help out with our house as well. While Lesley was sleeping, Mom would clean the house and prepare supper for us. Holly still walked to Sittie's house when she was finished school.

Here's a picture of Sittie holding Lesley on her living room couch one Friday evening. Sometimes, we'd all gather there for a Lebanese meal that Sittie would make. Usually she'd cook for her son and his family, but at times there would be Mom, Carol, Holly, me, Frank, Paul, Denise, Frankie and Darrin. Cooking never seemed to faze Mary Cromwell.

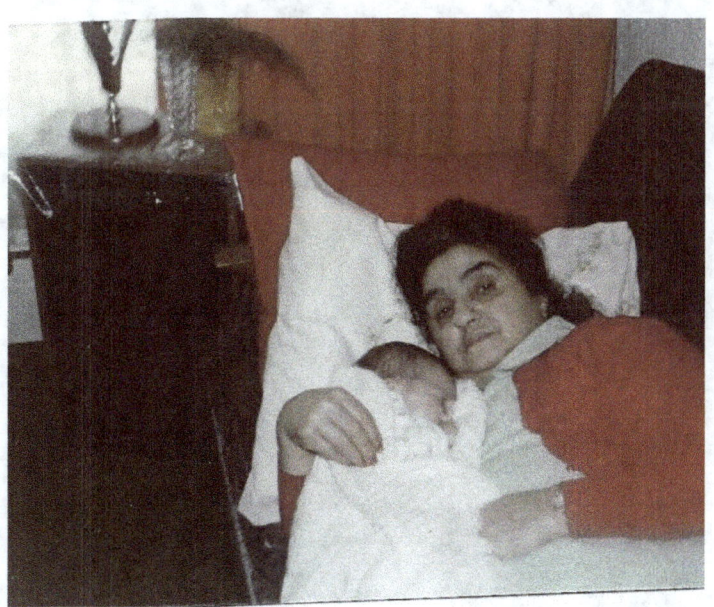

Lesley was precocious and took her first steps at nine months of age. Carol had her standing alone in our hallway and stepped back a bit holding out her hands. Lesley walked 3 steps toward her hands. Carol yelled loudly to me to come and watch. Her very excited and LOUD yell caused Lesley to promptly sit down and crawl again. She didn't walk by herself for two more months.

A few months after Lesley was born, I decided to grow a beard. It was a full beard with different coloured hair, brown, red, and black. I liked it, Carol liked it, Holly didn't care and the students at the NSD didn't mind. As for my beard, well all was well for two years until I got involved in a drama production at the NSD. I was to play a native American in the trilogy *Rare Earth*. Since "Indians" didn't have facial hair, I had to shave my beard off. Lesley was about three then, I believe. I cut off my beard in our bathroom, then shaved my face clean. When I left, Lesley was walking down the hallway to her bedroom when I went to pick her up and give her a hug.

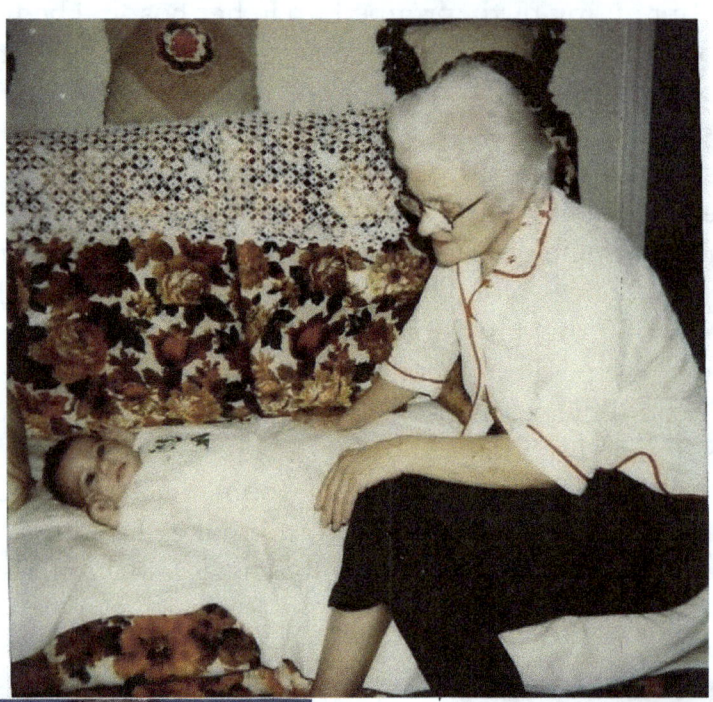

She screamed, "NO, you're not my Daddy!" Then struggled out of my arms and ran to her mother. All during supper, she stared at me. That night, I read her a book and put her to bed; she finally accepted that I was really her father.

I brought Lesley to the NSD right after Carol got home from the hospital and just before I returned to teaching full time again. Huh, did I say I was a very proud father? I still am. Carol dressed her up in her favourite colour, yellow. I think she might have had some pink on as well, don't really remember very clearly, but I brought her all around the school and even over to the residence, where I had some friends and colleagues. Naturally, I was looking for compliments about how good I did and how beautiful our daughter was. I got what I wanted, then went home.

A picture of Carol holding Lesley after she was christened.

That's how small she was when I took her to NSD. This was one of the happiest times in my life. I had my mother living with us, a beautiful, accomplished wife, two daughters, a job that I really enjoyed, good health, the ability to do house repairs, a couple of friends, nice home, freshly cut lumber for a new back deck, some success at handball tournaments, and knowing that my sister and her family were planning a summer time visit. As Aku used to say, "Life, you are SOOO sweet."

Mom Could Be One Of The Golden Girls - Sophia:

As I said previously, Mom developed a strong relationship with Carol's sister, Rita. On Friday nights, Mom used to love going down to Rita's bar for a drink or two, help out behind the bar, and talk to the Spanish and Portuguese fishermen who frequented the place when they had shore leave. Mom spoke fluent Italian, studied Spanish in high school, and could get by in Portuguese, and she absolutely loved to listen to the men's stories about their home and fishing in the North Atlantic.

Well, one Friday after supper in the summer, I drove Mom down to the Night Cap. She usually would call me for a ride home around 1:00 after the bar closed, but this night, no phone call. Carol and I waited for another hour, then called the bar. Got no answer. Just after we hung up, our phone rang. I thought it was Mom calling back. Nope, it was Ed, Rita's husband, asking if Rita was with us. We told him she wasn't, but I would drive down to the bar and check things out. And that's what I did. There was no sign of them, the bar was locked up, and looked as if it had been cleaned and was ready for the next day. Now I got worried!

I went back home and called Ed back to let him know that when we heard something, we'd call him. Then we waited, and waited, and stayed up all night waiting for my mother to contact us. Around 10:00 that morning, a taxi stopped in front of our house, Mom got out, holding her purse on her right arm, walked to the door, but before she used her key, we opened the door for her. Before we could ask her where she was all night, Mom said, "Pay the taxi, I'm going to bed." Now if you ever saw the television show *The Golden Girls*, Mom looked and acted just like the mother figure of the show, Sophia, especially at that moment. So I got my wallet and paid the taxi, over $20.00.

Carol followed her up the hall to her room and said, "Here, you can't just go to bed and not tell us where you were. We stayed up all night, worried to death."

Mom said, "I'll tell you later," and went to bed.

Finally, around 2:00 in the afternoon, Mom got up, made coffee, had her usual spoon of rye, and came into the living room with us. Carol said, "So, where were you until 10:00 this morning?"

"On board a Spanish ship."

"On board a Spanish ship until 10:00 in the morning?!!"

"Yep. Well maybe more like 9:30," said Mom.

Carol said, "Why did you go on to a Spanish ship?"

"Well, I couldn't let Rita go by herself, besides I was having fun talking with them."

"Why did it cost so much for the taxi?"

"I took Rita home first."

Then Carol said, "Do you realize that if anybody saw you getting off a Spanish ship at 10:00 in the morning, do you know that half the people in St. John's know your son? It would have been a scandal."

"We had a good time, and they were really nice to us."

A week or so later, we all got really sick and I kept saying, "You got the Spanish flu and shared it with all of us." We were so sick that Carol asked her brother-in-law, Buddy, to pick up the medicine we needed. He did and handed it to us through the door; he was taking no chance of getting it himself.

We were ill, the girls, Carol, Mom and me, for over a week.

Later that summer, my sister and her family came to visit. With the help of Skeets, I had the back deck finished, except for the stairs. I was trying to figure out how to build them when Robert and MaryLou, Buddy, Kathy, LeeAnn and Debbie arrived.

After getting the family settled, we made a large supper and went out on the deck for a liquid dessert for the adults and ice cream for the kids. I told Robert about my dilemma with the stairs, and he said that in the morning, we'll get the necessary lumber and build the steps. The morning arrived and we went out to measure the area where the steps would go. We then had some coffee and with LeeAnn and Buddy with us, Robert and I went to Chester Dawe's to get what we needed. We finished the stairs over the next two days, and they were strong enough to have lasted longer than the deck as a whole. As a matter of fact, I still use two of the steps to hold open my shed doors.

Both Buddy and LeeAnn passed their driver's license test that year before they came up for a visit. At that time, I had a yellow 1974 Pontiac Astre, four on the floor, that I allowed both LeeAnn and Buddy to drive.

One day, they asked to borrow my car to drive around downtown St. John's. They wanted to look for souvenirs to take back with them. When they returned, Buddy, who was driving, said there must be something wrong with the transmission because it was running very slow. So Robert and I went out to check on the car. I got in, started it up, and drove off. The clutch seemed to be slipping, so I took it directly to the mechanic Carol and I had been using since we tied the knot. Vic took a look and said the clutch needed to be replaced soon. Since the car was only a couple of years old, I wondered why that had happened. So I made arrangements to bring it in after my sister's family returned to Pennsylvania.

Later that day, LeeAnn told me that Buddy used to put the hand brake on when they were stopped at an intersection on the many hills in this city. The car seemed to lose speed after stopping on the road to Signal Hill. So what probably happened was that Buddy never fully released the hand brake and ruined my clutch as well as the hand brake. Just another financial setback that we had to handle.

My Fiftieth Birthday - Ouch:

Although my nieces and nephews never got back to Newfoundland and Labrador, ML and Robert would visit us again—for my 50th birthday in 1996.

That birthday was memorable for a number of reasons: their visit, the end-of-the-year party at Sue and Ann's house, and pulling a muscle in my back while helping a colleague out of their home via the back door. We had to use the back door because Jane's mobility was in a wheelchair, and the front door was inundated with shoes, so couldn't get through. I helped Jane for over twenty years and knew I'd have no problem getting her to her car; unfortunately, Ann's back stairs were broken. When we reached the missing step, I nearly threw Jane out of her wheelchair, but by avoiding that accident, a muscle in my back was pulled.

I have a fairly high tolerance for pain, and the pulled muscle didn't bother me for nearly a week. BUT, after ML and Robert got here, the back began to really hurt. Robert and I were cooking steaks on the BBQ and having a beer, but I couldn't sit down or carry on a conversation with him due to the pain. Finally, I went into my bedroom and got into a bastardized fetal position for relief. ML came in, saw me, and said, "Enough! I'm calling an ambulance." She did, and I was transported to the Health Sciences Centre. ML, Carol, and Robert followed and accompanied me to the emergency room.

There, a resident doctor evaluated me and decided that the best way to treat me was with a shot of Demerol. I was lying on my side, in a similar position to that in the bedroom, when this young doctor approached with a needle. He exposed my buttocks, wiped an area with an alcohol swab, and proceeded to poke that area with the needle. Unfortunately, my muscles were so tight that the needle bent, much to the surprise of all who witnessed it. The poor guy just smiled, shook his head, and got another needle. Then, after massaging a part of the buttocks, he cleaned the area and tried again. Success! Thirty minutes later, my pain was gone. What a welcome to my senior years!

Development Professionally:

Professionally, my forties and fifties were extremely good. In 1987, Jane Peters and I became the editors and distributors of *The Association of Canadian Educators of the Hearing Impaired (ACEHI)* newsletter. We gathered information related to Deaf education around the world and wrote articles about it; persuaded other educators of the Deaf from the eight other provincial schools for the Deaf to write stories about their classroom experiences; and took turns writing editorials. We did this for seven years.

I was elected as the Newfoundland Director for ACEHI in 1989. Jane House was the previous director and laid the groundwork for NSD to host the association's Biennial National Convention. Traditionally, the host province of the ACEHI convention also had the National Director of the Association, and Mr. Harkins was nominated for the position in 1987. He ran against Joyce Gillis from Nova Scotia. I assume that because she was better known by the 450 members from the other provinces, she won, and Mr. Harkins became the first host of the convention without being the National Director. In my opinion, a grave misjustice.

I was responsible for inviting various representatives from governmental agencies. I wrote letters to the Minister of Education, the Member of Parliament for St. John's East, as well as the MP for St. John's West, and the mayors of St. John's and Mount Pearl. Only the Minister of Education rejected our request—initially. I got this changed serendipitously.

My neighbour, Norm Kipnis, had a yacht that was moored at the Royal St. John's Yacht Club. Often, I was his crew member. The Premier at the time, Clyde Wells, also stored his yacht there. One early spring day, I was with Norm at the club and spotted Premier Wells tying his yacht to the dock. I meandered over and offered to lend a hand, and he accepted. I introduced myself and asked if he had received our invitation to welcome our keynote speakers at the convention. He said that he had not read it, but because it was an educational issue, he forwarded it to Minister Warren.

I told him who they were and their significance and importance to the research and application of Deaf studies worldwide. I told him who our keynote speakers were:

I.   Dr. I. K Jordan, Ph.D. – President of Gallaudet University
II.   Frank Bowe, Ph.D., LLD. – Professor at Hofstra University in New York
III.   Dr. E. Ross, Ph.D. – Director of the Office of Integrated Research at the National Technical Institute for the Deaf in Rochester, New York

I also told him that this was an international convention with over 150 delegates already booked to participate. I then asked him directly if he would honor us with his presence by welcoming the guest speakers and opening the conference. He asked when it would be. I told him the dates, and he said that he had to attend the Premier's meeting in Ottawa but would send the Minister of Education in his stead. He did, much to the chagrin of Mr. Warren, whom I had initially asked to attend and who had rejected the invitation.

The convention was a four-day affair. Most of the attendees arrived on Wednesday evening. We had set up a greeting committee to meet the attendees at the airport and bring them to their hotels or to the residence if they had previously requested and paid for it. As I stated earlier, we had nearly 150 participants, and about 75 stayed in the residence. Our three keynote speakers had the option of staying in one of our honors students' apartments or in one of the hotels. They all stayed in our apartments.

We had the best sign language interpreters in Canada for the conference, and they earned their pay as well as added to their reputation. One of our socials was a "Screech-In." All three of our keynote speakers participated, two of whom were Deaf. David Still, the man NCCD hired to train and establish their interpreter services, had the distinction of interpreting for this event.

Dr. Frank Bowe   *Dr. I. K Jordan*

"Screech-Ins" consist of four parts: Kiss a Cod, Eat" Newfie Steak" (Maple Leaf Bologna), drink a shot of Screech (rum), and repeat a Newfoundland saying, which usually ends with "Long may your big jib furl." Newfoundlanders have a distinct accent and unique colloquial language, and the people from Ontario, BC, NB, and especially the USA have a difficult time understanding what is being said. But the really difficult part was Dave interpreting the saying so that the Deaf participants, including me, King Jordan and Frank Bowe, could TRY to repeat it verbally and in sign. Suffice to say, it was one of the highlights of the convention.

At the convention of 1989, candidates for National Director were brought forward, and the winner was Loretta from Quebec. Her brother was Deaf and became the first Deaf Principal of the Alberta School for the Deaf, and as far as I know, the first Deaf principal of a school in Canada. Loretta was National Director from 1989 until 1991.

After the '89 conventions, I needed a break and decided to take Lesley on a trip to see my sister and other family members. In 1987, there was a movie called Planes, Trains, and Automobiles. We all went to see it and really liked it; so much so, that when it became available on VCR, we rented it a number of times. So for our trip to Pennsylvania, I decided to take Lesley on our own Planes, Trains, and Automobiles adventure. I booked us airline tickets to Boston's Logan Airport with the idea that we could take a train to New York's Grand Central Station and from there rent a car to drive to Martin's Creek.

Lesley and I at Uncle Earl's

The flight into Boston was perfect, but we arrived too late to take the train into New York and arrive with enough time to rent a car and drive to Pennsylvania, so we got a room at the Holiday Inn. I then got the hotel receptionist to help me book two tickets on the computer train to New York. At 8:00 the next morning, we got a taxi to the train station and boarded the commuter to New York. Three and a half hours later, we walked through Grand Central Station into the bright sun, looking for a car rental place. There were taxis at the station as well as a limousine. I asked the driver how much it would cost us to take that to Pennsylvania. Surprisingly enough, the cost was $60.00 an hour, so for $180. 00, we could take that to Easton and have my sister pick us up. The car rental with a drop off was only a few dollars cheaper, so we took the limo.

Back To Work Prepare To Retire From Nsd:

The next ACEHI convention was held in Calgary, Alberta. Three of the keynote speakers were people I knew fairly well: Jerome Schein, who held the David Piekoff Chair of Deafness at the University of Calgary, and the person I met and discussed in depth the pros and cons of using educational interpreters. He and I shared the opinion that they were great in a university setting and sometimes in high school; however, they were not appropriate to use any earlier in the child's education. He published an interesting study of educational interpreting in Northern Alberta and Northern Manitoba. It was very revealing.

Roger Carver was a Deaf man with an M.Ed. and worked as the Executive Director of the Deaf Children's Society of British Columbia. He was also at the conference we hosted in '89 and thoroughly enjoyed being Screeched-In. We shared a few beers together while discussing a variety of topics.

Finally, there was Dr. Ann Kennedy, who at that time was the Director of Services for the Calgary Board of Education. During one of our private talks over a beer for me and a glass of Sherry for her, she said that she was very grateful that I didn't drop out of the LAC program and had passed the oral exams. She also said that I surprised her with my accomplishments with ACEHI and NSD. And, finally, she said, probably because she got a little drunk, that I became her favorite graduate. Yeah right…But I have to admit that I was pleased she said that to me.

At that convention, I had the great opportunity to do some team interpreting with the only person who, very probably, was a more skilled interpreter than David Still, Debbie Russell. We stood on each side of the corral in which the Calgary Covered Wagon Race would take place and described the rationale for such a race, what was about to happen and what to look for. Let me tell you, the place was hot, dusty, and smelled of horse and cow manure; however, I really enjoyed that experience.

Earlier that year, I was nominated for National Director by Irvin McDonald from the Maritimes. Again, because I was a known name due to my work as co-editor and co-publisher of the Newsletter, as well as being the Newfoundland Director for four years, I was elected.

The people with whom I'd be working consisted of a variety of expertise in Deaf Education: from Alberta - Kathryn Britton, who was an educational research instructor at the University of Alberta; Manitoba - Nancy Schenkeveld, who was a teacher at the Manitoba School for the Deaf and adhered to the bi-bi form of instruction; Maritimes - Irvin McDonald (Deaf teacher of the Deaf at ISD) and Barry Imber, teacher and administrator at ISD; Newfoundland - Dianne Mark, experienced kindergarten teacher from NSD; Ontario - Jean Staley and Jean Biro, both teachers of the Deaf at two different schools in Ontario; Pacific - Karen Taylor (hard of hearing who had her own preschool program (I believe) and Claire Anderson, teacher of the Deaf at the Jericho Hill School for the Deaf; Quebec - Penny Packard, bi-lingual teacher of the Deaf at the Montreal Oral School; and Saskatchewan-North - Helen Galbraith teacher at the School for the

Deaf in Regina and Lois Roberge, an itinerant teacher. Finally, there was Loretta, an administrator at two different schools for the Deaf and me, who taught a variety of courses as well as an administrator, albeit in a residence. All of these positions demonstrate that this executive was very diverse in our chosen field. We had representation from the Deaf community, the Hard of Hearing community, teachers who used the oral method with their children, teachers who used the bi-social/bilingual method, teachers who used the concept of total communication, and representation from the administrative aspect of schools.

The picture is one of the many meetings of my colleagues of ACEHI: bottom left, Nance, Kathryn in red, Penny in green, Barry at the head of table, Loretta, past national director in white, and last Jean Biro. I believe we were discussing the concept of writing a Statement of Values that the organization believed in.

To my everlasting gratitude, Kathryn asked me if I wanted to see some of the tourist sites Alberta has to offer. I gladly accepted.

Here's Catherine picking me up at my hotel.

These are pictures of the places we visited.

Fairmont Hotel at Lake Louise

The National Director is responsible for overseeing all the money that is received and distributed by the Association. In the past, the spouse of the Director acted as the accountant, and so did Carol. Her expertise in bookkeeping is second to none, and Carol's report stunned everyone on the executive team in its comprehensiveness.

During my term, a number of interesting things happened. First, the membership grew to 473, the most ever, even though the R.J.D. Williams School for the Deaf had closed the previous year. However, that closure had a silver lining for ACEHI; the alumni and staff gifted us enough money to create the R.J.D. The Williams Scholarship was to be presented to the educator who developed a unique educational program for the Deaf. Carol set up an account with that money so that the interest accrued from the initial donation would be sufficient to cover the amount of the award. The first recipient was Karen Taylor.

Second, we created the ACEHI Statement of Values, which in part was derived from the NSD philosophy of education. In my opinion, the first two statements are the most important:

1. ACEHI advocates optimal education of deaf and hard-of-hearing students. This is a placement where: *Ability to Achieve = Possibility to Achieve.*
2. ACEHI advocates the involvement of a qualified educator of the deaf and hard of hearing (an ACEHI-certified educator) in any decision-making regarding the education of deaf and hard-of-hearing students.

Third, we got the constitution translated into French by our Quebec representative.

Fourth, we developed an amendment to the constitution to change the name of the Association to better reflect the importance of the Deaf Community in their children's education.

Oh yes, fifth, we revised the requirements for teacher certification from the Association and presented them to the participants of the 1993 Biennial Convention in Montreal. They were not adopted at this convention, but they must have been fair because they stirred the ire of both the Deaf community and the oral teachers of the Deaf. However, they were distributed to the members in attendance and sent to all the universities that provided a degree in Deaf Education. They were officially adopted at the next convention that was held in Amherst, Nova Scotia, in 1995, as was the name change.

In 1993, I became the Past National Director and was required to keep the minutes of the meetings held for the Directors. The National Director was Mary LaMont from Ontario. Our membership dropped to 385, so most of the meetings were held in Ontario since it was the least expensive way to bring all the Directors together. I quickly found out that I could not write the minutes of the discussions we had fast enough, nor could I read what I did write! So I quickly borrowed our Director's (Kelly Walsh's) laptop computer and typed the minutes from then on. At the next meeting, I brought along a portable printer, and before everyone left the meeting, they had the chance to read the minutes, make any needed corrections, and mail those minutes to the Directors.

In 1995, I was done with that part of my life. I was in my second year as Vice Principal of Residence and wanted to focus more on putting my mark on the students' second home. I established a positive reinforcement system of discipline for the students called the *Pat on the Back* or *PoB*. The way it worked was if a student received ten PoBs in a week, that student would be recognized with a short announcement and a gift of $1.50 in cash.

This cash was made available by getting donations from the various organizations that used our gymnasium. I never actually "rented" it out, but I made it known that we sure could use a donation to continue many of our residential activities. It worked out exceptionally well.

Another program I started was to buy a Polaroid camera and lots of film to give to the Junior Department. The counsellors there were to call the parents of the student who would be given the camera for that long weekend, with the instructions for them to take pictures of each member of the family with their names written in the white space underneath the picture. Also, the street and place where the father, mother, and siblings worked, if they could, and a picture of the student's bedroom at home. When we got those pictures, the Supervisory Counsellor would mount the pictures and descriptions on a poster board with the student's picture and name at the top. This would be displayed on the student's door or mounted in the living room for all to see. This method helped the students learn what hearing children learn incidentally. Also in 1995, at the age of 49, I began to take Taekwondo lessons. It was a no-brainer actually, Jane P set up a Taekwondo (TKD) program through the Hierhily Dojo with Graham Rogerson as the Sensei or instructor. Since Jane was doing the class, she found it hard to interpret and participate fully in the instruction, so she asked me to help out.

After a couple of classes, I decided to join up. I began as a white belt and began the slow process of advancing up the ladder. On October 25, 1995, I earned my first belt, Orange. In March of 1996, I participated in my one and only TKD tournament as a Green Belt, I came in second place in sparring and 3rd place in Poomse (forms). From then on, it was a steady progression until I was awarded a Black Belt on June 5, 2000. Master Chung putting the second dan black belt around my girth.

I retired from NSD in 2001, along with Mr. Harkins, who was the longest-serving principal of the school at 22 years. Charlie retired and eventually moved to South Carolina with his wife, Pat. Pat was a professor of Nursing at Memorial University of Newfoundland (MUN) and was accepted in that same position at the University of South Carolina in Spartanburg. Pat retired from that position in 2010, I believe, and they remain living in their beautiful house.

Back To California:

Since the NLTA settled a strike with the Liberal government by allowing them to claw back our Canadian Pension Plan benefits, I decided I could balance that out by qualifying for Social Security from the USA. I needed just 5 quarters of paying into it to reap their benefits, so I sent out my resume to various schools for the deaf in the United States. Four schools responded, Western Pennsylvania, Alabama School, South Carolina and California in Fremont. The first three schools paid for me to travel there for an interview, but CSD-Fremont sent a video interview along with a blank tape so my response to the questions could be returned to them via mail. I decided that I wanted my interview with them to be all in sign language, so I asked Jeanne if she would act as the interviewer and Wally Burke as the camera man. The interview was flawless, and I was very pleased.

I was offered a position in Alabama and Fremont, but California was my first choice since that was where my professional career as a teacher of the deaf was created. I had to report to the school by August 14, 2001. Since 2001 was our 25th anniversary, I thought it'd be nice to share it with my sister and perhaps renew our vows. However, because I'd be in California on the 27th, we'd have to do the ceremony early, and Carol wouldn't hear of it. So, that idea slid by the wayside.

During this period, Lesley discovered that the Outdoor Theatre in New York's Central Park was having a performance of Ibsen's *The Seagull*, which is one of the plays she was involved in while at Grenfell College, AND, it was free, AND, it featured: Meryl Streep, Kevin Kline, Philip Seymour Hoffman, John Goodman,

Marsha Gay Hardin, Natalie Portman, and Christopher Walken would be the cast.

The only caveat was that one had to get in line for tickets overnight. So on Tuesday, August 21st, we took a bus to New York to see the play on August 23rd, I believe. We went to the Theatre District on Wednesday, the 22nd and saw Riverdance at the Gershwin Theatre. Then we ate. And I dropped Lesley off at

Central Park where she got in line to get tickets for the play as soon as the box

office opened. I was a bit nervous about that, but she made friends quickly and settled in for a long night. I went back to the hotel, went swimming in the roof pool, took a shower, got dressed and took a cab back to where Lesley was in line. I asked the cabbie to just slow down enough so I could see my daughter. She seemed to be fine, so we went back to the hotel, and I took a nap.

I got up around 6:00, got some coffee, dressed and went back to Central Park. There I found Lesley and remained with her until we got our tickets. Went back to the hotel, and Lesley took a nap while I went for another swim. The play started at 8, so we decided to get a nice Italian dinner before getting in line for the play.

The doors opened at 7:30 and we found seats high up on stage left. They were next to the side and we could look down and see the actors entering the dressing rooms, some were actually doing their prep exercises. Very interesting for me.

We watched the first half of the play, and during the intermission, I had to use the rest room. So I left the theatre and found the men's room. When I tried to re-enter the theatre, I was banned. The ushers refused to honour my ticket, saying that once one left, they were not permitted to allow anyone back in. So I whistled up to Lesley and let her know I'd be waiting for her by the actors' entrance.

That was a good choice because after Lesley joined me, we got to meet Meryl Streep, who was very, very nice and chatty, but my daughter, who shared the experience with that particular play couldn't get a word out to speak with that great actress. We also meet John Goodman, whose hand engulfed mine when we shook and asked why we wanted to meet him, and Philip Seymour Hoffman. I'm pleased to say that Les lost her shyness with these two actors and had a nice conversation with them.

After this excitement, we returned to the hotel, had a couple of drinks and went to bed. Our return trip to ML's was calm and uneventful.

On August 11, 2001, I boarded United Flight 93 from Newark, NJ to SanFrancisco, California. One month later, that flight was hijacked by Osama BinLaden's terrorists and crashed in Shanksville, Pennsylvania. Serendipity again saved my life.

Unique 25th Anniversary Celebration:

I returned to Pennsylvania a week later to celebrate our wedding anniversary, and Lesley and I had the adventure described previously.

On August 27, our anniversary day, we took a Greyhound Bus to Philadelphia.

Our meal on that bus was Portuguese Buns and water. Great way to celebrate the Silver Anniversary, right? After we got to Philly, we got a hotel room, ate a nice dinner and the next day took their shuttle to the airport. My family began their trip back to Newfoundland and Labrador, and I returned to California.

Back To California. This Time As A Principal At Csd-F:

I was hired as the Principal of Special Needs Students at CSD-F. There were 60 students, who all had a variety of handicaps; ADHD, Fetal Alcohol Syndrome, children whose mothers were Opioid Addicts, and one child born with half of her brain non-functional.

They were in Elementary, Middle and Senior departments with no more than 8 students per class. That meant I was to supervise 7 teachers, 5 student assistants and a student placement or support coordinator.

Ann McIntyre filled that position and it was she who greeted me at the San Francisco Airport and drove me to the school grounds. Then she took me to a dormitory to show me my temporary quarters, and walked me around the grounds. Boy were they huge!

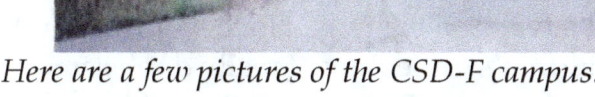

Here are a few pictures of the CSD-F campus.

This Clock Tower was a reminder of the CSD-F Campus in Berkely, which was impressive to me back when I volunteered there, but compared to this one, well, it was like comparing the NSD in Torbay with the new school on Topsail Road - there is none.

I was very impressed with their residential concept - cottages. It was almost the same concept as our Honours Residence, except that every student was enrolled. They had supervision, but also responsibilities accompanied by freedom. The school had 500 students, with 440 living on campus throughout the week. All went home each Friday because the transportation system there was a breeze.

I reported early so I could find a suitable apartment near the school. So the next day, I set out to get some personal transportation and find that apartment. Ann drove me to a bicycle store and dropped me off. I bought a Schwinn bike, much like the one seen in the movie "*Pee Wee* Herman's Big Adventure," and used that for the two and a half years I was there.

Then I rode around the city just getting my bearings and looking for signs that read "Apartments for Rent." I was fortunate to have found an apartment complex on Blacow Road that had such a sign, but it was completely enclosed with an iron fence. I rang the manager's bell and told her who I was and what I was looking for. She rang me in for an interview and to show me what was available. They had a bachelor apartment on the second floor, building 2SW, that was perfect for me, so I reserved it. I then went to the Bank of America in Irvington, a 20-minute bike ride from the apartment complex. There I opened a chequing account, deposited a couple of thousand Canadian dollars and went back to the apartment complex with a bunch of temporary cheques. I made one out, post-dated until I got my first pay cheque from the California Department of Education and returned to the CSD-F campus.

It's Really A Small World:

On August 14th, I participated in the first of many, many administrators' meetings. There were ten different departments at this school and each had its own 'principal' and assistant. My assistant was Ann. What stood out at this meeting was that it was interrupted by the parents of two of my students. They were looking to place their daughter into our program, and Ann and I went to meet them.

Boy, was I flabbergasted! The husband was a graduate of NSD, who met his wife while working as a heavy equipment operator in Minnesota. They moved to the Fremont area so she could work in the Tech industry and he found a job with a construction company nearby.

When he saw me, he couldn't believe it was 'Reade' and gave me a big hug. He then introduced me to his wife and began the story of their meeting and their children's difficulties. I really don't remember too much about how they met, and their children's difficulties are private, so that's all I'll say about that.

Setting Up An Apartment In A Hot Environment:

After the meetings were over, I gathered my few belongings and headed for 42010 Blacow Road to get the keys to my new home and think about how to furnish it. The apartment complex had all the necessary amendments, laundry, small gym, swimming pool and security. The one thing it didn't have was air conditioning, and that became a problem. Below is a picture of the pool and just behind the fence is the gym and laundry.

Since I had nothing in that apartment, I biked to Walmart, which took about an hour. There I bought utensils, two plates, a couple of bowls, coffee machine, filters, two glasses, 2 mugs, soap, a couple of wash clothes towels and a tiny micro-wave. I managed to fit them all into my basket and rode home. Then I rode to the local Safeway store and bought some coffee, various food items, coke and Canadian Club Whiskey (believe it or not, that imported whiskey was cheaper in California than in Newfoundland). On the way back, I stopped at a Taco Restaurant and bought some fast food to bring home. I didn't feel like cooking after all day. I stored my items, made a stiff drink and ate the taco and salad. Since I had no bed, or any kind of sleeping materials, I made myself as comfortable as possible on the floor and passed out.

The next day was Saturday, so I went to a furniture store and bought a futon to sleep on, a television, and a stand and arranged for the store to deliver them that afternoon. Then I went back to Walmart and bought bedding, a couple of pillows, and some hangers. That afternoon, I unpacked my suitcase, hung my clothes in the walk-in closet which was located opposite the bathroom and waited for the delivery of my furniture. After it came, I set up the futon and television; then went for a swim in 'my' swimming pool. Let me tell you, I was hot as hell and the pool was so cool, I remained in it for hours. Did a few laps, floated around, bobbed and found out that it was not sanitized by chlorine; rather they used a salt-based sanitizer.

I was lucky that the previous tenants still had their TV service connected, so I made supper and settled in to watch sports on TV. I had to get phone service as well as my own tv hook-up, and decided I'd do that on Monday from the school. After cleaning up from supper, I opened up the futon, threw on a sheet and a blanket and settled in for the night and some sleep. Unfortunately, the futon had a metal frame and was very uncomfortable. I threw the mattress on the floor and slept there that night.

Sunday, I returned to Walmart and bought a thick foam mattress to place underneath the one that came with the futon. I figured that thick foam would soften the metal frame and allow comfort that night. My apartment was on the second floor and was very warm, so I decided to buy a fan, one similar to an icebox. I saw it advertised on television, so I went to the store and got one. I also went to the nearest gas station and bought a couple of bags of ice. I put ice in the top, turned it on and sat in front of it. It cooled me down, a bit, but it wasn't the solution I needed. So I decided that after work on Monday, I'd ask Ann if she'd take me to a store to get an air conditioner. I gave Ann the ice fan.

Doing My Job At Csd-F:

I had only one new teacher for whom I had to mentor closely. The other 7 teachers were experienced and really good. I only had to sit in on their classes twice a year and put a mark on each matrix where the grade was "excellent."

One of the interesting perks of being an administrator at CSD-F was their tech department. All of us were provided with top-of-the-line cell phones. These phones had the ability to use email (remember this is in 2001), make long-distance calls (free to the user), and could be used on the Bay Area Rapid Transit (BART) system. So I could get on BART in Fremont and travel all the way to the University of San Francisco and not lose connection with my staff. And that's exactly what I had to do on October 6, 2001.

Tests To Work In California (I Thought I Was Finished Taking Tests):

To be a school administrator in California, one had to pass two tests; Math and Statistics Advancement Test (MSAT) and the California Basic Educational Skills Test (CBEST). I was advised by a number of my fellow administrators to schedule these tests separately because they are so difficult, and that only two people took them on the same day and passed, Pat Moore, our supervisor and my student placement supervisor, Ann McEntire. I decided to try my luck and take them both on the same day, which turned out to be my wife's birthday. Thought that was a good omen, again, serendipitous.

At 5:30 in the morning, I took the earliest BART to the University of California, San Francisco, which was actually the last stop on the line. When I left Fremont, the weather was sunny, warm and the forecast was for 78* weather; so I wore a loose Mexican shirt, shorts and sandals. Arriving in San Francisco, it was foggy, cold, and damp. I was freezing! It reminded me of the quote by Mark Twain, "The coldest winter I ever spent was a summer in San Francisco." I bought a large cup of tea and held it under the shirt until we were allowed to enter the auditorium.

One of the main rules about taking these tests was that once the test began, you were not permitted to leave your seat, even to sharpen your pencils, and you HAD to use a #2 lead pencil. So, before the test began, we all got in line at the pencil sharpener and got a whole pack of #2 pencils ready, and most also went to the bathroom, because to leave your seat even for that was not permitted.

After going over the rules, the ten of us sat down to begin our tests. The first set, the MSAT, was scheduled to begin at 9:00 and stop at 12:00. We were then given the opportunity to purchase a quick lunch, then return to the auditorium by 12:45. The next set of tests, C-BEST, began at 1:00 and were scheduled to last until 3:00. If you finished early, it was suggested that you review all your answers prior to leaving. I was so damned tired that when I finished the last question, around 2:30, I packed up and left for the BART station. It took only one week to get the results of these exams, and I passed each part of each one by being in the middle of the average score range. I was pleased.

Leftover Money? What A Concept:

In March of 2002, all the administrators had a meeting with the Superintendent Klopping about 'extra' money that had to be spent or it would be lost for the next year, $250,000 of Federal funds. It was decided that he'd distribute it equally between the ten different departments. so, I had $25,000 to use as I wanted.

At NSD, one of our teachers developed a strategy for teaching English to her intermediate students where she videotaped each student telling their story about their vacation, either summer, Christmas or Easter holidays. They used their preferred method of signing (remember back then, the term ASL was just beginning to be used), then transcribed it into English. It was a very successful method, so I decided to use a clone of that method.

I bought 3 of the best digital movie cameras the Technical Department could find and presented them to each department. I explained that the way to use them was to take their students on an outing, perhaps to Taco Bell, and film the teacher ordering a meal for each student or film the students ordering the meal for themselves, depending on their abilities. Then bring the video back to class and discuss it in ASL. Then the teacher could video each student talking about the experience in ASL and later write about it in English. Although it was a great technique, it was not very successful due to the fact that most of the students didn't have the ability to internalize what they had done.

For recreation, I joined the West Coast Taekwondo Club and continued training for a second-degree black belt. This club was different from the Chung Won Institute, from which I earned my first dan. I stuck with their training for 14 months, got in pretty good shape, continued developing my skills and maintained the flexibility (as bad as it was) that I had gotten. I also joined 24 24-hour fitness club, rode the stationary bike and lifted weights.

Part of the reason for joining that fitness club was that I was befriended by the nurse who most often attended to my students, Gerry, and her husband, Richard. I spent many dinners at their table with Richard's father and then sometimes shared my cooking skills with them.

After cleaning up, we would play Partner Rummoli, a card game similar to poker. We'd play for pennies and the game would last around two hours. After the game, I'd bike home, have a couple of drinks, watch TV and fall fast asleep. It was a good life, at first, but, naturally, I missed my own family.

Gerry and Richard were very supportive of me and invited me to many excursions they took with their friends and relatives. For example, I had Thanksgiving dinner with them where Gerry's mother and father brought their traditional Mexican-flavoured baked turkey; I think Norm called it a 'chocolate' turkey. That's them.

Here is a picture of Richard, Renata, Dick and Gerry playing Rummoli. I took the picture because I was making some tabouli as a snack while shifting partners around. And finally, Richard and Gerry introduced me to some of their friends with whom they went hiking and biking around the various trails in the Fremont area. Here we just finished climbing up the 5-mile trail of Mission Peak. Front is Moi, Renata, Jen, Gerry (in green), Richard, and Felix - don't remember the dog's name.

I Meet The Stones (Sort Of) And Sheryl Crow:

In November of 2002, my nephew Buddy was travelling with the Rolling Stones during their 40 Licks tour. When they got to San Francisco, he called me and said, "Hey, Unk, want to see and meet the Stones?" I said something like "Are you kidding me?"

But he wasn't and he made arrangements for me and a guest to get into the Pac Bell Stadium to see the Stones for free, and not only that, but to go backstage, and to attend each of the after-concert parties they had underneath the stadium.

So I thought of Richard and Gerry first, but Bud said he could only get the credentials for one other. So I asked Ann McIntyre if she was interested. Of course, she was, so it was arranged that we'd go on Saturday night. We'd meet Bud at his hotel room, The Hilton, around supper time and ride with him in his chauffeured van. Turns out Bud, better known in these circles as "Snake Castelletti," is a very well thought of stage manager, no stage builder. He designed their stage, supervised the setup of the Jumbo Screen, lighting and sound equipment. Here's Ann and Bud in his hotel room. All 6'3", 260 pounds of muscle and 5'10" Ann.

We arrived at the stadium around 4:30 PM and Buddy presented us with three different coloured wrist bands.

These allowed us to go anywhere in the stadium without any hassle from security. Then he took us backstage to show us his handiwork.

While there, the Stones came in to do a sound check and set up their playlist for the night.

All four of them walked passed Ann and me, close enough to smell their cologne; Mick, Keith, Ronnie and Charlie.

What surprised me was that they were all very short and thin. I doubt any of them came up higher than my chest, but you could tell that they were completely in charge. When they walked in, all the chatter stopped and Bud told us not to try to take any pictures of them, so, I hid my little throw-away camera.

After they walked by, Bud took us to the dining area. The spread was huge, a chef cut roast beef for you, different types of bread, a variety of vegetables, any kind of fruit you would want and the area that Buddy liked most, the smoothie machine.

The three of us made ourselves a plate, I got some milk and Bud made a smoothie.

Then he said, "Come on, let's sit with Cheryl." So we walked over to a table that had a very pretty, petite blond-haired woman who was eating alone and Bud asked if we could join her. Her response, "Of Course, Snake. Any time."

He then introduced me as his uncle from Newfoundland who was working at the School for the Deaf here. Then I introduced Ann and explained her position.

Well, we could hardly eat answering all the questions this woman had about working with 'handicapped' kids, etc., etc. The first thing we did was explain that Deaf people don't think of themselves as being handicapped. Then, between Ann and me, we filled her head with the various aspects of working with and within the Deaf community. When Cheryl was finished eating, she told us how interesting our conversation was, excused herself and left the table.

After eating, Bud showed us where the bathrooms were that we could use and continued our tour backstage and to the concert venue. The next few pictures are not of good quality, but do show Bud's work.

This is a picture of the Stones on stage with the Jumbo Tron video of them. That's one of Buds designs; it's made up of thousands of picture cells that are coordinated by a computer.

Turns out we were sitting with none other than Sheryl Crow. This picture of her was one used in the promotional material for her turn as the opening act for the Stones. Although this is a great picture, she is actually much more attractive in person and is a very down-to-earth, inquisitive person. I was very impressed with her talent, playing guitar, piano and the accordion, depending on which song she sang.

We were standing/sitting under the lights that were set up near the $1000.00 seats. Here's what very rich people or very dedicated fans were sitting on. Folding chairs were set up near

the stage and on either side of the ramp on which Mick and sometimes Keith would wander. Hard to see us, but Buddy, Ann, and I were seated in those seats to listen to Sheryl Crow. Then we moved underneath the light post.

Mick Jagger singing, I think, "Like A Rolling Stone," the song with which they opened the show.

Ann and I had just shared a joint, provided by my thoughtful nephew, and stood under one of the lights in the $1000.00 seat section. But before the Stones came on stage, we were surprised to see our supper companion being introduced to the stage.

In Trouble Again:

Turns out this was the best part of the month of November. There were a number of incidents that happened on a field trip to a science camp at Point Reyes National Park. A number of students got together and complained that I had hurt them. This was not true, but my supervisor decided that I needed to be disciplined. I vehemently disagreed, but she sent the necessary paperwork to the Department of Education. My punishment was to be put on leave for a week without pay. This angered me, and I decided to terminate my employment at CSD-F. Of course, I made sure that I had enough quarters to qualify for Social Security before I handed in my letter of resignation.

For those who might be interested, here's what happened to get me disciplined.

We took three vans of students to Point Reyes National Park. The principals of the two units, Special Needs and Middle School, drove two, and the vice principal of Middle School, whose name I don't remember, so I'll call him Dave, drove the third one. Upon arrival, the students were placed in cabins, with all the boys in one cabin with Dave, who is Deaf, and me as their supervisor. The girls were divided into two cabins, with the female teachers and mothers of the students taking turns as supervisors. The last cabin was for those ladies who were not on duty, so they could rest up. Two of the mothers in that cabin were on kitchen duty, which meant they were supposed to cook three meals a day for us all. Since I had a lot of experience cooking breakfast for a living, I volunteered to help them with breakfast. They readily agreed.

So my schedule was to watch the boys at night in the cabin, interpret and supervise a group during the science lessons provided by the park staff, and cook breakfast for all the participants in the morning. I actually did a lot of the prep work for the other meals. The ladies cooked, plated, and served the meal to the participants, then cleaned up.

On the last night at the camp, some students were disciplined by the staff in attendance. They were not permitted to participate in the special dessert and were confined to their sleeping cabin. They were also supposed to go to bed early. Most of the boys were very angry at this disciplinary measure and acted out. The staff, parents, and I managed to get them to settle down and get into their beds.

One boy, I'll call Tom, got out of bed and went to the bunk of another boy. I asked Tom what he was doing, and he said he had to go to the bathroom and wanted his friend to go with him. It's important to note that the cabins had no electric lighting, and flashlights had to be used. When Tom started to reach out to wake the other boy, I grabbed his arm and prevented that from happening. I did not grab hold with force, but I did not allow Tom to touch the sleeping boy. I told him that I'd walk down to the bathroom with him, and that's what we did. To make a long story short, Tom became a real pain, and I was up all night trying to get him to cooperate. He finally fell asleep around five in the morning. However, he later told his mother that I had hurt his arm.

Since I had been doing breakfasts, at six I woke Dave, who never knew what happened with Tom, to take over for me, then got a shower. After cooking and serving breakfast, I was assigned the clean-up task of sweeping out the four cabins that were used. My helpers were mostly from the special needs group and had no idea how to use a broom or sweep the dirt into a dustpan. I demonstrated how to do the task and assigned one of the "normal" middle school boys to be the team leader. I then split the group into three teams of two students, then assigned one team to a cabin to clean it up. I took them all into cabin number one and showed them how to roll up the rubber runner that went down the center of the cabin and divided the rows of bunks in half. Then I told them that one student would begin at the back wall of one section of bunks and the other would do the same with the opposite section. They would sweep the dirt into the center of the room, then down to the beginning of the next section of bunks and repeat the task until they were at the end of the cabin.

One duo consisted of two females who were not using the broom properly. As if I were instructing a person who did not know how to hold a golf club, I got behind one girl, took her hands in mine, and placed them on the broom in a manner in which she could use the tool to sweep the floor efficiently. She claimed I hurt her arm while doing this.

A number of students completed their last day tasks and decided to return to their respective cabins. Unfortunately, we were not done cleaning them, and they actually got in our way. So I asked them to leave the cabins until we finished. Most of them did just that, but two girls decided that they were going to ignore me and refused to look at me. Well, if Deaf students don't look at you, there is no communication. One girl was outside the cabin talking to the other one through the window. The other girl was lying on her bed. I tapped girl #1 on her arm and got her attention. I asked her to leave for a while until we finished cleaning the cabins. She did, but girl #2 just lay there and continued to refuse to look at me. So I took a broom and tapped her on her bum with the bristle part. That got her attention, and I asked her to leave until we finished. She did. Both girls said I hurt her — #1 on her arm and #2 on her bum.

The last complaint was with a boy who said that I hurt his chest. What happened was that he came into a cabin and stood around chatting with the duo who were supposed to be cleaning it. I asked him to leave, and he said that he was there to help. So I said, "Great, here's a broom, start sweeping." He laughed and sighed, "No way," and refused to take the broom I was offering him. So I held the broom in my right hand and put it about six inches from his chest, then let it go. It landed on his chest, and I told him to get to work. He actually did, but later was with the other kids complaining that the action hurt his chest.

It was obviously a setup by those students. It's interesting to note that the special needs students who were there never complained, but they did say they saw nothing, which didn't help me.

Setting A Teacher Straight:

However, it was another incident that really got my temper to flare up. After the situation in the cabins, it was around 11:30, and I hadn't had any sustenance since my morning orange juice, coffee, and pills. That is my normal schedule. I eat a brunch then a supper. At that time, I'd been doing that for over thirty years. I was eating my lunch while chatting with one of the parents who came along to act as a chaperone and had helped me cook breakfast that morning. The teacher who asked me to please accompany her class on this really important field trip actually yelled at me across the quad to stop eating my lunch. The parent with whom I'd been talking said that that was very rude of her. I said that I'd have a talk with her, and put the sandwich in the bag and walked to the main cabin where she was standing with a couple of colleagues. I asked her to accompany me around the corner for a private conversation. She did.

I then lit into her in sign only and explained my eating habits. I then told her I was her supervisor, and she embarrassed me in front of the parent I was speaking with, as well as the students and park supervisors. I was very displeased with her. Then she told me about the complaints being made by the students. I told her it was all nonsense and asked if she believed I hurt any of them. "Is that the impression you ever got from me in all the interactions I had with your students when you called me for help?" I asked.

She got a bit sheepish and said, "Not really, but I don't know."

"You don't know what? If I hurt those students either accidentally or on purpose? If that's what you think, then you really didn't get to know me, did you?" I walked away.

After packing up all the gear, we piled into the vans to return to Fremont. The plan was to stop at another park on the way back and eat the box lunches and discuss what the students learned over that weekend. Since I had already eaten my box lunch and the vans needed to be fueled, I brought each one to the gas station and paid for them all with the CSD-F credit card that was provided to the Principal of the Middle School. When I returned with my van, which was the last to be filled, we all piled in and drove back to Fremont and the school.

My Punishment And Enough Is Enough:

That was what happened to me to be disciplined by the California Department of Education. The bottom line was that there was a complaint made by a group of students about me, and my supervisor had to investigate said complaint. The students who made the complaint were all children of Deaf Adults, an important support for the school. So, for Pat and the other supervisors who heard my case to cover their asses and assuage the adults who were so important to the well-being of the school, my file was sent up the line. Thus was my discipline.

Interestingly enough, I found out after I had presented my resignation to Dr. Klopping that my week of suspension was to be spent over the Christmas holidays while I would be with my family in Newfoundland. So I guess I reacted too quickly and could have remained there for a longer period of time; however, I was glad to be home for good, and my serendipitous experience to end my Teacher of the Deaf career was completed.

When the teachers, student assistants, my secretary, and other principals learned of my situation and that I had handed in my resignation, many came up to me and expressed their sympathy and empathy to me. Two teachers and Gerry wrote letters of support for me. Unfortunately, the die was cast, and I was leaving. Before I packed up to go, my whole staff held a going-away party for me with craft gifts, which I have placed around my man cave, and the promise to keep in touch with me.

The youngest teacher, whom I monitored closely, Gerry, Rich, and the two oldest teachers did keep in touch via email. That lasted for nearly a year for my staff, but Gerry remained in touch until she passed away due to Amyotrophic Lateral Sclerosis (ALS), and Rich and I still share thoughts and laughs on Facebook and occasional emails.

CHAPTER 12:
WHAT NOW?

Upon arriving at my home and being warmly greeted by my wife and grandson, I asked about Lesley Marie. She was now at Memorial University's Grenfell College in Corner Brook. She had taken our green Dodge Colt with her for easy transportation home and to tool around the West Coast of Newfoundland. She was and still is a very good driver, safe, observant and forward-thinking.

However, she wasn't a mechanic and couldn't fix a specific problem with the Colt. A belt broke and she didn't have the money to take it to a local mechanic to repair it. So Lesley, being a student, parked the vehicle in a lot and left it there for a while.

Carol got a phone call from the owner of the lot right before I returned and told the owner that she'd take care of it within a week (I think that's how it went). After I got home and learned about the problem, I called our insurance company and arranged for it to be towed home to our mechanic, who, at that time, was Bides Comb's Service Station. There, the boys fixed the lovely little car and told us to teach Lesley to learn how to check the oil.

More Interpreting This Time For Pay:

So after that expense, I realized that I had better earn an extra dollar or two. The Newfoundland Coordinated Council on Deafness (NCCD) was still providing interpreting services for the Deaf Community, but had actually lost the contract for such with the government. That story is in itself a book, a tell-all book, but one I'll not get into here. Since I had been on the board before and had interpreted for them on many occasions, I let the president know I was available to interpret whenever they needed one.

My first job with them was for a former student who was planning to take a course at the Carpenters and Millwrights College, and contacted NCCD to get an interpreter. The job was for a full college year and paid me $35/hr while NCCD charged the government $45/hr. That was actually the same fee they charged when they first began providing interpreting services back in 1984. So for 2003 - 04, I worked 3 days a week at that college. I shared the duties with Des McCarthy, and I'm proud to say that the student passed easily.

Interpreting jobs were coming very sporadically and for one, a former student who needed to take a driver's education course, I was never paid. Although I submitted a bill to the appropriate division of the government, they said that I had to go through Interpreter Services NL, which was managed by a person who did not like me at all. The reason for her acrimony was that when she applied for a job working in the residence at NSD, I gave the position to a Deaf applicant and said that her signing skills were not adequate. So I never got paid for those 6 weeks of interpreting.

Back To Cab Driving:

I decided to make good on my claim that after retiring, if necessary, I'd drive a cab to make ends meet. So I got my taxi driver's license and went to work for Jiffy Cabs. This was 2005. I worked the day shift and was paid 50% of the meter after filling the cab with gas. This worked out to between $50 - 75 a day, not including tips. I called myself an independent contractor and got a tax break for all the money I earned interpreting and driving a cab.

Meanwhile, in 2003, Lesley completed her degree at Grenfell College. Her last few assignments were actually plays in which she had parts. Carol and her cousin by marriage, Sandy Cole, went to her graduation plays. A funny situation happened to them while sitting near the stage. One of the professors who was taking part in this play had a line he was supposed to say: "It's all the fuckin' same to me." He was practicing how to deliver that line and was saying it over and over again. Well, Carol and Sandy were close enough to backstage that they heard him.

I had the pleasure of actually attending Lesley's graduation ceremony, then renting a U-Haul truck and transporting all of her belongings back to St. John's. Although I admit to being prejudice, I think she looked beautiful in her cap and gown.

After returning home, Lesley got a job and decided to move out on her own. Naturally, Dad helped her move into her digs. Then helped her move again, then again and again until she finally found a place in which she decided to stay for a while. Fun times.

Interpreting Out Of The Country & Avoiding An International Conflict:

Then, in February of 2006, the man who took over as Vice-Principal of Residence, Chris, called me with a proposition.

One of our cadet students had been chosen to represent Newfoundland for the 90th anniversary of the Battle of the Somme in World War I.

This cadet would recite the Pledge to Remember by the Youth of Canada at the Memorial Service at Beaumont Hamel, France. I was very excited to have this opportunity to visit this unique place of honour to Newfoundland's fighting men. I was also pleased to see that my fellow Taekwondo student, Reneé, was chosen to represent the Canadian Cadets at the ceremony.

One of her grad pictures.

A Very Brief History Of The Battle Of The Somme Is As Follows:

In 1916, the Allies planned to make the "Big Push" to end WWI and the Somme River battlefield was chosen as the place to begin. On July 1, 1916, thousands of British and French troops advanced on the many German positions. They were ordered to *march* in the open and so were slaughtered. 57,000 soldiers died during this attack. The Royal Newfoundland Regiment was part of the British forces and was ordered to attack the German foothold in the area called Beaumont-Hamel. 801 Newfoundland Regiment soldiers went over the top of their trench; only 68 men answered to their names during the next day's roll call.

Although the first time Newfoundland organized a memorial to the Royal Newfoundland Regiment was in 1917, efforts to remember the fallen men of the Regiment were led by Lieutenant-Colonel Father Thomas Nangle, their Roman Catholic Padre during WWI in 1919. He decided what the Newfoundland Memorials would be like, oversaw their design, construction and location. By 1921, the people of Newfoundland had donated enough money for Nangle to purchase 30 hectares of the ground where the regiment was intrenched, including the "danger tree". The danger tree was a small, scraggly tree that marked the area of the deadliest line of fire by the German machine guns, and where most of the soldiers were killed.

British sculptor Basil Gotta was commissioned to design a statue that would be used for the various memorials. He chose the regiment's emblem, a majestic caribou, as the perfect statue for all five planned memorials.

The site at Beaumont Hamel was landscaped by Rudolph Cochins and has over 5000 trees native to Newfoundland, as well as many of the province's natural flora. This memorial is one of the only WWI sites in which visitors can walk through the actual Newfoundland and German trenches and see the area between those trenches - "No Man's Land." On June 7, 1925, the site was officially opened by British Field Marshal General Earl Haig, the same leader who caused the tragedy.

When I was contacted by an official of the Canadian Legion, I learned that this was actually a Pilgrimage, and we were to visit the five Caribou memorials in France and Belgium. There would be numerous dinners and official functions that I'd have to interpret for. So while everyone was eating, I'd be interpreting. While everyone was viewing the various attractions, I'd be interpreting the guide's description of each site. Whenever a dignitary would speak, I'd be interpreting. In reality, I was asked to interpret for Reneé almost all day, for the whole time we were there. So I requested that I be reimbursed for my time. The Legion Representative sent my request to the

Department of Veterans Affairs, and we negotiated a deal. So I was paid a total of $3000.00, as well as being provided with an official windbreaker, blazer, hat, shirt and tie.

The whole experience began four days before we were to depart. The Youth Group met for 4 hours daily in the Airport Inn to learn about the protocol, expected demeanour, and given a history and geography lesson about the region we'd be travelling and the information about the Battle of the Somme and specifically The Royal Newfoundland Regiment's participation at Beaumont-Hamel. In my opinion, I earned the money in those four days. Reneé is a very intelligent young woman who soaked up the information and participated in all the activities, but this 60-year-old man became tired fairly quickly and easily.

This is the City Hall of Lille. 16C, the back of it was WWI by artillery shelling. completely rebuilt after

Below is the Market Square of the of the food sold there is fresh and malls in Canada and the USA, you most anything you

At 5:00 in the morning on June 26, we all boarded a Department of National Defence (DND) transport airplane to fly to Lille, France. It took approximately 6 hours of flight time to begin our landing approach at their airport. After landing, we departed the plane and waited for our luggage. It was HOT! +37°C, sunny, and dusty. After about an hour, we boarded a local bus and made our way

to our home away from home for the next eight days. Our hotel was beautiful, very comfortable and situated so that we were only a few hours away from all the destinations we were to visit.

    After we all settled into our rooms, we had the rest of the day to see the sites of Lille, a city that was incorporated in the 15th Century. My job was to shadow Reneé and let her know what was being said, when she was interested, and interpret the banter of the various shop clerks we visited. Free days from then on were few. Nearly every hour was scheduled, including lunches and dinners with various dignitaries. I earned my $3000 and clothing.

    The pictures give an example of the architecture of this beautiful, historic city.

    The day after we got settled in, we made our first excursion to the various sites the youth group would learn about.

This is the youth group. Reneé is in the row of girls, 4th one from the left.

The Ulster Memorial Tower

One of the most moving sites we visited was the Ulster Tower. This was a Memorial erected in honour of the 34th Irish Regiment that fought for the United Kingdom since 1881.

Ulster historian, Paddy Corrigan, pictured here, explained what happened to this regiment in vivid and emotional detail. This regiment had over 5000 casualties in this battle on July 1, 1916.

The men were ordered to march into battle against the German Army, who were entrenched just yards away. German records state, "Why did they walk? They could have overrun us."

This visit took place on June 28th and it was one of the milder days, +35°C. After this visit, we had a Buffet lunch at the hotel during which I interpreted for Danny Williams, the Newfoundland and Labrador Premier and the Mayor of Lille. As normal, my eating was sporadic.

We were then given the opportunity to further explore Lille's shopping district if we wanted. Naturally, Reneé was raring to go shopping, and I tagged along. There wasn't a lot of interpreting for this excursion, but I did enjoy the architecture of the city.

June 29th was a full day, beginning at 10:30 with a trip to the Museum of the Great War in Peronne, France. Did a lot of interpreting here, as there were Museum guides who spoke of each of the exhibits. This was followed by a formal luncheon at the Museum. Then on to a memorial service at Monchy-le-Preux, Newfoundland Memorial. Here we had to wait under some trees until the Youth group was to make their entrance, and Reneé and I practiced our Taekwondo forms for our 2nd Dan test later this year.

Then a formal Reception hosted by the Mayor of Monchy-le-Preux and the Newfoundland Government. From there, we got some rest in the bus as we were taken to a Restaurant called Espace Gobelins, Roubaix, for another formal Dinner with more speeches. By the time this was over, I was exhausted and couldn't wait to get back to the hotel and some sleep. I really needed to rest up for the next day, as I was shown the schedule for June 30th.

Friday began a little later than the 29th, but went far longer into the evening. Suffice to say that the ceremonies began at 11:30 and continued through memorial ceremonies at 5 different places, each followed by a reception or formal lunch. The last place we visited was the Canadian Sunken Road Cemetery at 8:30. This was a candlelight ceremony that lasted for about 90 minutes, with speeches, of course. My hotel room was very welcoming that night and I slept long. I knew I needed some extra stamina for the July First Ceremonies.

Since we arrived in France, the whole country was in the midst of a vicious heat wave. The day we arrived, it was +37°C, as I said previously, and it only got hotter. France was also hosting the World Cup of Football (soccer) and a few of the games were cancelled due to the heat. At times it went as high as +42°C. In Fahrenheit, that would be 107.6°.

On July 1st, it was +41°C. All of the Youth contingent had to wear our blazers, shirts, ties and hats - no exceptions for the heat. Reneé and I had been practicing the Pledge by the Youth since we began this journey. She knew it by heart easily and signed it beautifully. It says:

They served, giving freely of themselves. To them, we pledge, amid the winds of time, to carry their torch and never forget. We will remember them.

The official ceremony was to begin at 10:00; however, the participants had to arrive much earlier. We got there at 8:30 and proceeded into the Beaumont Hamel trench that faces the monument. We were given a lot of bottled water and a parasol each so we'd have some relief from the unrelenting sun. There were no chairs for the Youth or their contingent, so we stood in the heat, in the trench, drinking warm water and holding parasols. Then, around 9:00, invited luminaries began to arrive. They were seated just above us, and complained to the ushers that they could not see the area where Princess Ann and the other Royals would be seated, so we were 'asked' to close the parasols.

So there we stood, dressed to the hilt, with the sun making us sweat like crazy. Reneé's face was becoming redder and redder. So I told her to take off her jacket and I held it over her head for a while, giving her a bit of shade. Some of the other members of the Youth group followed suit. The ushers kept bringing water to all of us standing in the trench, but it was warm, not refreshing at all. It did, however, keep us hydrated for a short time. Then one of the ushers came over to let us know that the ceremony would begin shortly and we should put our jackets back on.

Finally, Princess Anne and the other dignitaries arrived and took their seats. They were about 20 minutes late.

The ceremony began and I began interpreting the speeches for Reneé, but she told me not to bother. She just wanted to wait for her turn at the podium. After about 15 minutes, it was time for the Pledge by the Youth and Reneé took her place at the podium. She and Trevor, who gave the spoken version, completed their assignment and returned to the trench. Reneé's legs were shaky and Trevor helped her back, where she nearly fainted into my arms.

I tried to walk her to the first aid station, holding her up under her arm. We tried to leave the trench at the exit where she advanced to the podium, but one of the ushers stopped us and asked where we were going. I told him where and that Reneé was suffering from heat stroke and needed care quickly. He wouldn't let us through because we'd be walking in front of Princess Anne and ordered me to go through the trench. So that's what we did, but Reneé was now so weak that I had to carry her. When the people in the trench saw us coming, they made way for us to pass. It took me about 10 minutes to get her to the first aid station that way, whereas had I been permitted to carry her straight down the passageway, we'd have been there in less than a minute. Reneé was really having trouble now; she couldn't sweat anymore and complained about feeling cold and sick.

When we finally got to the first aid station, Doctor Batalion, who was the contingent's official doctor, followed us and advised that we get her to drink some cool water and put a cold cloth on her forehead, but the French EMT on duty wanted to give her intravenous saline solution. Dr. Batalion vetoed it, but the French EMT insisted and suggested we ask Reneé. However, by this time, she was becoming delirious and it was hard to talk to her, so I suggested that we call her mother in Newfoundland - I had it and gave it to the Canadian doctor.

So we made a trans-Atlantic phone call to Reneé's mother. After hearing my explanation of what happened, Mrs. Pardy gave the go-ahead for the intravenous saline solution. This worked wonderfully and Reneé started to come around. Unfortunately, Dr. Batalion insisted that she go back to the hotel immediately and get a cool shower. She didn't want to go. She really wanted to go to the reception and shake hands with Princess Anne. When the doctor got one of the top Youth Leaders to take Reneé back to the hotel and stay with her, she complied, albeit with tears. That left me on my own for the rest of the day and evening.

Celebrating My Sixtieth Birthday In France:

It was my sixtieth birthday and I decided to treat myself to a nice glass of Beaujolais wine and a prime rib steak dinner. I took the tour of the Memorial of Beaumont-Hamel and was astounded by how close the Newfoundland Trench was to the German Trench. You could literally toss a pack of cigarettes and/or a ball back and forth. And, according to the guide, that's exactly what happened between the fighting and killing. These were, after all, young men in their teens or early twenties who had to beef with each other, but had to follow the orders of their military superiors.

What a sad and haunting situation.

The picture is the French Trench. You can see the white flag in the distance. That's the German Trench.

After the tour, I returned to the hotel and took a cool shower, put on the television to watch some of the World Cup and rested for my birthday dinner. Around 5, I got dressed in some shorts, a loose shirt and sandals, then walked to a restaurant that I had noticed during our trips to the memorials. There, I had the wine and prime rib steak I craved. The wine was so good that I decided to buy one of their specials - a box containing 3 bottles of Beaujolais wine. But, I made a mistake and the waiter brought me three BOXES. Well, I thought, what the hell and bought them anyway. All in all, the meal and wine cost me 125.00 Euros, or approximately $175. I took my prize back to the hotel, preparing to share it with the other adults. I managed to share 2 full bottles, but that was all. So I packed the other 7 in my suitcase to bring home. Fortunately, we were travelling on a DoD aircraft and the border security never checked our baggage. However, my suitcase was so heavy with the bottles wrapped in clothing that the handle almost fell off.

In the period in-between, when some of the Newfoundland contingent found out that it was my birthday, they began to buy me shots of Jameson Irish Whiskey. Suffice to say, I had a fairly happy sixtieth birthday.

The following day, we had more memorials to visit and I was once again interpreting pretty well non-stop. We visited the famous Flanders Field, the place about which the poem by John McCrae was written. That day, it was still filled with red poppies. We had lunch with the Mayor of Ypres, Belgium, toured the Flanders Field museum, had dinner with various dignitaries at the Tweed Restaurant, and then went to a Last Post ceremony at a cemetery at Menin Gate. It was a long day for a 60-year-old man with a bit of a hangover.

July 3rd and 4th was more of the same. Visiting various memorials and cemeteries and participating in special luncheons and dinners.

One of the larger memorials we visited was the Thiepval Cemetery and Memorial. There are 72,337 missing British (including Newfoundlanders, Irishmen, and Scottish) and South African servicemen who died at the Battle of the Somme. All of the names are scribed on the walls inside the monument. One of the Contingent found his great-grandfather's name. July 4th was our farewell day. This day we had a special breakfast at 8:00, but then we had a day in which we could choose our activities. Reneé decided she wanted to shop at the city centre stores in Lille. It was still very hot, but we could dress for the weather and not have to wear our official clothes until the Farewell Dinner Event at Fort de Mons. More speeches, but they were easy to interpret and were filled with sentiment for the visit by Canadians.

On July 5th, we flew to Ottawa and checked into the Lord Elgin Hotel. This flight was from 8:30 am French time until 1:30 Ottawa time. The following day, all the Newfoundland contingent boarded an Air Canada Airbus to return home. Reneé was warmly greeted by her mother, who thanked me for taking care of her daughter. I told her that Reneé took care of herself except for July 1. Carol and my family greeted me and took me home. I really had an interesting experience, learned a lot, earned a bit of money and was exhausted.

The Road Trip To End All Road Trips":

The next big adventure I had was with my grandson, Lezlie. When he turned 17 and got his license, I promised him that we'd take a road trip through the United States.

I planned to visit my sister first in Pennsylvania, then Charlie Harkins and his family in South Carolina, then spend a few days at Disney World, and then go west until we decided it was time to come home. So in 2010, I bought tickets to Disney World for a 4-day stay from July 30th to August 2nd. That meant I had to book the ferry from Argenta to North Sydney for a couple of days after Lez graduated. Here's Lezlie Robert Reade after receiving his graduation diploma. I doubt that he was as proud as his Sittie, Mother and I were.

At the end of June, Lez brought his girlfriend, Makayla, over to the house to get ready for his prom

night. They were, and still are, a handsome couple. Soon after Lezlie's graduation ceremony and the closing of Gonzaga High School, we packed a couple of suitcases and started out for Argentia to get the ferry to North Sydney.

On the way, I thought I'd give Lezlie a history lesson related to the development and settlement of Newfoundland. So we stopped at Castle Hill and took a picture of the story board before we went into the museum. We had a two bed cabin on the Blue Puttee.

It was comfortable, had a television, private bathroom with a shower (small!), comfortable beds, and easy access to the rest of the ship.

Lez and I went to the bar, and he decided that he'd drink whatever I was having; so, we both had double Rye and coke - 2 of them. Lez had a hangover, so I told him I'd drive and he could get some sleep in the car.

After the ship docked, we bought gas and began our drive to the States. I planned to take Route 95 through Maine and down eat eastern coast; however, as we were driving, the road to Bangor, Maine,

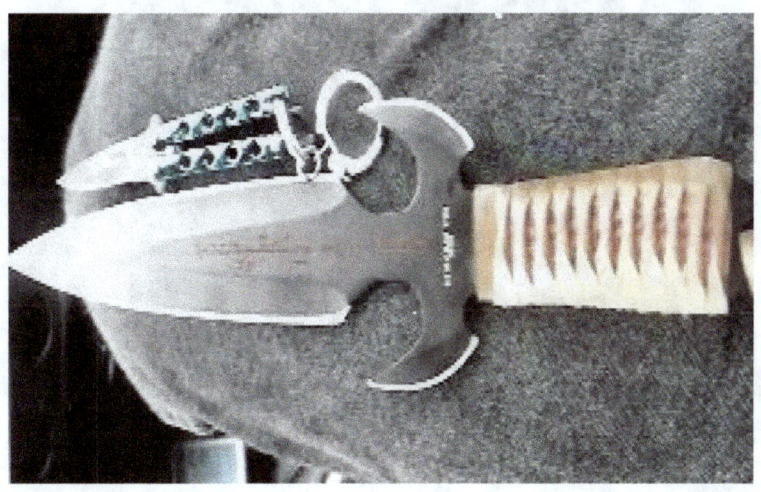

was under construction, so I changed plans and drove through Houlton, Maine. As we were driving through Truro, Nova Scotia, we had to stop for gas and some food.

Lezlie saw a knife that he liked and that became his first purchase.

These are the states we wound up travelling through: Maine, New Hampshire, Massachusetts, Rhode Island, New York, New Jersey, Pennsylvania, Maryland, Delaware, Virginia, North Carolina, South Carolina, Georgia, Florida, Alabama. Mississippi, Louisiana, Texas, New Mexico, Arizona, Colorado, Utah, Wyoming, Nebraska, Iowa, Illinois, Indiana and Michigan back into Canada.

It took us only two days to get to my sister's house in Martins Creek, Pennsylvania.

One day on the ferry, a sleepover in Maine, and then we arrived there. It was HOT, the temperature was around 35 - 40° C. So Lelie and I spent a lot of time in the air conditioned house, mall, or their swimming pool. Of course, we had to get a Jimmy's Hot Dog and a Philly Cheese Steak, no matter how hot it was.

Our Visit To New York:

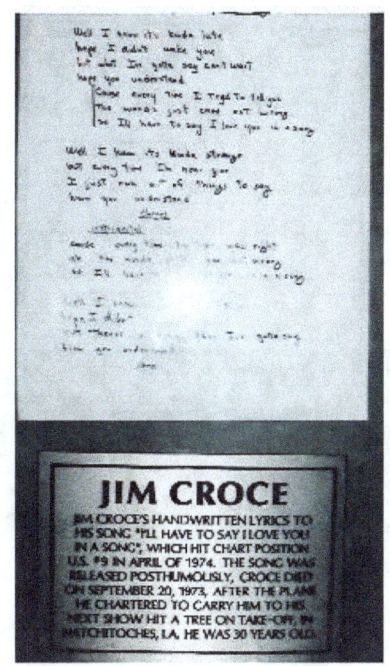

I thought he would like to see New York City, so we took a bus to the Big Apple and checked into the Holiday Inn Express on 29th Street.

I was familiar with this hotel because Carol, ML, Robert and I stayed there many years ago, and later, Lesley Marie and I stayed there for our Central Park Theatre experience.

We took a bus to New York and then a cab to the hotel. One of the first pictures Lezlie took was of the Big Apple Meat Market.

It was very hot and in New York City, with all the surrounding buildings, it felt hotter than 37°C. The air conditioned room was great, but Lezlie wanted to waste no time exploring Central Park. So that's where our first stop was. We rented bicycles so we'd get to see a lot of the park quickly. The first site we saw was the outdoor theatre, again where Lesley and I met Meryl Streep and the others. Then we saw John Lennon's tribute called "Strawberry Fields."

We did the full circle of the Park, and although I bought

copious amounts of fluids, I had to get back to the hotel and air conditioning, perhaps a short nap as well. After returning the bicycles, we took a pedi-cab back to the hotel. On the way, we passed the Empire State Building, Hard Rock Cafe and the Bubba Gump Shrimp Company.

We got back to the hotel, and I rested. I needed to coolness of the room as well as something to drink. Lez didn't want to stay with me, so I gave him a S100 and told him

to not get lost. He returned in about 2 hours with a number of purchases and a caricature charcoal of himself. On his adventure, he lost our camera at a tourist shop. So he retraced his route stopping in each shop that he was in looking around until he found the cameras.

That night we went to the Hard Rock Cafe for supper and a couple of drinks. This place was like a rock and roll museum. It had walls filled with guitars that were given to the place from musicians like John, Eric, George, Bo and Tom. Other very interesting exhibits were handwritten lyrics to some famous songs, such as Bruce Springsteen's Natural Magic and Jim Croce's I'll Have To Say I Love You In A Song, of which I took a picture.

The next day, we visited the Empire State Building after walking past the construction site of the Memorial to the Twin Towers and all the First Responders of the attack that happened on September 11, 2001.

The Empire State Building is also museum-like, something I completely forgot about. There are pictures of the building being constructed, of workers sitting on the I-Beams eating their lunch or standing without any safety equipment, hammering rivets to attach some I-Beams together. And, naturally, a souvenir shop. Lez and I took our time and looked at all the exhibits and walked the last couple of flights to the top of the Building.

Before we got the bus back to Pennsylvania, I had to give him one more unique experience. There are a few subways in Canada, and one of the most infamous is in New York, so that's where we went next.

We returned to Pennsylvania, where my nephew by marriage took us to a Philadelphia Phillies Baseball game. Greg Knaus did the driving and got us tickets through his workplace, a bargain for sure. Lez, Robert, Greg and I had a wonderful afternoon watching Cole Hamels pitch a one-hitter

against the San Diego Padres in a Phillies win. After the game, Greg brought us to the famous Pat's Steak Shop outside the ballpark. I must say that the steaks were good, but still not as good as Mizero's in Easton.

After celebrating my 65th birthday with a Reade Family reunion and a pool party, we played a pick-up game of 2 on 2 basketball and Lez got the idea that from then on, he had to make a three-pointer in each state we passed through, and this 65-year-old grandfather would be the rebounder for him - in over 30°C weather. We began in Easton.

After a few more days enjoying ML's pool, we set out for Charlie and Pat Harkins' home in Spartanburg, South Carolina. To get down there from Pennsylvania and to make Lezlie's trip a bit more exciting, I decided to pass through a couple of extra states. So Lez got the opportunity to make three pointers in New Jersey, Delaware, Maryland, West Virginia, Virginia, and finally in South Carolina. Had I gone the direct route, we'd have travelled 640 miles, as it was, we put over 780 miles on our little, yellow Suzuki Aerio.

Lezlie did a fair amount of driving during this leg of our trip, but I drove us into Spartanburg and to Charlie's house because I had Lez controlling the GPS device I bought for this trip. Since he's a youngster, somehow this generation of people seems to know exactly how to use the newer gadgets that take old folks like me forever to learn.

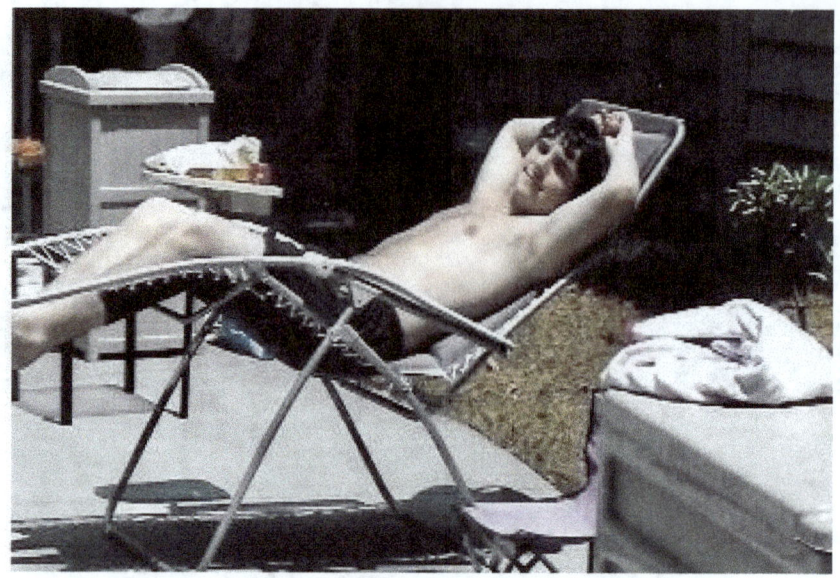

It was HOT, so we spent a lot of time sharing their pool with them.

We stayed with Pat and Charlie for 5 days. One day we took a trip into North Carolina to visit the Biltmore Castle/Estates. It was built by George Vanderbilt, the grandson of Cornelius (Commodore) Vanderbilt, who was a multimillionaire during the 19th century. As an aside, in 2024 dollars, his worth would be about $3Billion. George Vanderbilt built this castle between 1889 and 1895. The many features within this fairytale place include an indoor swimming pool with electric lights that illuminated the floor of the pool, 46 bathrooms with indoor flush toilets, 35 bedrooms, a large Italian garden, a vegetable garden, livestock, a pantry as big as a small house and it is completely self-sufficient. George began building his dream home at the age of 25. Due to an inheritance of over $2 million at the age of 21 and another $5 million after his father died, he never had to work for a living. Rather, he spent his time collecting artworks and building his castle, with the help of architect Morris Hunt, who also designed the New York Tribune building, and landscape designer Frederick, who is also famous for designing Central Park in New York.

So after our visit to the castle, Lez had to find a court and make another 3-pointer. We left Pat and Charlie's on a Wednesday and drove down to Orlando, Florida. Naturally, we had to find an outdoor court in Atlanta, Georgia, for him to make another shot. Here it is around 34°C and this 66-year-old grandfather is trying to get rebounds for the 17-year-old. For some reason, Lez was off his game, and I got a workout. When he finally made it, we went to an ice cream shop and I had a lot of water and a cone, Lez just a double-decker cone.

Walt Disney World And Daytona Beach:

Wednesday evening, we entered Orlando and followed the signs to Disney World. It wasn't hard to find at all. We got to the check-in counter, where they had our reservations ready and waiting. We were given a large room in Jamaica.

Let me tell you, Disney World is HUGE and a lot of fun. Jamaica was just one of five Caribbean areas in which there were hotels. Our room was on the second floor and was surrounded by palm trees and geckos. After we took our suitcases into the room, we changed into bathing suits and made our way to the nearest pool, which was designed to look like a lake. The water was cool and was just what the doctor ordered to cool off and prepare for our first dinner at the resort.

I planned to stay here for four days, paid for it back in January and am pleased that I did, but wish I'd have paid for a full week. There was so much to see, participate in and do that 4 days really just gave us a taste of the experience. Epcot Center was one of the main venues with many interesting things to try.

Here's Lez riding a Segway.

Walking down the street was another busy experience. There were all kinds of Disney Characters walking around and letting the customers take selfies with them; various street performers - one acrobat balanced himself on one hand on many table chairs, culminating on two of ten; then there were jugglers, and one of my favorites, a Street Theatre. The play was called "King Arthur's Quest for the Holy Grail." As you might think, judging from my childhood play, like being Tarzan and Captain Midnight, I would have loved to be an actor. With this Street Theatre, I got my chance. The professional performers chose people from the crowd to participate as different characters, and I was chosen to be King Arthur.

Again, it was an unbearably hot day, +40°C, but I was hyped to do it, and the pros provided a lot of water, sometimes provided in a goblet to go with the script.

Here I am as King Arthur, or as I prefer, King Grandad. This picture doesn't have all the cast or the professionals, and I apologize for that, but you get the idea. I'm the one in the middle wearing a kind of crown. Most of the dialogue was ad-libbed, with the professionals giving cues as questions that were easy to answer once you got into the idea of the play. We got a standing ovation, probably because there were no chairs available. Hehehehe…

Lez, being the handsome young man that he is, was given the opportunity to take his picture with many of Disney's Princesses, but the one that I liked best was when the young woman playing Pocahontas requested, no insisted, that he stand next to her and get the picture done.

This is a great picture of them, I think, and you can see why he had no hesitation to wrap his arm around her, with her encouragement, of course.

We also spent a lot of time in the Wild Kingdom. This is a zoo like no other I have ever been to. The animals were in their natural habitat, roaming free and living as instinctively as possible. The way visitors experienced this phenomenal place was on a train. Yep, from what I was told, the train tracks were installed before the rest of the exhibit was set up. This was done in order to acclimate the animals to this foreign accessory to their home. The place is HUGE! The ride took 2 hours to complete and we got to see and take pictures of as many animals as we wanted. We have pictures of a giraffe drinking water, an African elephant, an African Big Horned Cow and an ostrich.

When our Disney World experience was over, we headed north to Daytona Beach. There Lez went for a dip I the South Atlantic Ocean, talked me into eating at the Red Lobster Restaurant, where he bought a Caribbean Lobster, which is different from our wonderful Newfoundland lobsters, but still tasty and very expensive. We found a basketball court and he made his three-pointer.

Then, as we were looking for a hotel just before we had to find a hotel for the night, we saw a go-kart race track. So, naturally, we had to have a race. I guess because I weighed so much more than him, he beat me easily. We had a great time and it was worth the money and time.

We left Florida by Route I-10 and travelled into Alabama.

Stopped in Monroeville at the Spanish Fort High School and found their outdoor court. Lez made his three-pointer after a few warm-up shots and we hit the road looking for a hotel in which to spend the night.

The next day, Sunday, we drove into Mississippi. Again, it was a wonderful HOT day. Route 10 took us into Hattiesburg and we began looking for a basketball court. We needed gas, so we asked the gas station attendant where there was an outdoor basketball court. He directed us to the local YMCA. We found it with little problem and walked in. The female at the desk asked us what we were doing there. So I showed her my Y card from Newfoundland and told her our story. After a nice chuckle, she called down to the gym and asked the leaders there if they would come up and meet these two, handsome travellers from Canada.

Basketball In Hattisburg, Mississippi:

I have to say that after our experience in Disney World and sharing time with my family, this was THE highlight of our southern trip. The counsellors at this YMCA were both college players at the University of Mississippi. They were holding a practice session with their youth group and introduced themselves as Red and Junior.

Red was around 6'8", Junior 6'4" and both were in tip-top shape. I told them about Lezlie's quest to make three pointers, so they invited Lezlie and me to join their practice sessions. Lez jumped at the chance, but I said, "I'll just watch." I told them I was suffering from a case of the "toos." Junior said something like, I'm sorry to hear that, but what are the twos? I told them that it was a Newfoundland problem, I was too fat, too tired, too old and too lazy to participate. That brought a laugh and Red put his arm over my shoulder and led us to the gym.

They introduced us to their group as the travellers from Canada, Lezlie and his Pops. They also said that Lez would be practicing with them. Except for the woman at the front counter, we were the only white guys there. Turns out that Hattiesburg,

Mississippi is over 51% African American, so it's no wonder we were in the minority there.

As the group continued to warm up. Red began shooting three pointers from the top of the key. They were all net, one after another, again and again. So I challenged him, I told him that if he could make one with his eyes closed, I'd give him a Toonie. He said something like he didn't want a case of the "toos" like I had, but I assured him that it was good Canadian money that he could spend when he came up for a visit. Believe it or not, he made three in a row before missing.

I got a toonie and tossed it to Red is in the yellow shirt, Junior the hat. He looked at it, smiled and pocketed it.

Red was the player/coach of the Shirts and Junior the Skins and a full-court game began. They all were quick, good ball handlers and fair passers. I'm proud to say that Lezlie more than held his own in those games. Yep, they played three full-court games before some of the boys had to leave.

The teams dwindled down to 3 players each, so they switched to half-court ball when Red and Junior began to needle me. They kept saying, "Come on, Pops, get off your butt and join us. You're not too old to play. We'll make the kids take it easy on you. Your grandson needs your help." Finally, I changed into sneakers and joined them. We all played for another 30 or 40 minutes. All the other local boys had to go home for dinner and Junior had to get the Y ready for the Monday activities.

Junior, "Pops," came and went at the end of each shift, and he wore out expression on the old man. These two young men showed us a great time and let us make a couple of those pointless trips to Mississippi.

Lez and I got a drink of water from the fountain when Red asked us to join them in the lobby. Then Junior came in with a couple of YMCA 'T' T-shirts and two water bottles. Lez watched his lay-up go in.

From Mississippi, we went into Louisiana, where we stopped at the University of Louisiana/Monroe for the three-pointer and on to Marshall, Texas. We spent the night there, then found an outdoor park where he made his shot.

Little League Baseball Game:

I then called my cousin, Jimmy, to find out where he lived so we could pay him a visit. Turned out he and LaNor were following their grandson's Little League Team, Pearland. Jim's grandson, Coady, pitched the championship game for Pearland and won.

To celebrate, we all went to the Golden Corral all-you-can-eat restaurant. Coady's father, Craig, ate two 'T" bone steaks with a baked potato and creamed vegetables. Most of us ate over conservatively, but still were there for a couple of hours. Then we joined the family in their hotel for more celebration.

Those two days were HOT! Each day, the temperature was between 42° and 45°C, but Leslie still had to make his three pointers. He did. From Waco, we drove into Roswell, New Mexico, where legend has it that Aliens landed and settled.

Again, it was hot as hell, but Lezlie still made his shot; this time in a high school parking lot. We took our time driving through New Mexico and visited a number of great places, the Petrified Forest, Route 66, the Painted Desert, and got a picture of an old car, probably a 1930s Ford. It looked like the one Bonnie and Clyde were shot up in.

From there Lez fulfilled his quest at the Spencer Karol Memorial Park in Holbrook, Arizona, which is about 180 miles from the Grand Canyon. We found a small motel along the Route 66 so we could get an early start to the Grand Canyon.

The Impressive Grand Canyon:

We got to the Grand Canyon around 8:00 the next morning. Driving into the tourist lodge was a lovely experience as we passed deer and elk along the way.

Unfortunately, our desire to take the mule ride to the bottom of the canyon and return was quashed when I weighed in at 225 pounds.

Yep, they actually weighed Lezlie and me before completing the transaction for the ride. The weight for these rugged little animals was 220, so I was banned from the experience.

Lezlie had no weight problem; however, the age limit for riding alone was 18 years. Joe became very angry with me when I told the Park Ranger his actual age when asked.

We left the office very disappointed, but I then thought about taking a helicopter ride across the Canyon.

Nope, too damned expensive - $240.00/person for a 45-minute trip at that time.

Now the cost is $549.00. So we did the only thing we could do, we took the bus around the Canyon and stopped at various observation points.

These sites were breathtaking experiences.

The view of the trail   going into the canyon.

Lezlie standing on a rock
& overlooking the Colorado River

The Colorado River
flowing through the Canyon to
dispense water to California.

A few pictures of the Grand Canyon.

We left the Grand Canyon and travelled north toward Wyoming so we could spend a couple of days with my cousins, Nancy and Arlene. As we were driving, I saw a sign that said "The four Corners." I wondered what that could be, so when I needed to get gas, I stopped at a station that had Navajo paraphernalia. I thought that maybe

Lez might want to get something for his girlfriend, Makayla. He didn't see anything he thought she'd like, but while chatting we learned of a place that I never heard of before; the Four Corners. This is where four states, Arizona, Colorado, New Mexico and Utah all meet. Since that was not too much out of our way to Wyoming, we stopped there.

At first it was fun to see the signs that welcomed us to one state or the other, but the constant steering was very tiresome. Lezlie began the drive, but was soon overcome with arm weariness and asked me to take over. So I did, naturally, and continued on the miserable journey until we saw a sign that said,

"Welcome to Monticello, Utah." We stopped at the Monticello Inn, got a room for the night, ate supper and crashed. In the morning, I phoned my cousin, Nancy to let her know where we were and she was delighted to share that we were only about an hour's drive to Green River; Whoppity Doo! After eating a light breakfast, we went We left Monticello renewed and decided to take our time and look at some of the scenery that Utah had to offer. We were not disappointed, we saw a place called Domed Rock and that's exactly what it was. Fascinating as all get up and it looked as if there was a cave built into its base.

Look closely at the picture.

There were other interesting sights, but this was so interesting that we just had to stop and explore it after taking this picture.

Lez sat in all four
even though the
was hotter than hell.
he didn't burn his
beyond my
I, on the other hand,
to show off my
skills and stood on
one foot in all four

Naturally, when we were in
stopped at the Colorado Court High
fuled his goal - another three pointer
man fetched his misses until he had
Fortunately, it wasn't in the 40-degree
area, nope, only 33°C. Not too

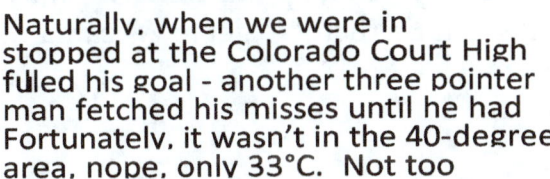

From here, we consulted the
system the most direct route to Green
Wyoming so we could visit my cousin
route we were given took us on a two
was one very long switchback that
Utah and

We got to Green River later that afternoon and found Nancy's home relatively quickly. After making our way into the house, we decided on who would shower first and what we'd have for supper. I told Nancy that we haven't had a home-cooked meal since we left ML's and would really enjoy something cooked from her kitchen. Well, it turns out that she's not much of a cook, so our 'home-cooked' meal was spaghetti and meat sauce. When her husband, James, got home from work, he was pleasantly surprised to have supper waiting for him.

We talked about growing up in Reiglesville, Nazareth, Easton and Belfast, married life, children, just about everything you can think of. Then Lezlie explained about his quest for making three pointers in every state we went through and if there was a court where he could get one. Nancy told us about the gym she worked out in and her friends there. She said that's where we'd go the next day. She then set us up with a make-shift bedroom in her den. It was cool and comfortable, of course, it didn't hurt that the temperature had dropped to a balmy 25°C.

The next morning, I made a light breakfast of eggs and toast for the three of us. James had already gone to work and missed out. Nancy then told us to get ready and we'd go to her gym. We did.

While there, she introduced us to a number of her friends and took us to the gym so Lez could make his three-pointer in Wyoming. Lez was a big hit with all the women at that gym.

A picture of him with Nancy and one of her girlfriends.

We stayed there for a couple of hours, and I said that we should probably get on the road so we could reach Arlene's house in Wheatland. We returned to Nancy's and packed up our things. Nance gave us really good directions as to how to get to Arlene's home. It wasn't difficult to get to Wheatland, but we needed to navigate a couple of back roads to find Arlene's ranch.

My cousin Arlene was a very talented artist throughout most of her life. She married a really good farmer and made a decent living farming in the eastern part of Wyoming. Arlene decorated their home with some of her paintings and other crafts that she made. Unfortunately, she contracted a disease that left her partially blind and caused her hands to become stiff, making it difficult to do intricate work like painting or her other crafts. She was able to keep house, do some yard work, and cook, but her career as an artist was finished.

When we got to her place, her husband had passed away, and she was living alone with her dog and some farm animals. She welcomed us warmly and showed us to our room. Then we asked her if there was anything she would like us to do for her around the place. She declined our offer and asked what we'd like for dinner. Arlene was unlike her sister in the cooking department, and she made us a great dinner of beef stew and a salad from vegetables grown in her garden. Her plans were to sell the farm and move into a seniors' complex in the capital city of Laramie.

While there, we got a call from Carol, who told us that she was going to Sardinia, Italy, with Lesley to attend Lesley's girlfriend's wedding, so we should cut the rest of our road trip short. Well, to be honest, Lez and I were both beginning to get tired of the traveling, and I readily agreed. The next day we thanked Arlene for her hospitality and began our trip back to Newfoundland.

Home Again:
We had to return to Newfoundland quickly, so we only stopped in each state long enough for his three-pointer, to gas up, and to rest for the night.

Our journey back took us through four more states: Nebraska, Iowa, Illinois, and Michigan. We crossed back into Canada via the Sault Sainte Marie International Bridge into Sault Sainte Marie, Ontario. From there, we drove all the way into Montreal and stayed with Lesley Marie for the night.

We made reservations for the ferry trip back to Argentia.

I figured that we could get to North Sydney in four days if we didn't waste any time, so I thought we'd stay at Lesley's for a couple of days so Lezlie could make his three-pointer and Lesley could show us her place of work and a bit of Old Montreal. That's exactly what we did.

We left Lesley thinking we'd see her again in St. John's.

We got to Edmundston, New Brunswick, and got a motel room.

The next morning, I asked the desk clerk if there was a basketball court nearby.

We found one, and Lez made his three-pointer before breakfast.

We then took the CTH East into Moncton and got to the Confederation Bridge into Prince Edward Island.

That bridge is huge! It's also a bit scary. It spans eight miles over icy seawater, rises as you enter it, and, I swear, moves sideways while driving across it. It is built on concrete pillars and is tall enough to allow ships to pass underneath. It cost us $36.00 to cross over.

We got back to St. John's just in time for Lesley and Carol to get on the plane bound for Sardinia, Italy.

BLURB

Serendipity is the story of a boy who grew up in a small Pennsylvania town and ended up living many lives in one. From a childhood filled with close calls, wild curiosity, and a knack for finding trouble, to the discipline and grit of the U.S. Marine Corps, to the free spirited years that followed, and finally to a long career teaching students who are deaf, John Reade looks back at it all with humor, honesty, and heart.

His journey takes you through the homes he lived in, the people who shaped him, the mistakes that toughened him, and the unexpected moments that pushed him forward. It is a reflection on family, courage, stubbornness, luck, and the strange way life can open new paths at the exact moment you think there are none left.

Written with the plainspoken charm of someone who has lived fully and remembers the details that matter, this memoir offers an easy, engaging read for anyone who enjoys real stories about real people.

ABOUT THE AUTHOR

John Reade is a baby boomer who lived a life full of various experiences, which he has tried to share in this memoire. He has been happily married to Carol Anne Cromwell since 1976, and they have lived in the same home since they joined forces. His immediate family consists of two daughters, Holly and Lesley, his grandson, Lezlie and great-grandson, Jayce.

www.ingramcontent.com/pod-product-compliance
Lightning Source LLC
Chambersburg PA
CBHW081532120626
46550CB00009B/2696